Researching Language and the Law

Linguistic Insights

Studies in Language and Communication

Edited by Maurizio Gotti,
University of Bergamo

Volume 121

PETER LANG
Bern · Berlin · Bruxelles · Frankfurt am Main · New York · Oxford · Wien

Davide Simone Giannoni & Celina Frade (eds)

Researching Language and the Law

Textual Features and Translation Issues

PETER LANG
Bern · Berlin · Bruxelles · Frankfurt am Main · New York · Oxford · Wien

Bibliographic information published by Die Deutsche Nationalbibliothek
Die Deutsche Nationalbibliothek lists this publication in the Deutsche Nationalbibliografie; detailed bibliographic data is available on the Internet at ‹http://dnb.d-nb.de›.

British Library and Library of Congress Cataloguing-in-Publication Data:
A catalogue record for this book is available from *The British Library*, Great Britain.

Library of Congress Cataloging-in-Publication Data

Researching language and the law : textual features and translation issues / Davide Simone Giannoni & Celina Frade (eds).
p. cm. – (Linguistic insights ; v. 121)
Includes bibliographical references.
ISBN 978-3-0343-0443-6 (alk. paper)
1. Law–Language. 2. Legal composition. I. Giannoni, Davide S. II. Frade, Celina
K213.R47 2010
340'.14–dc22
2010019498

This volume is part of a national research project on *Tension and Change in English Domain-Specific Genres* supported by the Italian Ministry of Education (COFIN Grant No. 2007JCY9Y9) and is published under the auspices of the University of Bergamo – Dipartimento di Lingue, Letterature e Culture Comparate.

ISSN 1424-8689
ISBN 978-3-0343-0443-6

Hochfeldstrasse 32, CH-3012 Bern, Switzerland
info@peterlang.com, www.peterlang.com, www.peterlang.net

Printed in Switzerland

Contents

Issues in Translation and Interpreting

D.S. GIANNONI / CELINA FRADE

Introduction

1. Legal discourse and its analysis

Like other domains of specialised language use, legal discourse is subject to the converging pressures of internationalisation and of emerging practices that destabilise well-established norms and routines. For this reason, the metaphor of globalisation can be fruitfully applied also to the law and its textual embodiment. Although viewed primarily as a feature of international commercial transactions, globalisation has rapidly spread to areas of human activity such as politics, education and the law. In broad terms, it implies an interdependence among organisations, institutions and individuals belonging to different national contexts as they attempt "to promote global coordination of activities in (but not necessarily across) different functional subsystems" (Jessop 2000: 203).

To mediate relations among these actors across national borders, globalisation relies on two symbolic communicative resources: law and language. It is law-driven in its overall effort to cover all relations within a global society and is discourse-driven insofar as it creates new language resources for conveying its ideas, constructing its practices and constituting its identities. It is plausible, therefore, to adopt the term 'legal globalisation' for the process that creates the legal conditions for such interchange on a global scale (Frade 2008). Although clearly influenced by the common law tradition primarily rooted in English, legal globalisation asserts its operational autonomy *vis-à-vis* national laws by not excluding the possibility of reciprocal influence or resistance to "attempts to brake or guide it through various forms of strategic coordination" (Jessop 2000: 329).

In an integrated, interdependent context, institutionalised expressions of supranational laws, rules and procedures are being developed and harmonised to regulate issues that can no longer be dealt with by national laws in isolation, as in the case of the European Union (EU) and its legislation. At the same time, the tendency to adopt English as a *lingua franca* is introducing linguistic, cultural and procedural features that were previously unknown in many contexts. This trend is especially challenging for legal practitioners in civil law countries and for those whose native language is not English, who are confronted with various communicative problems. At another level, legal linguists worldwide are increasingly engaged in interdisciplinary work on the language of legal communication and are expected to interact with legal practitioners on a global scale.

Early research on the language-law interface dates back to the 1960s (Mellinkoff 1963; Crystal/Davy 1969; Gustafsson 1975) and was particularly concerned with the status of *legal English* as a sub-language with its own style, syntax and terminology. Subsequently discourse analysis and genre analysis have targeted the common features of legal texts such as contracts and statutes, focusing on their lexico-grammatical and rhetorical features (cf. Bhatia 1993; Trosborg 1997). Legal English remained the main focus of most studies, without much consideration of other languages or of how language functions across different legal systems. More recently, as a consequence of emerging legal globalisation, studies on language and the law have developed a multicultural, multilingual approach extending to the use of legal English in non-Anglophone nations and in supranational legislation promoting the harmonisation of laws, rules and procedures (Bhatia *et al.* 2003; Frade 2008; Gotti 2009; Šarčević 2009). The creation of an 'International Round Table for the Semiotics of Law' (2004) and research on the semiotics of law in a global setting also provide evidence of scholars' efforts "to analyse the law from different perspectives than those of the traditions of European and Anglo-Saxon Jurisprudence" (Wagner *et al.* 2005: 9).

A topical example of the internationalisation of legal and linguistic practices is the discourse of arbitration, which has been the object of two international projects coordinated by the City University of Hong Kong (see <http://gild.mmc.cityu.edu.hk> and <http://enweb.

cityu.edu.hk/arbitrationpractice/index.html>). Its investigation shows how similar provisions dealing with international commercial arbitration are implemented in the statutes and regulations of different legal/cultural contexts and languages (Bhatia/Candlin 2004; Frade 2004; Giannoni 2005; Gotti 2005; Bhatia *et al.* 2008, 2010).

Since the establishment of the European Union in 1993, a growing amount of multidisciplinary work has concentrated on legal translation, interpretation and lexicography. Although a quick look at the official website of the EU (available at <http://europa.eu/index_en.htm>) gives the impression that English is the Union's *lingua franca*, all of its contents are available also in the other 22 official languages. The EU is required to publish its legislation in each of these and to communicate with authorities and the public of Member States in their own languages. Such a diverse linguistic arrangement is made possible by the complex translation facilities provided by EU institutions.

The contributions included in this volume reflect the interests of scholars specialising in the linguistic and legal aspects of normative texts across languages (English, Danish, French, Italian, Spanish) and legal systems. They were presented at an international conference organised by the Centre for Research on Languages for Specific Purposes (<http://www.unibg.it/cerlis>) at the University of Bergamo in June 2009. We are grateful to all the authors for patiently implementing our recommendations for revision and to the series editor, Maurizio Gotti, for general oversight of the project.

2. Outline of contents

The first part of this volume deals with textual features that are of special significance either because they single out legal communication from other types of professional discourse or because they highlight emerging tensions in the language of the law and its practitioners. In an in-depth, widely documented exploration of the subject, ESTRELLA MONTOLÍO DURÁN (Discourse, Grammar and

Professional Discourse Analysis: The Function of Conditional Structures in Legal Writing) describes the role and use of conditional logical connectors in statutory texts ranging from Babylonian law to modern-day Spanish legislation. Her diachronic analysis shows that conditional clauses are a recurring feature of such texts. The most frequent of these is the postponed structure [q, *if* p], which restricts the scope of the previous statement in order to anticipate an excessively broad (and, therefore, erroneous) interpretation; less often legal drafters rely on the structure [*if* p, then q], whereby possible consequences are pre-empted by turning information from the prior discourse into a supposition. The historical evidence presented in this study points to a striking continuity in legal reasoning across different ages, languages and cultures. What follows is a contribution by SUSAN KERMAS (English Legal Discourse and the French Continuum) charting the influence of French on English legal language in Europe. Its results, drawn mainly from the EUR-Lex archive, suggest that efforts to harmonise legislation in the EU often lead to the adoption of French loanwords – as in Middle English legal discourse. At the same time, English words lacking equivalents in Romance terminology tend to be replaced by new extended meanings of cognates of French terms. As this trend is unique to Europe, it is widening the distance between British and American legal nomenclature, which in turn increases the ambiguity of English texts used in non-European contexts.

STANISŁAW GOŹDŹ-ROSZKOWSKI (*Responsibility* and *Welfare*: Keywords and Semantic Categories in Legal Academic Journals) introduces the reader to new developments in keyword analysis, used as a resource for mapping genre-specific textual features. His study compares keyword data from journal articles and a range of other genres in a large legal corpus, with a discussion of the value of the different statistical tools employed. The results, based on the top 100 types, indicate that there are five categories of keyword whose presence is significant in journal articles: those associated respectively with citation, self-mention, legal terminology, legal knowledge structures and general language. In the next study (Linguistic and Legal Vagueness in EU Directives Harmonising Protection for Refugees and Displaced Persons) VANDA POLESE and STEFANIA

D'AVANZO explore how linguistic and legal vagueness is instrumental to ideology in EU directives dealing with the rights of migrants and asylum seekers. By managing the quantity/quality of vague lexicalisations in such texts, drafters construct an ideologically-biased discourse whose purpose is not to grant rights but to strengthen the role of Member States in controlling migration. While adjectives are the main lexical resource encoding vagueness, the analysis also considers adverbials and phrases that reflect the power relations underlying EU directives. Turning to the relationship between spoken and written usage in the law, ROSS CHARNOCK (Traces of Orality in Common Law Judgments) challenges the view that legal language is invariably complex in terms of syntax and terminology. In English common law courts, for example, the fact that most judgements are still delivered orally and then 'transcribed' reinforces the presence of features more typical of the spoken register, such as conversational connectives, performatives, deixis and dialogue. The corpus assembled in this study points to a historical trend towards increasing simplification and wordings that highlight the oral origin of this written genre.

The linguistic implications of European harmonisation are explored by JUDITH TURNBULL (Harmonisation of the Law and Legal Cultures in the EU: A Linguistic Approach), who shows that the rhetoric of the European Court of Justice is influenced by the cultural background of its judges. After assembling a sample of Opinions drafted by British and Italian advocates general in their respective languages, her study investigates the role of first-person markers, expressions of agreement/disagreement and politeness in such texts. Alongside evidence of accommodation to a supranational audience, the results predictably reflect the dratfers' language background. This means that EU Opinions may be classified as hybrid texts, insofar as they merge diverse linguistic and cultural conventions.

The second group of contributions addresses emerging issues in legal translation and interpreting, with insights that can improve our awareness of current practices and their linguistic dimension. PATRICK LEROYER and KIRSTEN WØLCH RASMUSSEN (Accessing Discursive Data Types in Legal Translation Dictionaries: The Case of *Sans Préjudice de*) test the common belief that bilingual dictionaries are of little value at phrase and sentence level. Using French>Danish legal dictionaries, the IATE multilingual term base and EUR-Lex, they describe a case study of textual difficulties encountered when translating the phrase *sans préjudice de* into Danish. Unlike printed dictionaries and their digital reproductions, these online resources contain evidence of 'textonyms' – that is of text-level discursive data types drawn from authentic documents – which could be usefully incorporated into legal dictionaries in the form of translational textual examples. In the next chapter, ÁNGEL M. FELICES LAGO (Axiological Analysis of Entries in a Spanish Law Dictionary and their English Equivalents) describes a method for mapping relevant values in various branches of legal discourse. A sample of terms and idioms reflecting widely-held social values linked to human behaviour was extracted from a Spanish law dictionary and investigated to identify which values are most prominent and how they are lexicalised. The results – revealing a marked prevalence of nouns over other parts of speech – provide interesting insights if contrasted with the axiological taxonomies proposed in the literature.

Turning from the text to the practitioner, CHRISTOPHER GODDARD (Legal Linguists: As (In)substantial as Ghosts and True Love?) offers a critical overview of a new profession, the 'legal linguist', which straddles language and the law. For this purpose he surveyed a number of EU academics, translators and students, to identify the difficulties and opportunities faced by practitioners capable of drafting, translating, editing and proofreading legal texts in various languages. The success of this emerging career option depends largely on the provision of specific academic programmes in legal linguistics and on the ability of trainees to secure a market niche distinct from that of legal translators or lawyer linguists. A similar interest underlies FRANCISCO VIGIER's contribution (Legal Translation and Interpreting in the UK Today), which provides a picture of working conditions for legal translators and interpreters in Britain. After describing some aspects of their training, accreditation and professional profile, it reports the findings of a survey of English-Spanish legal translators. This documents current conditions which, however, are likely to change as a result of European legislation regulating the recognition of foreign professional qualifications, competitiveness within the EU and the right to interpretation/translation in criminal proceedings.

The performance of liaison interpreters is analysed in a case study by IULIA DANIELA NEGRU (Acceptability versus Accuracy in Courtroom Interpreting). Her findings, based on a corpus of courtroom hearings and interrogations in Italian/Romanian, illustrate how a lack of professional training tends to produce 'acceptable', rather than accurate, translations. An overview of such features as choice of register, turn-taking, summarising and closeness to the source text suggests that in actual practice interpreters (who are often underpaid native-speakers) struggle to implement the detachment, responsibility and interpersonal skills recommended in the literature.

The last two chapters deal with the translation principles and strategies observed in international multilingual documents. ROCCO C. LOIACONO (The Translation of Bilateral Agreements between Australia and Italy: Linguistic or Functional?) investigates eleven agreements signed by the Australian and Italian governments between 1963 and 1996. After analysing borrowings, calques, approximate equivalents, paragraph length and use of register in such texts, the author concludes that *legal equivalence* is the preferred strategy adopted by translators. This means that they sought to ensure that both language versions produced the same interpretation, without too much concern for the target text's comprehensibility for the general public. CORNELIS J.W. BAAIJ (Translation in EU Legislative Procedure: A Receiver-Oriented Approach) offers a critical evaluation of receiver-oriented translation in EU legislation; this means that a translator adjusts the target text to account for its 'legal effect', i.e. its interpretation and application in national courts. Evidence gathered from EU guidelines and policy documents – as well as interviews with translators, editors and jurists – suggests that the ideal advocated by theorists is unlikely to be implemented. Because of the limited legal expertise of translators and the special nature of EU law, which is supranational and equally authentic in all its language versions, it is not easy to envisage an alternative to the current source-oriented approach.

Despite the growing amount of literature on the subject (cf. Collins/Hattenhauer 1983; Levi 1994; Morris 2000; Geeslin 2004), the study of language and the law deserves greater recognition in academic circles. Tiersma (2009) has recently noted, among other things, that its interdisciplinary nature is of special value in such related areas as semiotics and forensic linguistics. In line with this view, the research presented here sheds light on recent developments whose implications may be of interest not only to the discourse analyst but also to legal practitioners, drafters, translators and interpreters in Europe and elsewhere.

References

Bhatia, Vijay K. 1993. *Analysing Genre: Language Use in Professional Settings*. Longman: London.

Bhatia, Vijay K. / Candlin, Christopher N. 2004. Analysing Arbitration Laws across Legal Systems. *Hermes* 32, 13-43.

Bhatia, Vijay J. / Candlin, Christopher, N. / Engberg, Jan (eds) 2008. *Legal Discourse across Cultures and Systems*. Hong Kong: Hong Kong University Press.

Bhatia, Vijay K. / Candlin, Christopher N. / Gotti, Maurizio (eds) 2003. *Legal Discourse in Multilingual and Multicultural Contexts: Arbitration Texts in Europe*. Bern: Peter Lang.

Bhatia, Vijay K. / Candlin, Christopher N. / Gotti, Maurizio (eds) 2010. *The Discourses of Dispute Resolution*. Bern: Peter Lang.

Collins, Terence / Hattenhauer, Darryl 1983. Law and Language: A Selected, Annotated Bibliography on Legal Writing. *Journal of Legal Education* 33/1, 141-151.

Crystal, David / Davy, Derek 1969. *Investigating English Style*. Longman: London.

Frade, Celina 2004. Generic Variation across Legislative Writing: A Contrastive Analysis of the UNCITRAL Model Law and Brazil's Arbitration Law. *Hermes* 32, 45-75.

Frade, Celina 2008. Implications of Legal Globalisation for Brazilian Legal Practice. In Bhatia, Vijay J. / Candlin, Christopher, N. /

Engberg, Jan (eds) *Legal Discourse across Cultures and Systems*. Hong Kong: Hong Kong University Press, 275-290.

Frade, Celina 2009. Generic Variation in Cross-Examination across Legal Systems. In Šarčević, Susan (ed.) *Legal Language in Action: Translation, Terminology, Drafting and Procedural Issues*. Zagreb: Globus, 377-392.

Geeslin, Will 2004. Language and the Law: Selected Readings. *Legal Reference Services Quarterly* 23/1, 37-46.

Giannoni, Davide S. 2005. 'Any Dispute Shall Be Settled by Arbitration': A Study of Vagueness in International Model Arbitration Clauses. In Bhatia, Vijay K. / Engberg, Jan / Gotti, Maurizio / Heller, Dorothee (eds) *Vagueness in Normative Texts*. Bern: Peter Lang, 437-469.

Gotti, Maurizio 2005. Vagueness in the Model Law on International Commercial Arbitration. In Bhatia, Vijay K. / Engberg, Jan / Gotti, Maurizio / Heller, Dorothee (eds) *Vagueness in Normative Texts*. Bern: Peter Lang, 227-255.

Gotti, Maurizio 2009. Legal Drafting in an International Context: Linguistic and Cultural Issues. In Šarčević, Susan (ed.) *Legal Language in Action: Translation, Terminology, Drafting and Procedural Issues*. Zagreb: Globus, 277-300.

Gustafsson, Marita 1975. *Some Syntactic Properties of English Law Language.* Turku: University of Turku.

Jessop, Robert 2000. The Crisis of National Spatio-Temporal Fix and the Tendential Ecological Dominance of Globalizing Capitalism. *International Journal of Urban and Regional Research* 24/2, 323-360.

Levi, Judith N. 1994. *Language and Law: A Bibliographic Guide to Social Science Research in the U.S.A.* Chicago: American Bar Association.

Mellinkoff, David 1963. *The Language of the Law.* Boston: Little, Brown and Company.

Morris, Ruth 2000. *Bibliography on Court and Legal Interpreting.* Geneva: International Association of Conference Interpreters. Available online at <http://www.aiic.net/ViewPage.cfm/page 235.htm>.

Šarčević, Susan 2009. Introduction. In Šarčević, Susan (ed.) *Legal Language in Action: Translation, Terminology, Drafting and Procedural Issues*. Zagreb: Globus, 9-23.

Tiersma, Peter 2009. What is Language and Law? And Does Anyone Care? In Olsen, Frances / Lorz, Alexander / Stein, Dieter (eds) *Law and Language: Theory and Society*. Düsseldorf: Düsseldorf University Press.

Trosborg, Anna 1997. *Rhetorical Strategies in Legal Language: Discourse Analysis of Statutes and Contracts.* Tübingen: Narr.

Wagner, Anne / Summerfield, Tracey / Vanegas, Farid 2005. Law's Garden of Forking Paths. In Wagner, Anne / Summerfield, Tracey / Vanegas, Farid (eds) *Contemporary Issues of the Semiotics of Law. Cultural and Symbolic Analyses of Law in a Global Context*. Oxford: Hart Publishing, 1-16.

Textual Features

Estrella Montolío Durán

Discourse, Grammar and Professional Discourse Analysis: The Function of Conditional Structures in Legal Writing

1. Introduction

The aim of this chapter[1] is to describe and account for the functional importance of a specific linguistic structure within Spanish legal documents [*if* p, then q]. This is an essential feature of legal and legislative texts, as other specialists have already pointed out,[2] especially for English legal discourse. I shall try to demonstrate here that the relevance of this construction can be seen in present-day legal documents as well as in the earliest known legal records. For this purpose I will analyse the discourse-textual functions of the frame [*if* p, q] and those of the construction [q *if* p], while the last section extends the analysis to other varieties of conditional constructions, in particular those introduced by particles which in previous studies (Montolío 1991, 1999, 2000a) I refer to as complex conditional connectors: *siempre que* [provided that], *salvo que* [unless] and *a no ser que* [unless]. I shall also note the significant presence in texts drawn from the legal world of constructions such as *en caso de* (*que*) [in case of], as well as elliptical conditionals such as *de (no) ser así*

1 This work belongs to the project *Linguistic and Pragmatic Analysis of Expert Recommendation in Professional Documents* (Reference: FFI2008-00823), financed by the Spanish Ministry of Science and Innovation. I am greatly indebted to my erudite colleague Dr Joaquín Sanmartín, Professor of Assyriology in the Department of Semitic Studies at the University of Barcelona, who is a world specialist in Sumerian and Akkadian. I wish to thank him for the valuable information he has provided on the subject.

2 For instance, Trosborg (1995) and especially Bhatia (1993).

[otherwise], *en caso contrario* [should this not be the case] and *en su defecto* [failing that].

Having noted the recurring presence of conditional structures, generally introduced by *si* [if], although other connectors are used as well, the questions that I raise here, and which I then go on to attempt to answer are: Why do conditional constructions recur with such frequency in the writing of legal texts? And, consequently: What discourse functions do constructions of this type fulfil in the texts of the legal community and, above all, in the writing of laws?

Interestingly, the legislative style of the earliest legal codes of the Western world, written in Sumerian and Akkadian sometime in the 18th century BC, is based precisely on conditional sentences of the type: 'If any one does P, they will be punished with Q'. Thus, the well-known *Code of Hammurabi* (18th century BC) is a collection of laws that uses the conditional form, as exemplified by its first article:

(1) *Si un hombre acusa a otro hombre y le imputa un asesinato pero no puede probarlo, el acusador será ejecutado.*
If any one ensnare another, putting a ban upon him, but he can not prove it, then he that ensnared him shall be put to death.

As we shall see, the conditional structure [*if* p, then q] represents, in certain ways, a progress on a more ancient and elementary legislative style, based on the use of apodictic formulas of the type: 'Thou shalt not do X'. Providing for possible situations (generally presented using the particle *if*) in order to establish rules that match each case, constitutes an essential cognitive and linguistic mechanism for the legislator. This cognitive mechanism is expressed by means of a grammatical mechanism: the conditional structure. In the formulation of laws, an accumulation of conditional structures is not infrequent.

The first part of this study concentrates on the analysis of conditional structures in ancient legislative texts (Babylonian law and the *Code of Hammurabi*). This is followed by an analysis of conditional sentences and a description of their discourse functions in present-day legal documents. Given the discursive and cognitive relevance of conditional constructions in the drafting of laws, it seems more convenient to approach these from the theoretical perspective offered by discourse grammar, which focuses on the relationship between the grammatical structure of the language and its discourse functions (Chafe 1984, 1986; Ford/Thompson 1986; Fox/Thompson 1990; Ford 1993).

2. Material and method

For the purposes of this study, a double corpus was used: to exemplify Babylonian legislation, the *Code of Hammurabi* in Sanmartín's Spanish translation (1999) and King's (1910) English translation;[3] to exemplify contemporary legal texts, the body of laws passed in Spain during 2008, which amounts to some 150,000 words. As a tangible example of the importance of conditional structures in legislative writing, I randomly selected one of the laws making up the latter corpus, i.e. Law 1/2008 (13,693 words), which contains the following conditional structures:

Particles introducing conditional structures	Occurrences
si (*if* p, then q)	22
en caso de (que) (in case of)	6
siempre que (provided that)	3
salvo que (unless)	3
a menos que (unless)	1
en el supuesto de que (in case of)	1
Total	36

Table 1. Occurrences of conditional structures in Law 1/2008.

By contrast, if we look in the same law for another type of complex sentence – for example, causal sentences, which are known to express a more basic cognitive notion and as such are very frequent in general language – we find the following data:

3 These are both available online at <http://www.wsu.edu/~dee/MESO/CODE.HTM>.

Particles introducing causal structures	Occurrences
porque (because)	2
ya que (since/as)	1
visto que (since/as)	1
dado que (since/as)	0
puesto que (since/as)	0
Total	4

Table 2. Occurrences of causal structures in Law 1/2008.

Thus the structural importance of conditional sentences is more than self-evident in the writing of any law. These data lead me to formulate one of the hypotheses of this study: since ancient times, the drafting of legislation has been based on a consideration of plausible situations – possibly situations already experienced on one occasion or another by the community that is codifying its laws so as to anticipate equivalent legal actions.

3. The legal codes of the Babylonian tradition[4]

The Mesopotamian collections of law – of the Sumerian, Babylonian and Assyrian traditions – are the most ancient in the history of humanity. They do not constitute the earliest forms of social regulation, because there is evidence of earlier rules and judgments, but these collections are an example of the efforts made by a society to maintain order, stability, a sense of security and social cohesion, quashing disintegrative tendencies and making timely corrections to any imbalances. From a purely formal perspective, the legal articles of Babylonian tradition present the following variants: price lists, tariffs, and laws. The laws, in turn, may be (a) apodictic laws, (b) relative casuistic laws, or (c) conditional casuistic laws.

4 Section 3 is based on Sanmartín (1990). On this topic, also see the work of Sasson (1995) and Roth (1995).

3.1. From apodictic to conditional formulations

The formulation of an apodictic law embraces a necessary truth – it is unconditional. In other words, it is a categorical linguistic expression conveying evidence of a conceptual system which is considerably more elementary than that revealed by a conditional structure. In the *Code of Hammurabi*, characterised by what is basically a conditional form, we find a few cases of laws expressed in an apodictic form:

(2) *El campo -o el huerto o la casa- de un soldado -o de un militar o de un colono-* ***no pueden ser puestas a la venta.***
The field, garden, and house of a chieftain, of a man, or of one subject to quit-rent, **cannot be sold**. (CH 36)

This linguistic and cognitive contrast between the apodictic and the conditional formulation is of great interest, since the apodictic form presupposes the expression of a simple, basic notion that does not consider the situation in abstract terms (of possible contexts or circumstances), but rather in terms of strict prohibition.

Apodictic laws in their purest form do not usually include explicit punishment, but rather limit themselves to mere prohibition (*Thou shalt not do X*). Often, however, such a limited expression is insufficient and there is a need to anticipate different types of punishable situations. It is at this juncture that the conceptual and linguistic need arises for a conditional formulation: the conditional structure presents and facilitates at the same time a degree of conceptual, and even moral, sophistication that is much more elaborate.

By contrast, the Mosaic Law and Jewish laws in general are essentially apodictic in their formulation. They are legislative products developed from the traditions of nomadic peoples dedicated to shepherding their herds and not organized in complex social structures as the Babylonians, for example. Thus, the type of apodictic formulation in the example below, which is so frequent in Hebrew texts, is not surprising:

(3) *Seis días trabajarás y harás tus obras, pero el séptimo día es día de descanso, consagrado a Dios,* ***y no harás ningún trabajo*** *ni tu, ni tu hijo, ni tu hija, ni tu esclavo, ni la tu esclava, ni tu ganado, ni el extranjero que sea dentro de tus puertas.*
Six days you shall labor and do all your work, but the seventh day is a sabbath to the Lord your God. On it **you shall not do any work**, neither you, nor your son or daughter, nor your male or female servant, nor your animals, nor any foreigner residing in your towns. (*Exodus* 20: 9-10)

In the next section, the conditional formulation will be examined, since this is the most frequent, by far, in the Babylonian legal codification. To do so, we shall concentrate our analysis on the *Code of Hammurabi*.

3.2. The 'conditional style' in Babylonian legal writing

In the *Code of Hammurabi* another step is taken towards increased elaboration of thinking and instead of apodictic laws it has conditional laws, very often of the type that we would refer to in grammar as real *if*-conditionals (i.e. the condition is considered of probable fulfilment). In these laws, the protasis (the condition) is introduced using a formula based on 'if'. In all of these, the legislator first introduces a 'criminal' or punishable situation and then presents the solution or sanction that restores the social balance.

Frequently the law combines more than one conditional protasis. In other words, an article presents different circumstances that need to be considered together before establishing the corresponding punishment.

(4) ***Si*** *un hombre que ha perdido alguna cosa suya encuentra lo que ha perdido en manos de otro hombre, y el hombre en cuyas manos encuentra la cosa declara: "un vendedor me lo vendió; lo compré ante testigos",* ***y si*** *el dueño de la cosa perdida declara: "voy a presentar testigos que conocen la cosa perdida por mí",* ***y si*** *el comprador presenta al vendedor que se la vendió y a los testigos ante los que realizó la compra y el dueño de la cosa perdida presenta también sus testigos que conocían la cosa perdida por él, los jueces examinarán sus respectivas declaraciones; además, tanto los testigos ante los cuales se realizó la compra como los testigos que conocían la cosa perdida*

perdido declararán lo que saben en presencia de(l) dios. Según ello, el ladrón es el vendedor; que sea ejecutado. El dueño de la cosa perdida recuperará lo que perdió. El comprador recuperará el dinero que pagó del patrimonio del vendedor.
If any one lose an article, and find it in the possession of another: **if** the person in whose possession the thing is found say "A merchant sold it to me, I paid for it before witnesses," **and if** the owner of the thing say, "I will bring witnesses who know my property," **and if** the purchaser *brings* the merchant who sold it to him, and the witnesses before whom he bought it, and the owner shall bring witnesses who can identify his property, the judge shall examine their testimony – both of the witnesses before whom the price was paid, and of the witnesses who identify the lost article on oath. The merchant is then proved to be a thief and shall be put to death. The owner of the lost article receives his property, and he who bought it receives the money he paid from the estate of the merchant. (CH 9)

Often two or more articles are linked to present a broader panorama of hypothetical situations in order to state what the due punishment should be. This is the case of article 9 in the Code, which we have just seen, and which is followed by the article quoted in (5):

(5) ***Si** el comprador **no** presenta al vendedor que se la vendió ni a los testigos ante los cuales realizar la compra, mientras que el dueño de la cosa perdida presenta los testigos que reconocen la cosa perdida, el ladrón es el comprador; que sea ejecutado. El dueño de la cosa perdida recuperará lo que le perdió.*
If the purchaser **does not** bring the merchant and the witnesses before whom he bought the article, but its owner bring witnesses who identify it, then the buyer is the thief and shall be put to death, and the owner receives the lost article. (CH 10)

(6) [*Si un hombre compra o recibe en depósito plata, oro o un esclavo o esclava, o un buey o una oveja o un asno, o lo que sea, de manos de un hijo de un hombre o del esclavo de un hombre sin testigos ni contrato, ese hombre es un ladrón*]; ***será ejecutado***.
[If any one buy from the son or the slave of another man, without witnesses or a contract, silver or gold, a male or female slave, an ox or a sheep, an ass or anything, or if he take it in charge, he is considered a thief and] **shall be put to death**. (CH 7)

As example (6) shows, an important feature of casuistic laws expressed conditionally is the imbalance between the protasis, which tends to be long and protracted, and the apodosis (the consequence), which is quite short in most of the articles.

4. The form and function of conditional constructions

4.1. The notion of conditionality

Conditionality constitutes a very broad semantic notion, which may be expressed using a rich set of syntactic constructions that can vary greatly. So much so, in fact, that most specialists agree that conditionals are, probably, the most complex class of subordinate structures.[5]

Conditionality and its expression constitute a fundamental cognitive mechanism. Conditional structures are one of the main linguistic means we have as speakers for expressing, for example, our ability: to imagine situations that are distinct from reality (*If I were a millionaire*); to create possible worlds (*If we could fly*); to dream about how things might have turned out differently (*If we had met ten years earlier*); or to hide what is a fact behind an appearance of contingency (*If you're as tired as you just said you were*).

The notional and formal complexity of the phenomenon means we need to adopt an interdisciplinary perspective in which four types of analysis should play a role: grammatical, semantic, cognitive, and pragmatic.

---

5 The bibliography on conditional sentences is really vast. See, among others, Comrie (1986); Johnson-Laird (1986); Stalnaker (1986); Dancygier (1990); Dik (1990); Sweetser (1990); Ford (1993); Montolío (1999); Declerck/Reed (2001).

4.2. The meaning of the structure [if p, then q]

Specialist studies[6] agree that the relationship of implicature established between the two clauses of a conditional sentence does not link two existential phenomena, but rather between two speech acts. The *if*-particle contains a strong pragmatic value that consists of the interactive instruction 'Suppose p so that the declaration of q makes sense'. In other words, the connector *if* asks the interlocutor to accept provisionally the proposition contained in the protasis or antecedent, based on which the content of the consequent q must be interpreted.

Therefore, when a speaker uses a construction of the type [*if* p, then q], he is establishing a supposition and a pragmatic implicature between two utterances. First, the speaker uses a pattern with *if* to establish a supposition, insofar as the value of this element is precisely that of asking the interlocutor to suppose certain information in a given period of time. Secondly, the same speaker encodes a pragmatic implicature because, insofar as he/she is asking the listener to accept hypothesis p before showing the consequent q, so that a certain dependence is established between p and q.

4.3. The biconditional interpretation in natural language

The long tradition in studies of conditionals in the field of logic has produced an abundant literature interested abstractly in the semantic aspects of truthfulness but not in the use of conditionals in real interactions. In contrast, the study of conditional structures as they are used in daily speech has highlighted that speakers typically interpret these structures understanding the two elements (p and q) to be true, or that the truth of p is deduced from the truth of q. In this way, a conditional statement such as the following leads to a deduction that in the case of favourable climatic conditions, the speaker will indeed take a trip to the coast. In other words, it is generally understood that [*if* p, then q] implies [p true and q true]:

---

6 Especially the work of Ducrot (1971, 1972, 1973, 1980). From another perspective, cf. van der Auwera's (1986) and Sweetser's (1990) proposals.

(7) ***Si mañana hace sol**, iré a la playa*
If it is sunny tomorrow, I will go to the beach

The fact that it is communicatively adequate for the speaker to use more than one *if*-clause when there is more than one condition to be fulfilled explains why in legal language conditional forms containing more than one *if*-clause are frequent, as the following example and (1-4) make clear:

(8) ***Si** ya se ha abonado una parte de la sanción en el Estado de emisión, **o si** le consta a la autoridad que emita el Certificado que la ha pagado en cualquier otro Estado, se ha de indicar el importe abonado.*
[**If** a part of the penalty has already been paid in the Issuing State, or if the authority issuing the Certificate has notice that it has been paid in any other state, the sum paid must be declared.] (Law 1/2008, 4 December 2008)

It appears therefore that from an [*if* p, then q] construction the speaker deduces at the same time, via an inferential interpretation, that [*if* not-p, then not-q]. This interpretation is known in the literature as an 'invited inference' (Geis/Zwicky 1971). Thus, speakers make a biconditional interpretation of conditional statements, because a conditional structure is perceived as assuming that the propositions contained in the protasis and apodosis are both true or, thanks to their biconditional interpretation, both false.

4.4. Biconditional interpretation in legal discourse

The biconditional interpretation found in any statement of the type [*if* p, then q] is especially relevant to legal discourse, since it is made implicitly but is not signalled explicitly in the statement. Therefore, legal texts – which should necessarily be characterized by their clarity, objectivity and non-ambiguity – need to avoid interpretations induced inferentially and, consequently, they should, wherever possible, explicitly formulate any possible extensions of, or restrictions to, their interpretation (Montolío 2000b). As Bhatia (1982, 1987a, 1993) points out, the main function of these inserted conditions is to make the provision precise, clear, unambiguous and all-inclusive.

Let us consider a possible example. If the heir to certain goods were to die unexpectedly, it would be important to make it quite clear that the inheritance would pass on to the second-named beneficiary in the will; however, if the first heir were declared insane, the inheritance would not change hands. A connector of the type '*only if* the heir dies...' solves a legal-linguistic situation of this type:

(9) ***Sólo si*** *muere el primero de los herederos designados en el testamento, el segundo podrá hacerse cargo de la herencia.*
[**Only if** the first of the heirs appointed in the will dies, can the second receive the inheritance.] (Law 3/2008)

The inferential interpretation of the construction [*if* p, then q], which involves the simultaneous consideration [*if* not-p, then not-q], corresponds to the value that the connector *only if* expresses semantically by itself, with no need for any additional inferential value, and therefore clearly and unambiguously, as statement (9) shows. The non-ambiguity of the conditional expression *only if* explains why this construction is much more frequent in legal and administrative texts than in colloquial language.

However, the fact that it is communicatively inadequate for a speaker to combine the assertion [*if* p, then q] together with the possibility of [*if* not-p, q all the same] is corroborated by the existence of a series of syntactic constructions whose purpose is to warn the interlocutor not to make the usual biconditional interpretation. This is the case, in particular, of 'alternative' concessive-conditional constructions (König 1986; Haspelmath/König 1998):

(10) *Asimismo, serán deducibles las contribuciones de personal que se correspondan con pagos basados en instrumentos de patrimonio, utilizados como fórmula de retribución a los empleados,* ***tanto si*** *se satisface en efectivo* ***como si*** *es mediante la entrega de dichos instrumentos.*
[Similarly, personnel contributions corresponding to payments based on equity instruments, used as a means for remunerating employees, will be deductible, **whether** they are satisfied in cash or by the delivery of said instruments.] (Law 4/2008, 25 December 2008)

This concessive-conditional construction may be schematically represented as:

Whether *p* or *not p*,
Whether *p* or *r*, all the same *q*

The construction presents two possibilities: a given situation and, at the same time, a situation of the opposite polarity or another possible circumstance (Declerck/Reed 2001).

4.5. Clause order and discourse function of conditional structures

In accordance with Greenberg's (1966) 14th language universal, languages that possess the conditional construction characteristically have the protasis preceding the apodosis, that is [1st: *if* p, 2nd: then q]. The initial position of the *if*-clause constitutes therefore the usual, unmarked frame of conditional utterances in a language. This prototypical sentence-initial position of the subordinate clause comes as no surprise if we bear in mind that the function of the protasis is to create a supposition or, in other terms, a state of things, a possible world, a discursive frame through which the information that follows can be interpreted.

The typical initial position of the protasis and its function of introducing information that must be mentally present in order to interpret the following clause means that the value of this clause has been associated with the grammatical concept of 'theme', understood as the information of an utterance that is given or shared (Haiman 1978, 1983, 1986; Schiffrin 1992). Indeed, it would seem acceptable to assume that there exists a prototypical initial position of the protasis with a thematic value, where the protasis serves the function of introducing information that is already known to the interlocutors or which the speaker is going to use as the informative base on which the information contained in the apodosis will have to be interpreted.

However, this association between protasis and shared information depends on the fact that the subordinate clause does indeed occupy the prototypical initial position, that is, according to the frame ([1st: if p, 2nd: then q]), a position that is also characteristic of informational themes in an utterance (1st: theme -known information, 2nd: rheme -new information). Now, grammatical description has often neglected to examine the protasis in second position, where its contribution to the meaning is not easily understood as shared information. In a sentence such as

(11) *Los créditos de inversiones se entenderán adecuados para la contratación de personal eventual* ***si*** *no existe crédito suficiente para ello en el concepto presupuestario destinado específicamente a dicha finalidad.*
[Investment credit will be understood suitable for the contracting of staff **if** there is not enough credit to do so in the budget specifically destined to this purpose.] (Law 2/2008)

it does not seem appropriate to argue that the *if*-clause constitutes given or shared information, but rather that this is the new information.

In utterances such as these, the discourse function of the *if*-clause is not concerned with the provision of an informational base from which the information in the main clause can be interpreted. On the contrary, the function of the protasis in the frame [(1st): q, (2nd): if p] is related to the mechanisms of specification or restriction of the meaning of the main clause.[7]

4.6. Initial position if-clauses

It is no surprise that the discourse functions realised by the protasis differ depending on whether the clause is in initial or final position. Placing the clause first, as we have seen, constitutes a discourse frame or background whereby the information that follows is interpreted. For this reason, the most frequent discourse function of an initially placed protasis in legal and administrative languages will be one of the three illustrated below (cf. Montolío 2000b).

---

7 See Linde (1976), Chafe (1984), Ramsay (1987) and, especially, Ford/ Thompson (1986) and Ford's work (1993), based on an oral corpus, that analyzes the use of conditional constructions and other types of adverbial sentences in spontaneous conversation.

4.6.1. Selecting information from the prior discourse and turning it into a supposition

The first discourse function of those fulfilled by this construction [*if* p, then q] is that of selecting information from the prior discourse and turning it into a supposition, so as to explore the possible implications of choosing it as an option. This is illustrated in the following example:

(12) *En aquellos* ***supuestos*** *en que un mismo titular perciba dos o más pensiones públicas, la suma del importe anual íntegro de todas ellas, una vez revalorizadas las que procedan,* ***no podrá superar*** *el límite máximo a que se refiere el apartado anterior.* ***Si lo superase****, se minorará proporcionalmente la cuantía de la revalorización, hasta absorber el exceso sobre dicho límite.*
[**In cases in which** the same holder receives two or more state pensions, **the sum** of the full annual amount of all of these pensions, following their revaluation, **may not exceed** the threshold referred to above. **If the sum were to exceed it**, the amount will be reduced in proportion to the revaluation, to absorb the excess over that limit.] (Law 2/2008, 23 December 2008)

As example (13) shows, the *if*-clauses that realise this first discourse function present a marked anaphoric character since they take up an earlier point of information. For this reason they usually include a grammatical element of anaphoric character, such as the Spanish neutral pronoun *lo* (English *it*).

This function of taking up information present in the earlier discourse to convert it into a supposition (*if*), and to, thereby, introduce the consequences deriving from it, is a recurring feature in the *Code of Hammurabi*. This is the case when two legal articles that follow immediately from each other in the Code are related and the second expands, comments on, draws a distinction or restricts the scope of the former. In the following examples we shall see how the regulations governing the capture of slaves are linked through various articles:

(13) *Si* ***un*** *hombre captura en el campo un esclavo o una esclava fugitivos y los lleva a su dueño, el dueño del esclavo le dará 2 sicles de plata.*

If **any one** find runaway male or female slaves in the open country and bring them to their masters, the master of the slaves shall pay him two shekels of silver. (CH 17)

(14) *Si* ***el*** *esclavo no quiere dar el nombre de su dueño, que lo lleve a palacio; allí se estudiará su caso y luego será llevado a su dueño.*
If **the** slave will not give the name of the master, the finder shall bring him to the palace; a further investigation must follow, and the slave shall be returned to his master. (CH 18)

(15) *Si mantiene retenido a* ***ese*** *esclavo en su casa pero después el esclavo es descubierto en su poder, entonces aquel hombre será ejecutado.*
If he hold **the** slave in his house, and he is caught there, then the finder shall be put to death. (CH 19)

As can be seen, both in modern-day legal texts and in the earliest legal writings that have survived, more often than not the basic structure of these constructions responds to the following frame: [*X* must be done. If *X* is not done, then *Z* will happen].[8]

4.6.2. Contrasting different possibilities and their consequences

A second basic function of *if*-clauses is to compare and contrast different suppositions or possibilities and their respective consequences:

(16) ***Si*** *en virtud de las características técnicas de la emisión no es aplicable ninguna canalización entre las indicadas, se tomará el ancho de banda de la denominación de la emisión* ***o, en su defecto****, se aplicará la totalidad de la correspondiente banda de frecuencias destinada en el CNAF para estas aplicaciones.*
[**If** by virtue of the technical characteristics of the emission none of the channel frequencies among those indicated is applicable, then the bandwidth of the denomination of the emission shall be adopted **or, failing that** all of the corresponding frequency band provided in the *CNAF* for these applications shall be employed.] (Law 2/2008)

8 Bhatia (1993), following Cristal/Davy's (1969) proposal, also pointed out that most legal sentences have one of the two following forms: [If X, then Y shall do Z], or [If X, then Y shall be Z], where 'If X' stands for the description of case(s) to which the rule of law applies. Although they do not say so explicitly, 'Y' is meant to be the legal subject and 'Z' the legal action.

This type of alternative conditional construction responds to the following frame of legislative formulation: [If *P*, then *Q* // If *not-P*, then *Z*].

On occasion, the contrast between hypothetical situations is based not on the affirmative/negative polarity of the same proposition but on that between two contrasting concepts. This is the case in the following article, where the contrast is based on a given age limit: *less than 52 years old // more than 52 years old*:

(17) *En los **casos** de percepción del subsidio por desempleo cuando se trata de trabajadores fijos discontinuos:*
*(a) **Si son menores de cincuenta y dos años** y el beneficiario haya acreditado, a efectos del reconocimiento del subsidio, un periodo de ocupación cotizada de ciento ochenta o más días, la entidad gestora ingresará las cotizaciones a la Seguridad Social correspondientes a la contingencia de jubilación durante un periodo de sesenta días, a partir de la fecha en que nazca el derecho al subsidio.*
*(b) **Si son mayores de cincuenta y dos años**, la entidad gestora ingresará las cotizaciones a la Seguridad Social correspondientes a la contingencia de jubilación durante toda la percepción del subsidio, a que tuvieran derecho, una vez cumplida la edad indicada.*
[In **cases** of the receipt of unemployment benefit for fixed-term employees:
(a) **If they are under fifty-two years of age**... the entity will pay the contributions to the Social Security corresponding to the pension for a period of sixty days...
(b) **If they are over fifty-two years of age**, the entity will pay the contributions to the Social Security corresponding to the pension during the period in which the benefit was received...] (Law 2/2008)

The *Code of Hammurabi* also has this function of drawing a distinction between different possible circumstances and their punishment. Often, as in present-day legal style, the comparison of different circumstances and possibilities is based on an affirmative/negative polarity. This is the case of the following examples from the *Code*, where (19) presents the possibility of a polarity contrary to that presented previously in (18):

(18) ***Si un hombre arrienda un campo para explotarlo** pero luego no produce cebada en el campo, que le prueben que no lo cultiva adecuadamente, y él le dará al amo tanta cebada como produzca su vecino.*

If any one take over a field to till it, and obtain no harvest therefrom, it must be proved that he did no work on the field, and he must deliver grain, just as his neighbor raised, to the owner of the field. (CH 42)

(19) ***Si no explota el campo*** *y lo deja yermo, dará al amo tanta cebada como produzca su vecino, y el campo que había dejado baldío, se lo devolverá, una vez lo haya limpiado, a su dueño.*
If he do not till the field, but let it lie fallow, he shall give grain like his neighbor's to the owner of the field, and the field which he let lie fallow he must plow and sow and return to its owner. (CH 43)

Earlier examples from the *Code* (4-5) can be viewed in the same way. There are also instances of articles that are linked together using a contrast relation that is not one that depends on polarity but rather on the opposition between concepts. In the following example, the opposition is between *life (cure)* and *death*:

(20) ***Si*** *un veterinario realiza una incisión profunda en un buey o un asno y* ***le salva la vida****, el dueño del buey o del asno le abonará al médico 1/6 de sicle de plata como pago.*
If a veterinary surgeon perform a serious operation on an ass or an ox, and **cure** it, the owner shall pay the surgeon one-sixth of a shekel as a fee. (CH 224)

(21) ***Si*** *realiza una incisión profunda en un buey o un asno y le provoca la* ***muerte****, le abonará el amante del buey o del asno la cuarta parte de su valor.*
If he perform a serious operation on an ass or ox, and **kill** it, he shall pay the owner one-fourth of its value. (CH 225)

Thus the function of contrasting different suppositions constitutes a recurring function of the conditional structures in the formulations of the *Code of Hammurabi*.

4.6.3. Examining possible suppositions and their implied consequences

On occasion, suppositions under consideration can be deduced from the prior discourse; even when considered unlikely and, consequently, unexpected they are treated as plausible at a given moment of the statement:

(22) *Si, después de transmitir una resolución, la autoridad penal española recibiese una cantidad de dinero, sea porque hubiera sido pagada voluntariamente por la persona condenada o porque fuera resultado de actuaciones judiciales anteriores,* ***aplicará*** *el pago recibido en la forma legalmente prevista e informará inmediatamente de ello a la autoridad competente del Estado de ejecución...*
[If... the Spanish court authority should receive a sum of money... the payment received **will be dealt with** in the legal manner provided for this purpose] (Law 1/2008)

The function of examining possible suppositions and their implied consequences is, probably, the most frequent discourse function of those performed by conditional structures in legal texts, including the earliest known legal codifications. This can be corroborated by the following examples drawn from the *Code*:

(23) ***Si*** *en la casa de un hombre se declara un incendio y algún hombre que había venido a apagar, le hace gracia algún objeto y se lo queda, ese hombre será quemado en ese mismo fuego.*
If fire break out in a house, and some one who comes to put it out cast his eye upon the property of the owner of the house, and take the property of the master of the house, he shall be thrown into that self-same fire. (CH 25)

(24) ***Si*** *un médico rehace un hueso roto a un hombre, o le cura un tendón dañado, el paciente abonará al médico 5 sicles de plata.*
If a physician heal the broken bone or diseased soft part of a man, the patient shall pay the physician five shekels in money. (CH 221)

We shall now examine *if*-clauses in second position. This pattern is not found in the *Code* because in the languages of earlier Mesopotamian codes (Sumerian and Akkadian) the only construction used is *if* p, q (Sanmartín 1999). So my analysis will concentrate on contemporary legal documentation.

4.7. Second position if-clauses: the legislator restricts the scope of a previous statement

When, contrary to the standard pattern, the protasis appears in second place – [q, if p] – the discourse function of the subordinate clause changes and its value depends on the discursive operations that are prototypically performed by adverbial clauses in second place, such as specification or restriction. The protasis in sentence-final position may be given one of two distinct syntactic patterns, with or without a pause: [q if p] and [q, if p].

If-clauses in second place are considerably less frequent than those that occur in first position in spontaneous oral registers. Unlike spoken language, in legislative documents the postponed protasis [q, if p] is notably more frequent. The reason for this lies in the need, at the heart of legal discourse, to specify or restrict the reach of certain assertions and therefore the interpretation that the receiver has to make. Indeed, many examples of this construction [q, if p] are found in the legal documents of our corpus.

These two syntactic patterns correspond, in turn, to two slightly different functions. When the subordinate clause does not constitute a separated unit in itself (that is: [q if p]), it expresses semantic restrictions or modifications with respect to the main clause to which it is related, as the following example illustrates:

(25) *Tampoco estarán sujetas a dicho gravamen por tales operaciones las entidades cuya sede de dirección efectiva se encuentre en países no pertenecientes a la Unión Europea* ***si*** *su domicilio social está situado en un Estado miembro de la Unión Europea distinto de España.*
[Companies with their management headquarters in non-EU countries will not be subject to tax on the aforementioned operations **if** their registered address is in an EU member state country other than that of Spain.] (Law 4/2008)

The restrictive mechanism practised by this construction can be shown schematically as follows:

[Q *if* P]
{*assertion*} {*restriction or specification*}

In other words, the prior assertion is reinterpreted as being valid only under certain possible circumstances. According to my work with legal corpora, this frame with pause between clauses [q**,** if p] seems more frequent in legal texts than in everyday language:

(26) *Los Consejeros Permanentes de Estado causarán en su propio favor derecho a la pensión indemnizatoria establecida en la norma primera del número 5 del artículo 10 de la Ley 74/1980, de 29 de diciembre,* ***si se declarase***[9] *su incapacidad permanente en los términos que establece el artículo 32.1 del Reglamento Orgánico del Consejo de Estado, aprobado por el Real Decreto 1674/1980, de 18 de julio.*
[The Permanent Councillors of State will rule in their favour the right to a compensatory pension as established under the first norm, subsection 5, article 10 of Law 74/29 December 1980**, if their permanent incapacity should be declared** in accordance with the terms established by 32.1 of the Organic Regulations of the State Council, passed by Royal Decree 1674/18 July 1980.] (Law 2/2008)

In the frame [q, if p], the presence of a pause, signalled by a comma, also appears to express the idea of anti-expectation or an even smaller likelihood of the proposition contained in *p* being fulfilled.

4.8. The case of complex conditional connectors

This same restrictive function is carried out by those conditional clauses referred to in previous studies as *complex conditional connectors* (Montolío 1991, 1999, 2000a), including among others, *siempre que* (provided that) and *salvo que* (unless), both of which are very frequent in legal documents (cf. Geis 1973; Dancygier 1985; Montolío 2000b; Garofalo 2006):

(27) *La autoridad judicial penal española competente para ejecutar una resolución por la que se condene al pago de una sanción pecuniaria a una persona física o jurídica que posea propiedades, obtenga ingresos o tenga su residencia habitual o su sede social en otro Estado miembro de la Unión Europea, podrá transmitir la resolución,* ***siempre que ésta sea firme****, a la autoridad competente de dicho Estado para que proceda a su ejecución.*
[The Spanish criminal authority... will be able to transfer this decision, **provided that it is final**] (Law 1/2008)

---

9 Of course, in these cases, the imperfect of subjunctive tense collaborates, in addition to the postposition and the pause, to express low probability or anti-expectation.

(28) *Las entidades de gestión liquidarán el importe debido al titular, en concepto de derecho de participación, en el plazo máximo de un año a contar desde el momento del pago,* ***salvo que en dicho plazo el titular reclame la liquidación,*** *en cuyo caso ésta se efectuará en el mes siguiente a la reclamación.*
[The management bodies shall discharge the sum due to the holder, by way of participation rights, in a period no longer than a year from the moment of payment, **unless that within this period the holder demands discharge be made**, in which case this will be made effective in the month following the claim.] (Law 3/2008)

Complex conditional connectors (CCCs) are a more elaborate and sophisticated version of the contingent hypothesis. Three grammatical features distinguish these structures from those containing an *if*-clause: in the case of Spanish, they combine exclusively with verbs in the subjunctive mood; in terms of syntax, they prototypically occupy the position after the main clause; they are unable to combine with the anaphoric *then*. In their semantic-pragmatic sense, these structures have the following characteristics: rhematic informative value; biconditional value; exceptional (favourable or unfavourable) conditions for the fulfilment of *q* (Montolío 1999, 2000a).

Among complex conditional connectors, two groups can be identified: affirmative CCCs, including *siempre que*, *siempre y cuando*, *a condición de que*, *con tal de que* (provided that); and negative CCCs including *salvo que*, *a no ser que*, *a menos que*, *excepto que* and *excepto si* (unless).

Affirmative CCCs present the supposition required in order to permit the fulfilment of what is expressed by the main clause. In other words, the subordinate clause introduces the sole circumstances under which *q* will take place (Dostie 1987; Montolío 1991, 1999, 2000a; Athanasiadou/Dirven 1995; Visconti 2000). This is why they express exceptional conditions for the fulfilment of q.

(29) *Se encontrarán en situación de incapacidad temporal los funcionarios que acrediten padecer un proceso patológico por enfermedad o lesión por accidente que les impida con carácter temporal el normal desempeño de sus funciones públicas o que se encuentren en período de observación médica por enfermedad profesional,* ***siempre y cuando reciban la asistencia sanitaria necesaria para su recuperación facilitada por la Mutualidad General de Funcionarios Civiles del Estado y hayan obtenido licencia por enfermedad.***

[Those public servants shall be deemed to be in a situation of temporary incapacity that are able to present documents accrediting to their suffering a pathological process due to illness or injury resulting from an accident (…), **providing that they are in receipt of the necessary healthcare to ensure recovery**] (Law 2/2008)

In the next example, the legal paragraph contains a construction with *siempre que* (provided that) and another with *siempre y cuando* (provided that). In both cases the clause containing the affirmative CCC strictly limits the fulfilment of the main clause to that of the supposition introduced by the subordinate clause.

(30) *En relación con los Proyectos Concertados de Investigación de los Programas Nacionales Científico-Tecnológicos... se autoriza al Centro para el Desarrollo Tecnológico Industrial) para la concesión de moratorias o aplazamientos de hasta un máximo de cinco años...* [***siempre que*** *se presten garantías suficientes por parte del deudor...* y cuando la situación financiera justifique la imposibilidad de atender los pagos en sus fechas... {***siempre y cuando*** *se acredite documentalmente dicha situación...*}].
[In relation to National Scientific-Technological Research Projects... the Center for Industrial Technological Development is granted a moratorium for a maximum of five years... [**provided that** sufficient guarantees are offered by the debtor... and that the financial situation justifies the impossibility of paying on time... {**provided that** that the financial situation is confirmed by official records...}]] (Law 2/2008)

It is important to note that in this example the clause introduced by *siempre y cuando* expresses the only circumstance that allows the fulfilment of the supposition presented, in turn, by the clause headed by *siempre que*.

By contrast, the complex conditional connectors that I have referred to as being negative present the exceptional situation that they would impede the fulfilment of *q* or the main clause. That is, the subordinate clause introduces the sole circumstances under which *q* would no longer be fulfilled:

(31) *Las cantidades percibidas en concepto de ejecución de una resolución en España se ingresarán en la cuenta de depósitos y consignaciones judiciales,* ***salvo que se hubiese acordado otra cosa con el Estado de emisión*** *respecto*

de las cantidades que constituyan una compensación en beneficio de las víctimas a que se refiere la letra b) del artículo 3.2.
[The quantities received... shall be deposited in the corresponding court account, **unless a different course of action had been agreed with the Issuing State**.] (Law 1/2008)

Paraphrasing this, one could say that if the subject has agreed with the Issuing State to do something different, then the sums will *not* be deposited. The same occurs in the following example:

(32) *Una vez transmitida la resolución, la resolución será ejecutada de acuerdo con el ordenamiento jurídico del Estado encargado de aplicarla,* ***salvo que concurra alguno de los motivos de denegación o suspensión de la ejecución.***
[Once the decision has been transferred, the decision shall be enforced in accordance with the legal regulations of the State with responsibility for executing it, **unless any of the reasons for dismissing or suspending its enforcement should arise**.] (Law 1/2008)

Negative CCCs thus express the circumstances under which something will *not* occur. In other words (in line with Dancygier 1985, 1990; Montolío 1991; Declerck/Reed 2001), such a construction rejects *q*, not *p*. The underlying pattern is q *unless* p = q [(not-q) if p]. This is the only possible situation in which the supposition in the main clause will not be fulfilled and accounts for the fact that clauses with CCCs in general, and negative CCCs more specifically, are highly appropriate frames for formulating *reservations* (Montolío 2007).

The mechanism of reservation that conditional structures of this type express can be shown schematically as follows (cf. example 33):

Q	*unless*	P =
Q will be done.	(However)	If P Q will not be done
{Assertion}	{Restriction of the assertion: Reserve}	

(33) *La transmisión de las resoluciones por las que se exija el pago de una sanción pecuniaria con el Reino Unido y la República de Irlanda, se efectuará con arreglo a lo dispuesto en esta ley,* ***a menos que*** *estos Estados manifiesten mediante declaración depositada ante la Secretaría General del Consejo y notificada a la Comisión, que optan por la transmisión de sus resoluciones y del certificado correspondiente por conducto de su autoridad o autoridades centrales especificadas en la declaración.*

> [The transfer of decisions which require the payment of a pecuniary fine with the United Kingdom or the Republic of Ireland shall be carried out in accordance with the provisions in this law, **unless** these States demonstrate otherwise...] (Law 1/2008)

Indeed, clauses with negative CCCs are frequently employed to express legal reservations when the legislator wishes to make explicit the supposition for which a legal norm might not be fulfilled.

5. Summary and conclusions

The main purpose of this study was to explain why conditional constructions recur with such frequency in the writing of legal and administrative texts. What I hope to have shown is that conditional structures, in general, and, more specifically the structure [*if* p, then q] constitute an essential grammatical and cognitive mechanism in the codification of legal regulations, both in today's documents and in the earliest known legal records. By examining the legal documents of ancient Babylon, I have highlighted the evolution in the history of legal formulations represented by the change in legislative style from apodictic to conditional formulations (foreseeing the possible transgression and its social regulation).

Another objective was to identify the specific discourse-textual functions fulfilled historically by *if*-p clauses in the texts of law and government. Our corpus shows that the discourse functions of conditional sentences in ancient and contemporary legal texts are fundamentally the same.

The discourse functions fulfilled by these constructions vary substantially according to the order of clauses within the frame. The main function of the conditionals of type [*if* p, then q] is to provide for possible circumstances so as to determine their possible consequences (or legal actions) by selecting information from the prior discourse and turning it into a supposition; contrasting different possibilities and their consequences; and examining possible suppositions and their implied consequences.

In actual legal corpora, postposed *if*-clauses restrict the scope of the previous statement in order to anticipate an excessively broad (and, therefore, erroneous) interpretation by the receptor. This type of conditional clause serves, therefore, to express reservations. Related to this final position frame, are conditional constructions with complex connectors, which assume greater elaboration of the contingent hypothesis to provide for possible future punishments.

The theoretical perspective offered by discourse grammar, which focuses on the relationship between the grammatical structure of language and its discourse functions, provides a better understanding of the value of different types of conditional construction in legal texts and of the purposes of these professional texts. Adopting a similar approach, further research could help deepen our knowledge of the discourse functions of grammatical structures that characterize other types of professional text in the law and beyond.

References

Athanasiadou, Angelica / Dirven, René. 1995. Conditional Conjunctions and Conceptual Companions. In Dirven, René / Vanparys, Johan (eds) *Current approaches to the Lexicon*. Frankfurt: Peter Lang, 225-248.

Bhatia, Vijay K. 1982. *An Investigation into the Formal and Functional Characteristics of Qualifications in Legislative Writing and Its Application to English for Academic Legal Purposes*. PhD thesis. Birmingham: Universisty of Aston.

Bhatia, Vijay K. 1987. Language of the Law. *Language Teaching* 20, 227-234.

Bhatia, Vijay K. 1993. *Analysing Genre: Language Use in Professional Settings*. London: Longman.

Bhatia, Vijay K. / Candlin, Christopher N. / Engberg, Jan (eds) 2008. *Legal Discourse across Cultures and Systems*. Hong Kong: Hong Kong University Press.

Chafe, Wallace L. 1984. How People Use Adverbial Clauses. In Brugmann, Claudia / Macaulay, Monica (eds) *Proceedings of the Tenth Annual Meeting of the Berkeley Linguistics Society*. Berkeley: Berkeley Linguistics Society.

Chafe, Wallace. L. / Nichols, Johanna 1986. *Evidentiality: The Linguistic Coding of Epistemology*. Norwood: Ablex Publishing Corporation.

Comrie, Bernard 1986. Conditionals: A Typology. In Traugott, Elizabeth / Ter Meulen, Alice / Reilly, Judy Snitzer / Ferguson, Charles (eds) *On Conditionals*. Cambridge: Cambridge University Press, 77-99.

Dancygier, Barbara 1985. If, Unless, and Their Polish Equivalents. *Papers in Contrastive Linguistics* 20, 65-72.

Dancygier, Barbara 1990. Conditionals: Sequence of Events and Sequence of Clauses. In Fisiak, Jaeck (ed.) *Further Insights into Contrastive Analysis*. Amsterdam: John Benjamins, 357-373.

Declerck, Renaat / Reed, Susan 2001. *Conditionals: A Comprehensive Empirical Analysis*. Berlin: Mouton de Gruyter.

Dik, Simon 1990. On the Semantics of Conditionals. In Nuyts, Jan / Bolkestein, Machtelt / Vet, Co (eds) *Layers and Levels of Representation in Language Theory. A Functional View*. Amsterdam: John Benjamins, 233-262.

Dostie, Gaetane 1986. Etude sémantique de quatre connecteurs conditionnels: à condition que, pourvu que, en autant que et d'abord que.*Le français moderne* 55/3-4, 174-203.

Ducrot, Oswald 1971. L'expression en français de la notion de condition suffisante. *Langue française* 12, 60-66.

Ducrot, Oswald 1972. *Dire et ne pas dire*. Paris: Hermann.

Ducrot, Oswald 1973. *La preuve et le dire: Langage et logique*. Paris: Mame.

Ducrot, Oswald 1980. *Les échelles argumentatives*. Paris: Éditions de Minuit.

Ford, Cecilia / Thompson, Sandra 1986. Conditionals in Discourse: A Text-Based Study from English. In Traugott, Elizabeth / Ter

Meulen, Alice / Reilly, Judy Snitzer / Ferguson, Charles (eds) *On Conditionals*. Cambridge: Cambridge University Press, 353-372.

Ford, Cecilia 1993. *Grammar in Interaction: Adverbial Clauses in American English Conversations*. Cambridge: Cambridge University Press.

Fox, Barbara / Thompson, Sandra 1990. A Discourse Explanation of the Grammar of Relative Clauses in English Conversation. *Language* 66/2, 297-316.

Garofalo, Giovanni 2006. I connettivi condizionali complessi nei testi normativi spagnoli. *Rivista Internazionale di Tecnica della Traduzione* 9, 75-97.

Geis, Michael / Zwicky, Arnold 1971. On Invited Inferences. *Linguistic Inquiry* 4/2, 561-566.

Geis, Michael 1973. If and Unless. In Kachru, Braj / Lees, Robert / Malkiel, Yakov / Pietrangeli, Angelina / Saporta, Sol (eds) *Issues in Linguistics: Papers in Honour of Henry and Renee Kahane*. Urbana: University of Illinois Press, 231-253.

Greenberg, Joseph H. (ed.) 1966. *Universals of Language*. Cambridge, MS: MIT Press.

Haiman, John 1978. Conditionals Are Topics. *Language* 54, 564-589.

Haiman, John 1983. Paratactic if-Clauses. *Journal of Pragmatics* 7/3, 263-281.

Haiman, John 1986. Constraints on the Form and Meaning of the Protasis. In Traugott, Elizabeth / Ter Meulen, Alice / Reilly, Judy Snitzer / Ferguson, Charles (eds) *On Conditionals*. Cambridge: Cambridge University Press, 215-227.

Haspelmath, Martin / König, Ekkehard 1998. Concessive Conditionals in the Languages of Europe. In Van Der Auwera, Johan (ed.) *Adverbial Constructions in the Languages of Europe*. Berlin: Mouton De Gruyter, 564-640.

Johnson-Laird, Philip 1986. Conditionals and Mental Models. In Traugott, Elizabeth / Ter Meulen, Alice / Reilly, Judy Snitzer / Ferguson, Charles (eds) *On Conditionals*. Cambridge: Cambridge University Press, pp. 55-75.

König, Ekkehard 1986. Conditionals, Concessive Conditionals and Concessives: Areas of Contrast, Overlap and Neutralization. In

Traugott, Elizabeth / Ter Meulen, Alice / Reilly, Judy Snitzer / Ferguson, Charles (eds) *On Conditionals*. Cambridge: Cambridge University Press, 229-246.

Linde, Charlotte 1976. Constraints on the Ordering of if-Clauses. In Thompson, H. / Whistler, K. / Edge, V. / Jaeger, J.J. / Javkin, R. / Petruck, M. / Smeall, C. / van Valin, R.D. (eds) *Proceedings of the Second Annual Meeting of the Berkeley Linguistics Society*. Berkeley: University of California, 280-285.

Montolío, Estrella 1990. *Expresión de la condicionalidad en español*. PhD thesis. Barcelona: University of Barcelona.

Montolío, Estrella 1991. On Conditional Structures with Complex Connectors. In Van Der Auwera, Thomas (ed.) *Adverbialia*. Strasbourg: European Science Foundation, 33-52.

Montolío, Estrella 1999. Las construcciones condicionales. In Bosque, Ignacio / Demonte, Violeta (eds) *Gramática descriptiva de la Lengua Española*. Vol. 3. Madrid: Espasa-Calpe, 3643-3737.

Montolío, Estrella 2000a. On Affirmative and Negative Complex Conditional Connectives. In Couper-Kuhlen, Elizabeth / Kortmann, Bernd (eds) *Cause, Condition, Concession and Contrast*. Berlin: Mouton de Gruyter, 143-171.

Montolío, Estrella 2000b. Les estructures condicionals [*si p, q*] i la seva rellevància en les formulacions legislatives, administratives i jurídiques. *Revista de llengua i dret* 34, 67-92.

Montolío, Estrella 2007. Advising without Committing: The Use of Argumentative Reservation in Texts Written by Consultants. In Sarangi, Srikant / Garzone, Giuliana (eds) *Ideology and Ethics in Specialized Communication: A Discourse Perspective*. Bern: Peter Lang, 251-275.

Ramsey, Violeta 1987. The Functional Distribution of Preposed and Postposed *if* and *when* Clauses in Written Narrative. In Tomlin, Russell (ed.) *Coherence and Grounding in Discourse*. Amsterdam: John Benjamins, 383-408.

Roth, Martha T. 1995. *Law Collections from Mesopotamia and Asia Minor.* Atlanta, GA: Scholars Press.

Sanmartín, Joaquín 1999. *Los códigos legales de tradición babilónica*. Barcelona: Trotta – Edicions de la Universitat de Barcelona.

Sasson, Jack M. 1995. King Hammurabi of Babylon. In Sasson, Jack M. (ed.) *Civilizations of the Ancient Near East II*. New York: Simon & Schuster MacMillan, 901-915.

Schiffrin, Deborah 1992. Conditionals as Topics in Discourse. *Linguistics* 30/1, 165-197.

Stalnaker, Robert C. 1968. A Theory of Conditionals. In Rescher, Nicholas (ed.) *Studies in Logical Theory*. Oxford: Blackwell, 98-112. [Reprinted in Harper, William / Stalnaker, Robert / Pearce, Glenn (eds) 1981. *Ifs: Conditionals, Belief, Decision, Chance and Time*. Dordrecht: D. Reidel, 41-56].

Sweetser, Eve 1990. *From Etymology to Pragmatics: Metaphorical and Cultural Aspects of Semantic Structure*. Cambridge: Cambridge University Press.

Trosborg, Anna 1995. Introduction. *Journal of Pragmatics* 23/1, 1-5.

Van der Auwera, Jan 1986. Conditionals and Speech Acts. In Traugott, Elizabeth / Ter Meulen, Alice / Reilly, Judy Snitzer / Ferguson, Charles (eds) *On Conditionals*. Cambridge: Cambridge University Press, 197-213.

Visconti, Jacqueline 2000. *I connettivi condizionali complessi in italiano e in inglese*. Turin: Edizioni dell'Orso.

SUSAN KERMAS

English Legal Discourse and the French Continuum

1. Introduction

No scholar would deny that English is receptive to foreign influence and that French – particularly Norman French – has had a huge impact on English legal discourse. What perhaps has not been discussed is the re-emergence of French influence on the language of law today. Though the various efforts to simplify legal language have emphasized the necessity to avoid foreign words and phrases (cf. Gotti 2005; Williams 2005) – especially Latin – words of Romance origin common to many European languages have made English a particularly suitable vehicle for intercultural communication within Europe and at the same time made the language more vulnerable to change.

What I argue in this chapter is that the unique language contact situation within the EU (European Union) has triggered another phase of French influence. My examination of English and French legal documents in the EUR-Lex archive[1] published between the 1990s and today will demonstrate not only that many words have been influenced by French but, more importantly, that efforts to harmonise legal language within the EU may also be creating a further rift between British and American legal discourse and subsequently, ordinary language.

1 It includes over 3.6 million documents starting from 1951 and is constantly updated. Among these the European treaties, the *Official Journal*, international agreements, legislation in force and Parliamentary questions. Available online at <http://eur-lex.europa.eu/en/index.htm>.

2. Aims and historical background

2.1. French influence on legal language

Historical surveys of the development of English lexis give plenty of evidence of French influence on English legal discourse and on the profound effect of the Norman Conquest on the language of law and administration. We know from scholarly research on the history of English that "for three centuries English ceased to be the official language of the land, surviving only as the speech of a largely dispossessed people" (Hughes 2000: 110) and that French radically changed legal discourse in the following centuries.[2] The fact that words such as *gemōt,* and *scīr* were replaced by *parliament* and *county* marks not only the presence of a loosely organized politico-administrative system prior to the Norman Conquest[3] but more importantly the beginning of a special register accessible only to legal practitioners (cf. Wagner 2003).

The new terms for trials and offences – *judge* (dēma), *judgment* (dōm), *justice* ((folc)riht), *advocate* (forespeca), *suit* (sacu/sp•c), *perjury* (aÞbryce, 'oath-breaking'), *bigamy* (twiewifing), *arson* (hūsbryne), *larceny* (īef), *gaol* (carcern/cweatern) and *innocent* (unsynning) – in Pollington's Anglo-Saxon dictionary (1996) certainly attest the radical change from Anglo-Saxon to Anglo-Norman and Serjeantson's (1968) long lists of French loanwords entering English from that period to the 20th century are likewise important because

---

2 In effect, it even ousted the Latin previously used in written records. By the end of the 13th century, French had become the language of the Court, and between 1260 and 1535 all court reports (the Year Books) were written entirely in French (cf. Crystal 2004). By 1310 it had also become the normal language for statutes. Many attempts were made to adopt English again but it was only in 1650 that the Puritans passed a law requiring that all case reports and books of law be in English.

3 The Laws of Ine, King of Wessex, promulgated between 688 and 695 (cf. Hughes 2000), had been handed down to Alfred (and re-elaborated sometime between 885 and 899).

they testify the continuation of its influence in ordinary language on the one hand and in the field of diplomacy on the other.

The inclusion of legal terms of later periods in general overviews of the development of English lexis such as Crystal (1988) and Stockwell/Minkova (2001) and in texts more specific to the language of law (Wagner 2003; Williams 2005) demonstrates that words of French origin continued to enter English long after it was officially abolished in 1731 – suffice it to mention the verb *to sanction* (authorize) in the 18th century, *secretariat, surveillance*, *concessionaire* and *directorate* in the 19th, *travaux preparatoires* and *appellation controlee* in the 20th and *lèse-humanity* in 2001. However, current scholarship dealing with later developments of legal language is more concerned with textual features than with lexis (Williams 2005). Today the use of French forms and loanwords is often object of debate of English legal discourse critics aiming at plain English (cf. Gotti 2005); yet it is likewise undeniable that forms such as *directorate general* and *acquis communautaire* are a fundamental part of European law. The aim of this chapter then is to throw light on the role of French in forging a new variety of English.

2.2. Diverging legal nomenclatures

Another important aspect of legal discourse for this research topic is semantic variance, for "serious difficulties arise in interpreting law across countries and languages, due to the system-bound nature of legal terminology" (Peruginelli 2008: 12). The link between the language of law and the history and culture of each country is so strong that it has caused words to gain and lose connotations within different jurisdictions. Furthermore, these divergences can sometimes lead to confusion in general language.

As an illustration of semantic diversity already present in English, a lexicographic search of the terms *larceny* and *felony* demonstrated that the numerous competing meanings between the two in ordinary language are attributable to recent changes within the British and American jurisdictions. In effect, the term *larceny* was used in a parallel manner for five centuries in the two legal systems as indeed the distinction originally made between *grand* and *petty larceny* (the former to theft of personal property having a value above a legally specified amount, the latter to theft of a lower value) (OED).[4] The introduction of a distinction between *theft* proper ('felony') and *petit theft* ('larceny') in 18th-century America in contrast with the Law of England which considered both crimes to be felony (Giles 1744) certainly demonstrates that legal terms were already diverging in the two jurisdictions before the term *theft* replaced *larceny* in the British legal system in 1967.

The difficulty of harmonizing legal terminology within the EU resulting from the different conceptual meanings of words within the various legal systems at national levels is a subject of constant debate among experts drafting legal documents (European Communities 2003) and has been broached by scholars such as Catenaccio (2008) in their work on European legal discourse. My hypothesis that the use of English in Europe is diverging from British usage was confirmed by a search of the EUR-Lex database. While an initial search generated over a thousand instances of *theft* as opposed to one (in an American context) for *larceny*[5] and seemed at first sight to indicate that the language of law in Europe is opting for British nomenclature rather than American in the field of crime at least, a similar search of other related terms shows that there is an element of conflict with British legal usage. In the case of *felony* and *misdemeanour* – terms replaced by *indictable* and *non-indictable* offences in British law in 1967[6] – the number of instances certainly demonstrates that the same replacement has not occurred in European law. While there were 31 of *misdemeanour* and six of *felony* there were only nine of *indictable* and none of *non-indictable*.

---

4 According to Bouvier (1843) this distinction was only made in some states.

5 It occurs in a statistical report on the cost of inequity in education in the US sent to the European Parliament in 2006.

6 *Misdemeanour* is another source of confusion. Though in the language of law it is a non-indictable charge in general language it frequently collocates with words regarding indictable offences in both British and American English.

2.3. Method

With these premises then the thrust of my search will be to determine the influence of French on English legal discourse on the one hand and its role in furthering a rift with the language of law and ordinary language in Britain and America on the other. My hypothesis that French – more than any other Romance language – is influencing English is determined by its long-standing role as the language of diplomacy and its representativeness in working commissions within the EU.

The actual choice of lexemes was made following a search of the English version of the *Official Journal* of the EU on a variety of issues, aimed at finding French lexemes and words with new connotations. In order to countercheck my suppositions, I examined both the English and the French versions of the relative legal documents in the EUR-Lex archive and did a lexicographical search in the two languages. This was necessarily followed by a search of legislation in the United Kingdom (<http://www.hmso.gov.uk/acts.htm>) and France (<http://www.legifrance.gouv.fr>) not only because some terms were irretrievable in the dictionaries but also to see the relationship with national forms of legalese. As one of the ultimate aims was to determine any semantic deviations resulting from the culture/system-bound nature of legal terminology this particular part of the search was also useful for determining any incongruence with the European meaning of the terms analyzed.

A key word search of Webcorp (<http:///www.webcorp.org.uk>) was particularly useful, since it allowed me to search the web as a corpus and to shed light on the divergences between technical legal discourse and general usage. On the one hand I could check the presence of terms found in EU legislation in separate corpora of news discourse in British and American English, one consisting of five British broadsheet newspapers, the other of four American newspapers. On the other it gave me the possibility to compare usage in two separate corpora of British and American academic discourse. It was also useful for checking the use of the French equivalents in a broad search of French websites.

This chapter will first of all examine the presence of French lexis and words with French cognates which regularly turn up in European legal documents. It will then focus on neologisms and the inevitable creation of new false friends in less technical words and finally on resistance to English influence.

3. The Europeanization of English legal discourse

What Sweet (2003: 216) intends by Europeanization of law is "the impact of market integration (i.e. cross-border economic exchange) and supranational governance (i.e. EU rules, procedures, actors, and organizations) on processes and outcomes at the national level". Our concern here is the impact of these factors on legal discourse and the dominant role of French in this Europeanization process.

3.1. French influence in EU legislation

My hypothesis that French is regaining its hold on English is partly supported in the *Guide of the European Parliament, the Council and the Commission* written for people involved in the drafting of legislation within Community institutions (European Communities: 2003). Though it has few specific guidelines regarding the choice of lexis – except for the indication that words should be clear and consistent – it nonetheless anticipates the influence of French. The signatories of this document represent a variety of nationalities but their actual titles (*Jurisconsults* for the Legal Services of the Parliament and Council and *Director-General* for the Legal Service of the Commission) are of obvious French origin. The French in the Commission's Legal Revisers' Group's email address (<juristes-reviseurs@cec.eu.int>) is a further indication that French is influential, as indeed the corrigendum "version revisée par les juristes reviseurs" in a 2008 English document.[7]

Certainly, the use of the term *jurisconsult* is unique to EU law and was first introduced in the original Treaty of Paris of 1951 establishing the institutions of what was to become the European Union.[8] Although the term was already in use in British English in 1605 (OED), it has become far less popular than its equivalent *jurist*. Indeed, while *jurist* is used in the general newspaper sections of Webcorp (154 in the British, 33 in the American), there are no concordances for *jurisconsult* in the British section and only seven in the American and in both the British and American academic sections the occurrences are exclusive to historical and foreign contexts. In EU law on the other hand both terms have continued to be used as testified by the 152 instances of *jurisconsult(s)* from 1951-2008 and 58 of *jurist(s)* from 1981-2009. The strong preference for the more specific term *legal adviser* (3,433 instances between 1954 and 2009) is justifiable since the other two have accumulated meanings from 'expert in civil and international law' to 'law student' in British English and 'lawyer' in the case of *jurist* in American English.

An initial thematic search for documents regarding the recognition of diplomas and vocational requisites in the EUR-Lex database enabled me to identify French items which might be of interest from a translational point of view due to the different educational systems and the objective difficulty in finding exact equivalent terms. This was then followed by a quantitative search of the entire EUR-Lex database in order to ascertain their actual diffusion. In effect, what emerged was that all the French words identified were encountered in the opinions of advocates general relating to Court Case C-285/01 published in the European Court reports of 2003 and in draft documents and written questions to the

7 These French words were in the European Commission's *Proposal for a Directive of the European Parliament and of the Council amending Directive 1999/62/EC* on the charging of heavy goods vehicles for the use of certain infrastructures of 8/7/08.

8 It was the Treaty establishing the European Coal and Steel Community – Title II – The institutions of the Community – Chapter 4 – The Court of Justice – Article 32b dated 18/4/1951.

commission. More importantly, with exception of the word *concours* with no precise English equivalent,[9] the use of the French terms was in most cases unnecessary. Between 1996 and today, fifteen instances of *stagiaire* were identified in cases where *trainee lawyer* or *trainee nurse* could easily have been adopted. The two cases of *agent stagiaire* in the Court Report could have been rendered as *trainee agent*,[10] and the three instances of *domiciliataire* regarding service on behalf of companies could have been rendered as *domiciliary* service. Even though a Webcorp search demonstrates that most of these 'unnecessary' terms are having little effect on general language, this is not the case for *stagiaire* which generated 31 instances in British English and an exiguous number in American if we bear in mind that four of the eight instances were followed by 'or trainee' and one was in a European context.

Another search of EUR-Lex was interesting for two reasons. On the one hand the search for *appellation d'origine controlee* revealed the presence of a new French form (*appellation of origin*) present in EU law since the 1970s, on the other a parallel search in Webcorp revealed that this new form had in no way influenced general language in Britain. Indeed, while both forms are of the same frequency in EU law, with 47 instances of *appellation controlee* and 58 of *appellation of origin* only the former is used in general English. The only plausible explanation of the reticence to accept the 'European' anglicized adaptation of the term emerged from a qualitative search of documents containing both terms. Indeed, what transpired was that a more precise term *registered designation of origin* appeared in the 1970s, followed by *protected designation of origin* in the 1990s. The overwhelming use of the term – 400 instances

9 In the Court Report there is a definition: "that is to say a selection procedure in the form of a competition" (*European Court Reports 2003*, p.1-08219) and in questions to the commission we find possible equivalents including *public examination, competitive examination* and *competition.*

10 It is almost as if jurists feared that the word *trainee lawyer* may not be understood. In the Opinion of the Advocate General of 11/5/06 we even find the French translation *avocat stagiaire*, as if to explain what is meant by 'trainee lawyer'. There are indeed only eight occurrences of 'trainee lawyer' in the corpus.

since its first appearance in 1996 – may have been determined by the inadequacy of the truncated form *appellation of origin* in view of the specificity of the protective measures adopted.[11] A Webcorp search of British news discourse demonstrates that the newly coined *protected designation of origin* has become as popular as the older French form, generating 27 instances and 28 of *appellation controlee.*

Certainly, the results of my search of words in this section prove that French influence on English legal discourse is fairly strong in draft documents and questions to the commission written by the non-expert and that its influence on general language is different in the two main varieties of English. The fact that a search of the American section generated 13 concordances of the older French form *appellation controlee*, 14 of *appellation of origin* and 13 of the new term as opposed to an exiguous number of *stagiaire* can only be determined by the rate of interest in the topics. What is also important is that in their quest for precision and avoidance of foreignisms in the final documents European legal drafters and revisers are creating a new variety of legalese. The fact that none of the new 'European' English words treated in this section have entered either the *Oxford Dictionary of Law* (Martin/Law 2006) or the OED certainly points to the difficult process of updating dictionaries; however, it may also indicate that the emergence of a new European standard has not yet been perceived by lexicographers.

3.2. The burgeoning of terms with French cognates

The terms that seem to be gaining ground in European legislation are those that have cognates in French, words deriving from the same ancestral language (Latin) and whose meanings have developed in the same way. These are frequently specialized terms and are also encountered in other languages thanks to the dominance of this

11 Since the term has to specify that a product was produced in the region indicated in its name, using vines or foodstuffs and production methods which satisfy the regulating body, the loss of 'controlee' had made *appellation of origin* inadequate.

language as a cultural and scientific medium until the 17th century. Words such as *infraction, delict, contravention, violation* and *crime* have kept the same meanings in English and French and are of frequent usage in European legal discourse. On the other hand, words such as *larceny, felony* and *misdemeanour* (which are disappearing from British English legal terminology) have no corresponding French cognates today in spite of their Anglo-Norman origin and are hardly present in the EU law. In corroboration of my hypothesis, a EUR-Lex search produced 70 instances of *infraction,* 67 of *delict,* 1,036 of *contravention,* 2,813 of *violation* and 2,750 of *crime* as opposed to one instance of *larceny* in a working document on crime in the United States, six of *felony* and a slightly more significant 35 of *misdemeanour.*

This tendency to adopt words of a common etymon is even more important when there is a choice of words. At first sight, the presence of the near synonyms *obligatory, compulsory* and *mandatory* in European legal discourse simply reflects British usage, at least from a quantitative point of view (2,284 instances of *obligatory,* 5,730 of *mandatory* and 7,325 for *compulsory*). However, the fact that *obligatory* collocates with words normally requiring *compulsory* in both British and American English may be determined by the lack of corresponding cognates in French as indeed in other European languages.[12] In effect, of the three words available in English only *obligatory* has a corresponding cognate in French so it is only natural that a EUR-Lex search should generate instances of obligatory number plates for bicycles, obligatory collection of information on users by Microsoft.NET, obligatory BSE tests on cattle, and obligatory insurance which would normally collocate with *compulsory* in British and American English.

Interestingly, while a search of the British and American newspaper sections of Webcorp confirms the propensity to use *compulsory* and *mandatory* in general language, what also emerged was that *obligatory* is used more frequently in pleasantly compelling contexts

12 Thanks to the possibility of viewing texts in bilingual versions it was possible to note that *compulsory* was indeed translated with cognate forms of *obligatory* in Spanish, Danish, Latvian, Maltese, Portuguese and Romanian.

than in compulsory circumstances. *Obligatory* frequently collocates with *section* and *scenes* in both varieties and there are instances of *obligatory seasonal visits / open-top bus tours / pictures with the Acropolis* in British contexts and *obligatory appearance before cameras and reporters / exercises and exercisers / moments in all buddy movies* in the US, in contexts totally extraneous to law. With exception of a few references to European *obligatory warning triangles* and *health insurance* there were no instances of the *obligatory number plates for bicycles / insurance for cyclists / information to be displayed on egg packs* in the newspaper section of Webcorp. The only significant instances of *obligatory* in the sense of 'legally binding' were found in the academic section relating to international educational courses, the law and an Indian article on biotechnology.

4. Effects of harmonization on European legal discourse

One of the main aims of EU commissions and expert groups working on documents is the harmonization of legal language, at least from a conceptual point of view. Though there is no specific group working on terminology, as in Italy's German-speaking province[13] or in the Alpine Convention,[14] harmonized terminology is undoubtedly the ultimate result of the interaction of different legal cultures. This section focuses therefore on neologisms resulting from this need to harmonize terminology on the one hand and the new French/English

13 The Bolzano "Terminology Commission is in charge of determining and regularly updating the legal and administrative terminology used by the public bodies and institutions in the German language" (Chiocchetti/Voltmer 2008: 46) and validates equivalences between the Italian and German terms. For further information about problem areas, cf. Ralli/Stanizzi (2008).

14 This project aims at harmonizing terminology in the four languages of the Convention: French, German, Italian and Slovene (cf. Chiocchetti/Voltmer 2008) and has produced a term bank available at <http://www.eurac.edu/lexalp> (cf. Lanzoni 2008; Sérasset 2008).

false friends inadvertently resulting from the intensification of language contact within the European jurisdiction on the other.[15]

4.1. New forms of legalese

The quest for transparency in European legislation has given birth to new redundant forms, in spite of the worldwide tendency to avoid superfluous terms. While pleonasms such as *give and grant*, *had and received, goods and chattels, fit and proper, pardon and forgive* (Crystal 2004: 153) took hold in English at a time when English, French and Latin were competing for attention, today the emphasis on precision may be creating new forms of redundancy. A search for the term *burglary* in the European legislation corpus produced 39 hits, chiefly referring to alarm systems and insurance, but also the neologism *domestic burglary* – a new example of redundancy. This form occurs in a *Report on Social Inclusion* (2001) and in two *Communications* from the Commission to the Council and the European Parliament (2004). As a countercheck for general usage, I then carried out two searches of WebCorp: the British broadsheet section generated 105 instances, while the American newspaper section yielded none. In other words, the new term has already entered general usage in British English but not in its American counterpart.

The corresponding term *cambriolage domestique* in the French version of the European legislative texts is likewise redundant, as *cambriolage* specifically refers to household theft just as burglary does in general English. To corroborate this, a search of the general French section of Webcorp yielded no instances of *cambriolage domestique* and out of 213 instances of *cambriolage* only two referred to anything but housebreaking.[16] A similar search for *burglary* in the British section of Webcorp confirmed that both the French and the English words had the same conceptual meaning in general usage.

---

15 See, for instance, Garzone's (2003) account of the need to harmonize arbitration rules for the settlement of international commercial disputes.

16 The earlier example referred to a burglary at the Cypriot embassy in Paris (*Le Figaro,* 11/8/09) the other to a London jewellery (*Libération.fr*, 2/8/1995).

A search for *domestic burglary* in British lexicographical sources failed to uncover the source of this term. The only indication that it is present in British legal lexis emerged from a search of the Public General Acts of the Westminster Parliament, where the *Powers of Criminal Courts (Sentencing) Act* of 2000 defines this crime as "a burglary committed in respect of a building or part of a building which is a dwelling".[17] However, the actual need for a more precise term emerges from the English lexicographic search, which shows that the British Theft Act 1968 applies the term *burglary* alone both to housebreaking and to entering 'a building, ship or inhabited vehicle' (Martin/Law 2006), in other words to any property – private or commercial.

Until the introduction of the term *domestic burglary,* the distinction between household and business premises normally made in other European jurisdictions was not apparent in English statutory law. The conceptual difference between *housebreaking* originally referring to daytime and *burglary* limited to night time theft was unique to English common law and alien to other European jurisdictions.[18] Because of the pressure to harmonize European legal terminology from a conceptual point of view, English needed a new technical term to meet that goal, especially in view of the different meanings that *burglary* had already accumulated in English legalese. A strong move towards a common European legal basis for crime prevention began in the 1990s and many commissions have been set up to gain this goal.[19] We find the term *domestic burglary* in the *European Sourcebook of Crime and Criminal Justice Statistics* (2000)[20] drafted by a group of experts representing thirteen countries. The fact that the commission was chaired by a French speaker no doubt influenced the choice of term and the need to conform to the French concept of *cambriolage,* burglary in domestic premises. The

---

17 The full text is available online at <http://www.hmso.gov.uk/acts.htm>.

18 Technical legal terms often have different conceptual values in common and civil law systems (cf. Gotti 2008; Salmi-Tolonen 2008; Zimmermann 2008).

19 The Amsterdam Treaty, dealing primarily with organized crime, has been in force since May 1999.

20 Available online at <http://www.europeansourcebook.org/key_findings.pdf>.

reason why *domestic* was added to both the French and English terms was probably dictated by the need to follow the EU guidelines for drafting documents which states the necessity to avoid ambiguity with ordinary language and terms used differently within any of the national legal systems (European Communities 2003: 17, 21).[21]

Another interesting term is *volume crime*, first used in reference to 'non-organized crime' in a Communication from the Commission to the Council and the European Parliament on crime prevention in the European Union (12.3.04). This type of crime includes domestic burglary, theft from vehicles, common assault, street robbery and so on, which as stated in the document "can best be defined as volume crime because [... it] comprises all ranges of crime, which are committed frequently and where victims are easily identifiable" (COM(2004)165 final). There is no entry either in Martin and Law (2006) or in the OED. The relative French term *criminalité de masse* was irretrievable in French legislation[22] while in English it first appeared a year later, in the Serious Organised Crime and Police Act 2005 which specifies that *volume crime* applies to vehicle crime, robbery and domestic burglary.

A corpus search of Webcorp certainly demonstrates then that the use of this neologism is limited to Europe since it generated 65 concordances in the British newspaper section and only one in the parallel American section. The fact that both *volume crime* and the equivalent French term made their first appearance in European law means that a lexical gap was primarily perceived at a European level. The fact that both French and English continue to use the near synonym *petty crime* and *petite criminalité* in reference to drug-related offences and minor theft means on the one hand that in some cases the two languages have to adapt in a parallel manner, on the other the contact between the two languages is extremely strong. The actual choice of term *volume* rather than *mass* in English is no doubt

21 Indeed, both the OED and the ninth edition of the French Academy's official dictionary (Académie française 2000) indicate that the words can refer to theft in any building.

22 Available online at <http://www.legifrance.gouv.fr>.

connected with possible ambiguity stemming from its association with *mass killings* and *mass murder*.

4.2. New false friends stemming from language contact

If language contact and the harmonization process in the EU are creating a new variety of English (and French) legal terminology, what is also extremely salient is the impact on the general lexis of legal texts. Such words are less noticeable than the more specialized terms and can easily escape the notice of legal experts of different nationalities working side by side in commissions. Words of French origin have sometimes influenced meaning in their English cognate equivalents thanks to language contact situations.

To check for possible interferences between French and English lexis, a search was made for words that according to the guidelines for writers of English at the European Commission (Directorate General for Translation) might be used erroneously in such a multilingual situation as EU law. A quick title search for *capacity* demonstrated that the meaning 'ability, capacity' is so widespread in English that continuing was pointless. On the other hand, the results of my search demonstrate that since the end of the 1990s most words have been used correctly: *eventual* appears to be used in the proper sense of 'at the end of a process or period of time' rather than in the French sense of 'possible'; *candidate* has the correct British and American sense of 'applicant for a job or exam' and is not used in place of 'applicant country' for European membership; likewise, *opportunity* has not been influenced by the French meaning of 'advisability'. The only instances of misuse date back to the early 1990s and are often encountered in unrevised questions to the commission written by members of the general public.[23]

On the other hand, *dispose of* tends to extend its usage to the French meaning of *disposer de* ('to have, to hold'). For example,

23 For instance, in a Written Question about the *opportunity* to freeze the accounts of Haitian dictator Raoul Cedras published in the *Official Journal C320*, 26/11/1993.

"Member States do not *dispose of* sufficient funds the finance data access [... and] the winning tenderer did not *dispose of* the personnel offered", in a Working Document regarding the European Earth observation program (20.5.09). There are also instances of British usage with the meaning 'to get rid of' and 'to deal with', as in "the competent authority of the Port Member State may confiscate and *dispose of* the fish in accordance with national rules" in a Proposal for a Council Regulation amending Council Regulation No. 1386/2007 (16.4.09). This shows that *dispose of* has gained another meaning and become a potential source of confusion both in legal and general usage.

A term not mentioned in the guidelines (Directorate-General for Translation) that appears to be influenced by French is the word *competent.* In general English (British and American) it is normally used in the sense of 'efficient' or 'knowledgeable'. However, a search of European legislation gives 26,109 instances of *competent* collocating with *authorities, administrative bodies, courts, institutions, government departments* and *Member States*, in the sense of 'appropriate' or 'specific'. In WebCorp there are instances of *competent teachers, competent supervisors, workers* and so on and only one instance of 'competent authority' (*The Times*, 26.12.08). This is further proof of the subtle influence of French on English, though here the phenomenon is restricted to European legal usage.

4.3. Resistance to English influence within the EU

In the multilingual context of European legislation, mutual influences can possibly be unidirectional. Indeed, a search of the term *sanction* in European legislation shows that French is resistant to English in legal contexts. The verb originally meant 'ratify', 'authorize' and 'enforce a law'; however, since the mid-20th century it has become a source of confusion in both varieties of English due to the emergence of a new extended meaning ('impose sanctions' and 'penalize'). This appeared in the 1950s in English (though not sanctioned by the OED, which says it is of 'dubious acceptability'), while a search of British and American newspapers indicates that both the new meaning and earlier usage are current today.[24] A search of European legislation showed that while the noun *sanction* and its cognate French form have the unequivocal meaning of 'severe measure', the verb *sanctioned* has its French cognate restricted to the sense of 'impose sanctions'. To 'confirm by enactment' is rendered as *consacrer* in French, while its equivalent term meaning 'penalize' is *condamner* (in negative sentences also *impuni*). The cognate of *indûment sanctionnées* was used only in its sense of 'to enforce a law by attaching a penalty to transgressors', as in the phrase "to ensure that genuine establishments and transactions are not unduly sanctioned" (10.12.07). Interestingly, though a search of the French newspaper section of Webcorp demonstrates that in general usage the new meaning of 'to penalize' is paramount, it was only in 2001 that it was first included in French dictionaries (Robert). According to the *Dictionnaire de l'Académie française* (1935) – the latest edition for words with an initial 's' – and French dictionaries of the 1990s (cf. Robert 1992) the only approved meanings are indeed 'ratify', 'confirm' and 'approve'.

It would appear then that the new meaning is avoided in official French European documents, whereas it is used in English legal documentation in spite of lexicographers' reticence to accept a new form (cf. OED). Both in general English and French, on the other hand, the new form is extremely popular. Arguably the new meaning was first adopted as a result of the frequent occurrence of the plural form of the noun, which points to 'coercive measures', usually adopted to enforce a violated law or treaty in an international context – hence its use in both the French and English media.[25] There are other instances of English words, such as *procurement* and *rent*, which have not influenced French in spite of their common etymon. However, the reasons for the limited use of foreignisms, in French are beyond the scope of this chapter.

---

24 There is also evidence that usage evolved more or less simultaneously in the two varieties of English, as the American news discourse section of Webcorp also generated instances of news articles of the beginning of the 20th century where the meaning is restricted to 'approve/authorize'.

25 Partington (1998) noted the same diversity between meaning as sanctioned by dictionaries and real usage in Italian.

5. Conclusions

In conclusion, we can say that English legal jargon is particularly complex because of its use as a vehicular language and the strict link to social practices within various jurisdictions worldwide. In particular there seem to be three main trends emerging in European legal discourse subsequent to increasing consultations between legal experts from various European Union areas intent on furthering the harmonization process. Though most terms remain untouched in European law (also in view of the necessity to cooperate with countries outside its jurisdiction), there is an undeniable new wave of French loanwords; a substitution of nomenclature previously used in English-speaking jurisdictions in cases of ambiguity and lack of correspondence with Romance terminology; and the adoption of previously unknown extended French meanings in English cognate words. All three tendencies are unique to European jurisprudence and are therefore causing a rift between British and American legal nomenclature and creating, as a consequence, a further source of ambiguity in international contexts.

These trends are the product of increased cross-language contact within the European Union and are affecting general language too. The fact that English is used as a lingua franca worldwide makes it extremely susceptible to change and partly explains why it has readily adapted to foreign influence. My hypothesis that the influence is from French rather than any other Romance language is corroborated by the overt presence of non-adapted French loanwords and the emergence of parallel technical neologisms (e.g. *domestic burglary* and *volume crime*) in both English and French, resulting from the same need to meet the required conceptual clarity aimed at in European legal discourse. In the case of less technical terms (e.g. *competent* and *dispose of*), its influence may also be reinforced by the presence of similar cognates in other Romance languages. European law is after all a unique system operating in tandem with the laws of each of its 27 member states and reciprocal influences are inevitable.

References

Académie française 1935. *Dictionnaire de l'Académie francaise.* Paris: Fayard. Available at <http://atilf.atilf.fr/academie.htm>.

Académie française 2000. *Dictionnaire de l'Académie francaise.* Paris: Fayard. Available at <http://atilf.atilf.fr/academie9.htm>.

Bouvier, John 1843. *A Law Dictionary.* Philadelphia: Johnson [Reprinted 2004. Clark, NJ: The Lawbook Exchange].

Catenaccio, Paola 2008. Implementing Council Directive 1993/13/EEU on Unfair Terms in Consumer Contracts in Great Britain: A Case for Intra-linguistic Translation? Bhatia, Vijay K. / Candlin, Christopher N. / Evangelisti Allori, Paola (eds) *Language, Culture and the Law – The Formulation of Legal Concepts across Systems and Cultures.* Bern: Peter Lang, 259-280.

Chiocchetti, Elena / Voltmer, Leonhard 2008. LexALP – Harmonising Alpine Terminology. In Chiocchetti, Elena / Voltmer, Leonhard (eds) *Harmonising Legal Terminology.* Bolzano: EURAC, 45-55.

Crystal, David 1988. *The English Language.* London: Penguin.

Crystal, David 2004. *The Stories of English.* London: Penguin.

Directorate-General for Translation. *How to Write Clearly.* Luxembourg: European Commission's Translation Service. Retrieved from <http://ec.europa.eu/translation/writing/clear_writing/fight_the_fog_en.pdf> on 30 November 2009.

European Communities 2003. *Joint Practical Guide of the European Parliament, the Council and the Commission for Persons Involved in the Drafting of Legislation with the Community Institutions.* Luxembourg: Office for Official Publications of the European Communities.

Garzone, Giuliana 2003. Arbitration Rules across Legal Cultures: An Intercultural Approach. In Bhatia, Vijay / Candlin, Christopher / Gotti, Maurizio (eds) *Legal Discourse in Multilingual and Multicultural Contexts. Arbitration Texts in Europe.* Bern: Peter Lang, 177-220.

Giles, Jacob 2004 [1744]. *A New Law Dictionary.* Clark, NJ: The Lawbook Exchange.

Gotti, Maurizio 2005. *Investigating Specialized Discourse.* Bern: Peter Lang.

Gotti, Maurizio 2008. The Formulation of Legal Concepts in Arbitration Normative Texts. In Bhatia, Vijay K. / Candlin, Christopher N. / Evangelisti Allori, Paola (eds) *Language, Culture and the Law. The Formulation of Legal Concepts across Systems and Cultures.* Bern: Peter Lang, 23-45.

Hughes, Geoffrey 2000. *A History of English Words.* Oxford: Blackwell.

Lanzoni, Lisa 2008. Transnational Cooperation Activities through the Experience of the LexALP Project. In Chiocchetti, Elena / Voltmer, Leonhard (eds) *Harmonising Legal Terminology.* Bolzano: EURAC, 63-67.

Martin, Elizabeth / Law, Jonathan (eds) 2006 [1983]. *Oxford Dictionary of Law.* Oxford: Oxford University Press.

OED 1989-2009. *The Oxford English Dictionary Online.* Oxford: Oxford University Press. Accessed at <http://www.oed.com> on 5th October 2009.

Partington, Alan 1998. *Patterns and Meanings. Using Corpora for English Language Research and Teaching.* Amsterdam: John Benjamins.

Peruginelli, Ginevra 2008. Multilingual Legal Information Access: An Overview. In Chiocchetti, Elena / Voltmer, Leonhard (eds) *Harmonising Legal Terminology.* Bolzano: EURAC, 11-33.

Pollington, Stephen 1996. *Wordcraft.* Norfolk: Anglo-Saxon Books.

Ralli, Natascia / Stanizzi, Isabella 2008. Il dietro le quinte della normazione. In Chiocchetti, Elena / Voltmer, Leonhard (eds) *Normazione, armonizzazione e pianificazione linguistica.* Bolzano: LexALP, 61-74.

Robert, Paul 1992. *Dictionnaire alphabétique et analogique.* Paris: Le Robert.

Robert, Paul 2001. *Le Grand Robert de la Langue Française.* Paris: Le Robert.

Salmi-Tolonen, Tarja 2008. Negotiated Meaning and International Commercial Law. In Bhatia, Vijay K. / Candlin, Christopher N. / Evangelisti Allori, Paola (eds) *Language, Culture and the Law.*

The Formulation of Legal Concepts across Systems and Cultures. Bern: Peter Lang, 117-139.

Sérasset, Gilles 2008. La plate-forme 'jibiki' dans le projet LexALP. In Chiocchetti, Elena / Voltmer, Leonhard (eds) *Normazione, armonizzazione e pianificazione linguistica*. Bolzano: LexALP, 31-47.

Serjeantson, Mary S. 1968. *A History of Foreign Words in English*. London: Routledge / Kegan Paul.

Stockwell, Robert / Minkova, Donka 2001. *English Words – History and Structure*. Cambridge: Cambridge University Press.

Sweet, Alec Stone 2003. Integration and Europeanization of Law. In Craig, Paul / Rawlings, Richard (eds) *Law and Administration in Europe. Essays in Honour of Carol Harlow*. Oxford: Oxford University Press, 197-223.

Wagner, Anne 2003. Origins and Use of English Legal Terms through History. *LSP and Professional Communication* 3/2, 93-105.

Williams, Christopher 2005. *Tradition and Change in Legal English*. Bern: Peter Lang.

Zimmermann, Reinhard 2002. *Comparative Foundations of a European Law of Set-Off and Prescription*. Cambridge: Cambridge University Press.

STANISŁAW GOŹDŹ-ROSZKOWSKI

Responsibility and *Welfare*: Keywords and Semantic Categories in Legal Academic Journals

1. Introduction

One of the indisputable benefits of corpus-based analysis is that it allows researchers to objectively identify widespread patterns of naturally occurring language, which may be otherwise overlooked. Corpus linguists have access to a range of procedures that can be implemented in the analysis of text e.g. concordances, collocations, frequency lists, dispersion plots.

One statistical procedure that has proved to be popular involves the creation of keyword lists. The concept of a *keyword* is by no means new. In fact, it has two meanings. The original one is associated with a lexical item which is considered *key* because of its cultural, historical or social importance (see, for instance, Williams 1985). However, in present-day corpus linguistics, a keyword is understood as a statistically significant word form. Keywords have become popularized thanks to the computer software WordSmith Tools, devised by Mike Scott (2008). Keyword analysis is still a relatively new analytical tool although this seems to be changing. Recently, there have been a number of studies devoted to discourse analysis in which keyword analysis is proving to be extremely useful (see, for instance, Tribble 2000; Johnson *et al.* 2003; Baker 2004; Xiao/McEnery 2005; Culpeper 2009).[1] Generally, it is argued that

1 A comprehensive bibliography on various aspects of keyword analysis can be found at <http://www/lexically.net/publications/publications.htm>.

keyword analysis can reveal not only a great deal about the subject matter, the 'aboutness' of a particular text genre, but it can also help specify the salient features which are functionally related to that genre.

However, there are relatively few studies which use this analytical tool to examine disciplinary genres – one exception is Cacchiani (forth.), which treats keywords as cues to knowledge construction in the genre of research articles. This chapter aims to provide both quantitative evidence and qualitative analysis of salient keywords identified in legal journal articles in an attempt to characterize this genre in terms of its prevalent lexical patterns.

2. Data and methodology

In the help function of WordSmith Tools 5.0, Scott (2008) refers to keywords as "those words whose frequency is unusually high in comparison with some norm". Extracting keywords involves comparing two wordlists. One wordlist is based on the words from a particular genre, the other wordlist is a larger reference list.[2] Roughly, keyword analysis consists of two major steps. The first is largely automated and is performed by a computer programme. To that effect, the KeyWords facility of WordSmith Tools 5.0 was used in the present study. The other step is carried out by the researcher and it basically consists of examining the words generated by the programme and determining their discoursal functions in their contexts. The entire process should not be considered in any way as 'mechanical'. A lot depends on the type of data that the researcher selects and what parameters he or she adopts for the subsequent analysis. Culpeper (2009: 34-35) has a useful discussion of what decisions need to be made when performing a keyword analysis: he points out that in any keyword analysis, "the choice of data for comparison (the reference

2 See McEnery *et al.* (2006: 308-312) for a detailed description of the procedure.

corpus) is an issue". In short, the keyword results are bound to be affected by the reference corpus (and its subsets). In the present analysis, I decided against comparing my legal data with a large multi-genre corpus, such as the BNC (British National Corpus) or COCA (Corpus of Contemporary American English). In my view, comparing a range of specialized genres from the same domain against a general reference corpus would inevitably lead to obtaining findings which may be highly homogenous and probably valid for legal language in general but would not help identify features unique to a particular genre.

Since I am interested in studying variation within the legal register, the reference corpus was designed using text files from all legal genres minus the genre under examination. Thus, for instance, my keyword analysis compares a smaller wordlist based on all text files from the category of legal academic genres with a reference wordlist consisting of all the other genres *excluding* legal academic articles. As a result, one should obtain findings which could be interpreted as representative or indicative of the genre in question but *relative to* other legal genres. Table 1 provides the composition of the legal corpus used in this study. The keyword analysis documented in this chapter was carried out on an almost 600,000 word corpus of journal articles selected randomly from online resources at different US law schools. The journal article wordlist was compared against a larger reference wordlist created using six other legal genres grouped in a corpus of over 5.3 million words.

	Number of tokens (running words)
Academic articles	583,901
Reference corpus	5,308,424
- bills	1,369,344
- opinions	1,264,564
- contracts	1,182,616
- briefs	769,154
- professional articles	202,668
- textbooks	520,078
Total	5,892,325

Table 1. Composition of the legal corpus.

There are other parameters available in WordSmith Tools that prompt the analyst to make further important decisions before approaching the computer-generated output. One such parameter concerns the so-called minimum 'frequency cut-off point', which defines the minimum number of times a word must appear in a dataset to be considered as 'key'. The frequency cut-off point is a useful parameter which can be adopted to avoid obtaining too much data and it can also minimize the occurrence of highly local or idiosyncratic keywords. The minimum frequency cut-off point should be set bearing in mind the size of one's data. In this analysis, it was set at 25.

Another parameter which can be used involves applying tests for statistical significance. Such tests are intended to measure the significance of the unusualness of a keyword and enable the researcher to assess the strength of the differences in frequency of the word from what one might expect on the basis of the reference corpus. The log likelihood test was selected for this analysis. The analysis was repeated with the chi-square test but almost identical results were obtained, with only some minor differences in the ranking of keywords. The probability value was set at 0.000001 (1 in a million) since my major concern was that of selectivity. As Culpeper (2009: 36) stresses, "manipulating the *p* value is a useful way of controlling the quantity of keywords derived, and thus the number of keywords a researcher must interpret". Also, it is desirable to provide raw frequencies (as shown in the Appendix) of particular items in keyword lists, because this may be yet another factor helpful in reducing the risk of identifying words which appear locally.

Finally, it is advisable to consider *dispersion*. WordSmith Tools enable users to generate a dispersion plot for a given item. As Scott (2008) explains in the help function: "a dispersion value is the degree to which a set of values are uniformly spread". In the present analysis, this function helps to determine how the occurrences of a particular word are distributed across the dataset. By looking at the plot, it is possible to find out in how many different texts the word has been found and whether it tends to concentrate heavily, for example, at the beginning of a text or at its end, or perhaps in the middle. In the example below (Figure 1), the original keyword list for academic journals identified *Alaska* as the seventh keyword. This item had a raw frequency of 626 hits and keyness calculated at 1436.47. It is in fact found in only eight texts and tends to concentrate heavily in only four different documents. The dispersion value provides some mathematical support for this: plot dispersion ranges from 0 to 1, with 0.9 indicative of highly uniform dispersion and 0 or 0.1 of very irregular distribution. In addition, a further restriction was adopted whereby only words which are found in at least ten different texts are considered. As a result, *Alaska* was eventually removed from the list of keywords.

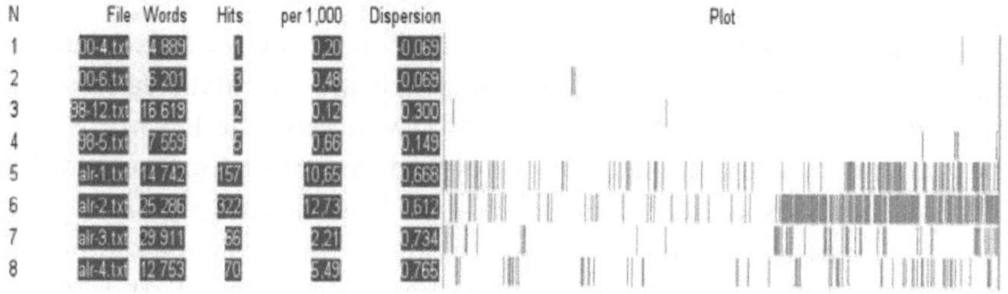

Figure 1. Dispersion plot of the candidate keyword *Alaska.*

Another example is that of the word *securitization.* It appeared as the ninth keyword in the original keyword list in academic journals, with keyness calculated at 1400.72. Its raw frequency is 310 hits in the academic texts, while occurred only once in the reference corpus. However, its distribution turned out to be restricted to only one text! Thus, the word *securitization* was not included in the final version of the keyword list. The scope of this analysis was further limited to one hundred keywords grouped in order of keyness (cf. Appendix).

3. Towards a categorization of keywords in texts

Scott (2000) maintains that there are essentially three types of keywords: proper words, keywords related to the text's 'aboutness' or content and finally, keywords which tend to indicate style rather than aboutness; he adds that aboutness can be linked to Halliday's (1994) ideational metafunction. In the case of legal texts, this type of keywords would include terms of art, such as, for instance, *company, agreement, shares* or *partner* in contractual instruments. Regarding key indicators of style, Scott (2000: 143) cites the example of high-frequency words such as *because*, *shall* or *already* and comments:

> These would not usually be identified by the reader as key. [...] But the fact that KeyWords identifies such words should prompt you to go back to the text [...] to investigate why such words have cropped up with unusual frequencies.

As Culpeper (2009) notes, it seems that aboutness keywords relate to open class words, i.e. lexical words which are the main carriers of meaning in a text (Biber *et al.* 1999: 55), while stylistic keywords can be associated with a closed class or closed system of function words. For his analysis of the character-talk in Shakespeare's *Romeo and Juliet*, Culpeper (2009) proposes a three-way categorization of keywords into ideational keywords, textual keywords, and interpersonal keywords. In what follows, a tentative classification of keywords in journal articles will be provided motivated by their functions in relevant contexts.

4. Results and discussion

Predictably, academic journals are marked by the presence of keywords that contribute towards the construction of academic discourse. They are all related to the academic register in that they identify and refer readers to relevant sources on which propositions made in the articles are based. Indeed, as Hyland (forth.) notes: "One of the most striking differences in disciplinary uses of language is in citation practices". Legal texts appear to have their own format for constructing legal citations. Understanding them is extremely important because they help locate the original documents. For example, in *See 43 U.S.C. 1603,* the interested reader is referred to Section 1603 of Vol. 43 of the United States Code. Any citation referring to a case will contain the name of the parties involved in the litigation, i.e. its heading (cf. Lee *et al.* 1999), as in another corpus example: *See Rice v. Rehner, 463 U.S. 713, 726 (1983).*

4.1. Citation keywords

Citation keywords form a relatively small but salient category. There are as many as four such keywords found among the top ten keywords: *Id., supra, note* (the latter two are very often used as one expression, i.e. *supra note*), and *see.* The other keywords include *citation, journal,* and *literature.* The word *supra* or the expression *supra note* are clearly unique to academic and legal citation practice. *Supra* is a Latin term for 'above'. It signals a situation where a writer wants the reader to look up a previously-cited source. Thus, *supra* is used to indicate that the current citation is from the same source as the previous one. This word is often used in legal research and is used to denote that matter under current consideration has already appeared somewhere before in the text or document in which the reference is made. For instance, if a writer wants to mention a source in his or her fifth footnote, then he would denote it in this manner: *see supra note 5* or *see supra text after note.*

Id. is the most common abbreviated form which stands for the Latin *Idem*, meaning 'the same' and it is used to indicate a reference made earlier in the text, as in the following corpus example (emphasis added):

(1) An exception to the Santa Clara Pueblo rule has emerged in the Tenth Circuit, in Dry Creek Lodge, Inc. v. Arapahoe and Shoshone Tribes, 623 F.2d 682 (10th Cir. 1980). There the court permitted federal judicial relief against a tribe when a non-Native lacked a tribal forum in which to litigate his claim. *See id.* at 684-85.

The extremely frequent occurrence of the directive *see* illustrates how legal academic articles are replete with references to statutes and cases. The frequent use of *see* is not confined to academic genres. It is also a key directive in briefs and opinions (ranking as 8th and 7th keyword, respectively). Interestingly, *see* is not found as a keyword in legal textbooks (Gozdz-Roszkowski, forth.). However, it appears that it is the preferred form of directing readers to other parts of a text or other texts in much of what we could refer to as the expository-persuasive mode of legal writing. Clearly, it is also a fairly common device in other disciplinary discourses (cf. Hyland 2009).

Words derived from Latin seems to suggest specificity in terms of language resources appropriated for citation in legal academic genres and they are all found in the top ten keywords (except for *article*). Legal academic articles tend to display the general tendency of legal writing to cite the authorities from which a legal principle has been drawn. Legal writers may draw the legal principle from one controlling authority or from several (Brostoff/Sinsheimer 2003). As Bhatia notes, this tendency is one of the reasons for "an extremely high degree of intertextuality and interdiscursivity in legal discourse, whether it is the case of textbooks, cases, judgments or legislation" (2004: 35).

4.2. The self-mention keyword 'we'

Self mention is another important feature which varies both *across* and *within* disciplines. It concerns how far writers want to intrude into their texts through the use of *I* or *we*, or by using impersonal forms. Hyland (forth.) argues that presenting a discoursal self is central to the writing process, and we cannot avoid projecting an impression of ourselves and how we stand in relation to our arguments, discipline, and readers. To some extent, this is determined by seniority, experience, confidence, personality, and so on, but the presence or absence of explicit author reference is a conscious choice whereby writers adopt a particular community-situated authorial identity. In our corpus, journal articles make frequent use of *we*:

(2) In the next issue of the Journal of Employment Discrimination Law, *we* will consider how an organization moves from a compliance culture based on rules of conduct to a values culture that is based on shared norms of behavior and relationships.

In the example above, the personal pronoun fulfils a text-organizing function by specifying how the author intends to arrange the content of the article and what aims are envisaged by him or her.

As can be seen in the following example, the first-person pronoun is used to express authorial stance quite unequivocally:

(3) *We* do not agree that the corporation's property interests settle the question. The State urges in effect that the corporation's right to control the inhabitants of Chickasaw is coextensive with the right of a homeowner to regulate the conduct of his guests. *We* cannot accept that contention.

Indeed, stance structures with a 1st person subject are frequently used, as shown by the co-occurrence between *we* and mental verbs (Biber *et al.* 1999) such as *assume, consider, find, know, see* and *think*:

(4) However, *we* think it more realistic to analyze the case in which there is a distribution of views and the government punishes only the extremist speech.

We is typically used even if an article is single-authored. An additional examination of its most frequent collocates reveals that there is also a strong co-occurrence between *we* and modal verbs such as *can, may, must, should* and the verb *need*:

(5) It is then that *we may*, in good conscience, begin the process of rationing our health care technologies. My position is that *we must* begin to set out our criteria for making these decisions now.

Excerpt (5) illustrates how *we* is employed as a useful device to engage the reader by signalling mutual obligation and commitment to shared ideas or values. Worth noting is the presence of an overt expression of author stance (*my position is that...*).

4.3. Legal terms as keywords

Compared to other legal genres, legal academic articles are clearly marked by their reliance on a relatively limited number of keywords denoting legal concepts. In our analysis, these include: *discovery, governor, harm, Miranda, penalty, prosecutors, sentencing, sovereignty, treaty.* Strictly speaking, this category also includes so-called 'semi-technical' or 'mixed' terms, i.e. words from the general language which "have acquired additional meanings by a process of analogy in the specialist context of legal activity" (Alcaraz/Hughes 2002: 17). If we look at the list of keywords provided above, *discovery* and *harm* are a fine example of this type of terms, which also includes words whose meaning does not differ substantially from their everyday meaning. For instance, the keyword *child* is defined in *Black's Law Dictionary* (Black/Black 1990) as "progeny; offspring of parentage. Unborn or recently born human being. [...] At common law one who had not attained the age of fourteen years". Thus, the legal definition may be more accurate in the way it specifies the age of a young person, his or her rights, etc.

What this analysis seems to suggest is that legal journals contain relatively few purely technical terms. At the same time, there is a fairly large category of words from the common stock such as *child, parents, higher, school, students, university,* etc. which seem to signal a broad range of issues embedded in the highly social context of much legal research.

4.4. Keywords used to signal and support legal reasoning

There is growing evidence to suggest that each disciplinary discourse may have its own knowledge-system structure, which in turn affects the preferred modes of communication (cf. Berkenkotter/Huckin 1995). To address this aspect I looked at keywords that are associated with the process of advancing argument in scholarly writing: *beliefs, estimates, model, probability, problems, results, responsibility, theory.* The two examples below corroborate the presence of empirical and social research trends in legal research with a clear focus on the evaluation of its outcome:

(4) Empirical evidence generally supports this idea with respect to the relative propensity of stock insurers to exist when future cash flows are more uncertain

or business income is generally more risky (Lamm-Tennant/Starks 1993). Through observation of the behavior of insurance companies involved directly in litigation, the *results* of this study are consistent with this idea as well.

(5) This paper *estimates* the effect of judicial characteristics (political affiliation, race, and sex) on federal criminal sentencing using variation in judicial characteristics at the district level. The *results* suggest that judges' race and sex have little influence on prison sentences in general but do affect racial and sex disparities.

The keyword *model* is also strongly indicative of how legal research is constructed and carried out. It signals the presence of logical tools employed to model legal argument:

(6) Robert Pollack has built a *model* in which the donor's utility depends on the recipient's consumption of certain goods, as opposed to the recipient's utility. In this 'paternalistic' *model*, the donor's utility rises if, but only if, the recipient consumes more of those goods that the donor wants the recipient to consume. Yet, in this *model*, as in Becker's, the donor might derive more utility from transferring a dollar to the recipient than by increasing his own consumption.

The keyword *beliefs* is noteworthy for its co-occurrence in rather atypical co-texts. In our corpus data, *beliefs* are discussed in the context of their *distribution* among the parties to a dispute as a result of a discovery procedure:

(7) In the wake of the papers by Shavell and Sobel, several authors have modeled the discovery process. Cooter and Rubinfeld (1994) develop a model of discovery in which plaintiffs and defendants have subjective *beliefs* about the outcome at trial. Settlement occurs if a contract zone exists, while a trial occurs when the contract zone fails to exist. The effect of discovery depends on how it changes the *distribution of beliefs* of the two parties to the dispute. In this context, discovery can either raise or lower the probability of trial depending on whether it makes the litigants more or less optimistic about the outcome.

Of course, this does not mean that *beliefs* do not co-occur with more predictable collocates. There is in fact evidence that these include *common, cultural, personal, philosophical, prior, religious, subjective,* etc., which indicate a very broad range of use for this keyword.

4.5. General language keywords

By far the largest category of keywords indicates the topics raised in the articles. These can be generalized, as health care (*care, patient, recipients*), education (*higher, school, students, university*), welfare (*poor, social, welfare*), family (*child, children, families, parents*), crime (*crimes, death, penalty, victim*), and ethics (*ethical, moral, morally, values*).

Inevitably, there is considerable overlap between these categories when, for instance, family matters are discussed in the context of social welfare or crime and capital punishment is viewed from the perspective of ethics. These keywords are, in my view, indicative of how the law, as a set of rules, may be examined at several different levels. At one level, it divides social behavior into actions that society regards as either obligatory and permissible or forbidden. It specifies when and how people are held responsible for shirking obligations, or for engaging in forbidden behavior. At another level, it organizes private processes of dispute settlement. At yet another level, it allocates *welfare* (understood here as things such as wealth, status, and social power).

The occurrence of *responsibility* as a keyword is perfectly understandable if we bear in mind that law is a process determining responsibility for socially consequential behavior (Lempert/Sanders 1989). Furthermore, allocating responsibility is a central legal task. Applying the law often involves deciding what people did or did not do, determining what they could (not) have done and distinguishing the intended from the unintended consequences of behavior. There is a consensus among legal theorists that the term *responsibility* is particularly hard to define: "One of the difficulties with discussions of responsibility is that the term *responsibility* has different meanings. We sometimes fail to distinguish these meanings and, consequently, the various ways in which individuals may be held responsible" (Lempert/Sanders 1989: 5).

Collocational analysis shows that *responsibility* tends to be qualified by such adjectives as *moral, personal* and *professional*:

(8) Taking responsibility for one's actions means taking responsibility for any foreseeable consequences of those actions. A doctor cannot shirk *moral* or *legal responsibility* for such consequences by saying that bringing them about was not the primary intention of his actions. It is inconsistent, therefore, for a doctor practicing active euthanasia to be seen as morally inferior to a colleague who is doing exactly the same thing while merely claiming he has different intentions.

Interestingly, the keyword *responsibility* also collocates with other keywords identified as belonging to the category of illustrating and supporting legal reasoning. In the following example, we can note how discussion in a legal journal revolves around different theoretical perspectives on the concept of responsibility:

(9) One recent critic, Jean Roberts, equating his *theory* of voluntary action with his *theory* of *moral responsibility*, goes on to argue that Aristotle holds a *theory of moral responsibility* that is alien to our modern conception of *responsibility*.

Responsibility appears to provide a glimpse into a complex and interrelated network of legal concepts characteristic of a great deal of legal thinking.

5. Conclusions

The main goal of this chapter was to compare the most frequent words in a corpus of legal academic articles with the most frequent words in a larger corpus of other legal genres in the hope of isolating the most characteristic, genre-specific words. The results provide evidence which enables one to propose the presence of at least five distinctive categories: citation keywords, self-mention keywords, keywords as legal terms, keywords signalling prevalent knowledge structures in legal discourse, and general language keywords. It is argued that these categories are unique to journal articles in quantitative terms, i.e. they are much more frequently employed in this genre than in any of the other genres grouped in the reference corpus. The present analysis focused on one hundred most salient keywords, i.e. keywords selected in order of their keyness. More work is needed, which could include a greater range of keywords perhaps resulting from different constraints than those imposed in this study (e.g. lower frequency cut-off point). This analysis could also be extended by comparing other legal genres against a larger reference corpus. For example, it would be interesting to examine keywords extracted from a corpus of legal textbooks in order to find out if or to what extent the two academic genres, i.e. journal articles and textbooks are similar or different.

References

Alcaraz, Enrique / Hughes, Brian 2002. *Legal Translation Explained.* Manchester: St. Jerome Publishing.

Baker, Paul 2004. Querying Keywords: Questions of Difference, Frequency and Sense in Keywords Analysis. *Journal of English Linguistics* 32/4, 346-359.

Berkenkotter, Carol / Huckin, Thomas 1995. *Genre Knowledge in Disciplinary Communication – Cognition / Culture / Power.* Hillsdale, NJ: Lawrence Erlbaum.

Bhatia, Vijay K. 2004. *Worlds of Written Discourse. A Genre-Based View*. London: Continuum.

Biber Douglas / Johansson Stig / Leech Geoffrey / Conrad Susan / Finegan Edward 1999. *Longman Grammar of Spoken and Written English.* London: Longman.

Black, Henry L. / Black, Henry Campbell [6]1990. *Black's Law Dictionary with Pronunciations*. New York: West Publishing Company.

Brostoff, Teresa, K. / Sinsheimer, Ann 2003. *Legal English. An Introduction to the Legal Language and Culture of the United States*. New York: Oceana Publications.

Cacchiani, Silvia (forthcoming). Keywords and Key Lexical Bundles as Cues to Knowledge Construction in RAs in Economics. In Goźdź-Roszkowski, Stanisław (ed.) *Explorations in Language and Corpora.* Frankfurt: Peter Lang.

Culpeper, Jonathan 2009. Keyness. Words, Parts-of-Speech and Semantic Categories in the Character-Talk of Shakespeare's Romeo and Juliet. *International Journal of Corpus Linguistics* 14/1, 29-59.

Goźdź-Roszkowski, Stanisław (forthcoming). *Textual Patterns of Variation in Legal Language. A Corpus-Based Study*. Frankfurt: Peter Lang.

Halliday, M.A.K. 1994. *An Introduction to Functional Grammar.* London: Edward Arnold.

Hyland, Ken 2009. *Academic Discourse.* London: Continuum.

Hyland, Ken (forthcoming). Corpora and EAP: Specificity in Disciplinary Discourses. In Gozdz-Roszkowski, Stanisław (ed.) *Explorations in Language and Corpora.* Frankfurt: Peter Lang.

Johnson, Sally / Culpeper, Jonathan / Suhr, Stephanie 2003. From 'Politically Correct Councillors' to 'Blairite Nonsense': Discourses of Political Correctness in Three British Newspapers. *Discourse and Society* 14/1, 28-47.

Lee, Debra S. / Hall, Charles / Hurley, Marsha 1999. *American Legal English. Using Language in Legal Contexts.* Ann Arbor: The University of Michigan Press.

Lempert, Richard O. / Sanders, Joseph 1989. *An Invitation to Law and Social Science: Desert, Disputes and Distribution.* Philadelphia: University of Pennsylvania Press.

McEnery, Tony / Xiao Richard / Tono Yukio 2006. *Corpus-Based Language Study. An Advanced Resource Book.* London: Routledge.

Scott, Mike 2000. Focusing on the Text and Its Key Words. In Burnard, Lou / McEnery, Tony (eds) *Rethinking Language Pedagogy from a Corpus Perspective.* Vol. 2. Frankfurt: Peter Lang, 103-122.

Scott, Mike 2008. *WordSmith Tools Help Manual.* Liverpool: Lexical Analysis Software.

Tribble, Chris 2000. Genres, Keywords, Teaching: Towards a Pedagogic Account of the Language of Project Proposals. In Burnard, Lou / McEnery, Tony (eds) *Rethinking Language Pedagogy from a Corpus Perspective.* Vol. 2. Frankfurt: Peter Lang, 75-90.

Williams, Raymond 1985. *Keywords. A Vocabulary of Culture and Society.* Oxford: Oxford University Press.

Xiao, Richard / McEnery, Tony 2005. Two Approaches to Genre Analysis: Three Genres in Modern American English. *Journal of English Linguistics* 33/1, 62-82.

Appendix

Top 100 positive keywords in academic journals, in order of keyness

Rank	*Keyword*	*Frequency*	*Keyness*	*Rank*	*Keyword*	*Frequency*	*Keyness*
1	Id.	2322	2649.48	51	speech	331	372.12
2	note	1269	2565.99	52	can	902	367.45
3	welfare	757	2486.53	53	firms	171	366.06
4	supra	1172	1816.25	54	social	415	360.17
5	see	2548	1418.98	55	poor	126	357.85
6	school	748	1148.28	56	some	700	343.33
7	citation	343	974.01	57	behaviour	182	332.94
8	death	581	840.44	58	guidelines	265	332.58
9	care	770	828.29	59	penalty	299	331.23
10	these	1061	787.75	60	families	196	328.73
11	self	436	745.17	61	accident	143	328.09
12	are	2955	692.42	62	we	1002	326.91
13	people	457	686.92	63	rhetoric	79	308.61
14	presidential	225	671.05	64	students	242	304.37
15	optimal	157	665.97	65	sovereignty	164	300.15
16	human	325	663.26	66	responsibility	296	292.95
17	model	361	654.84	67	most	498	292.76
18	sentencing	395	638.41	68	more	1089	289.43

19	environmental	460	638.10	69	estimates	115	289.09
20	ethics	207	610.25	70	parents	222	286.22
21	probability	198	584.40	71	however	777	284.30
22	journal	165	577.92	72	also	1018	281.15
23	reform	274	569.60	73	policy	512	276.66
24	president	523	564.29	74	morally	73	274.03
25	their	1502	541.15	75	recollection	65	272.51
26	prosecutors	174	532.73	76	problems	209	271.05
27	they	1178	525.64	77	aid	152	270.21
28	about	633	525.11	78	were	990	269.83
29	child	530	522.67	79	sanctions	131	267.28
30	bias	142	519.35	80	Miranda	97	260.87
31	university	260	510.71	81	results	268	259.12
32	recipients	184	488.60	82	beliefs	92	251.88
33	many	442	476.07	83	lawyers	174	251.12
34	economics	135	475.57	84	theory	197	251.10
35	defense	524	470.93	85	politics	83	247.14
36	ethical	141	463.36	86	article	574	246.83
37	none	281	458.63	87	society	160	246.37
38	supreme	500	434.41	88	governor	106	239.32
39	level	343	432.87	89	represented	183	238.06
40	crimes	237	419.27	90	patient	158	237.67
41	education	496	407.03	91	American	321	235.78
42	while	515	398.39	92	values	132	235.44
43	country	364	396.82	93	treaty	144	234.82
44	higher	277	386.45	94	harm	169	227.93
45	moral	167	394.40	95	voluntary	199	227.62
46	risk	394	394.01	96	literature	91	226.71
47	discovery	250	388.06	97	dependent	125	226.54
48	victim	182	388.04	98	powers	254	225.87
49	children	468	379.56	99	jobs	115	224.72
50	at	4436	374.34	100	legislation	214	220.55

VANDA POLESE / STEFANIA D'AVANZO

Linguistic and Legal Vagueness in EU Directives Harmonising Protection for Refugees and Displaced Persons

1. Introduction

The main aim of this chapter[1] is to investigate vagueness in EU directives harmonising Member States' efforts to grant refugees and displaced persons' civil and human rights. It focuses on linguistic and legal vagueness in the structure of directives viewed as normative texts and in the ideology underlying the EU's attitude in granting specific rights to migrants. The research questions are therefore: How and in what direction is the language of the directives under scrutiny accountable for the representation of migrants? How and to what extent are ideological implications accountable for vagueness in the directives? Can power roles be operationalised through vagueness?

In normative texts vagueness is a crucial issue. As Bhatia *et al.* (2005: 9) remark:

> People may not necessarily and not always be aware of vagueness in language use, while in other cases they choose deliberately to be vague. This holds particularly true for the use of vagueness in normative texts which are usually taken to have a high degree of precision.

Some vagueness may be determined by the need for all-inclusiveness and therefore appears as a necessary prerequisite for an efficient legal system. However, it leaves room for interpretation and communicative

1 Although it was planned and discussed jointly, Vanda Polese is responsible for Sections 1-6 and 9, Stefania D'Avanzo for Sections 7-8.

negotiation of the exact meaning of a word or expression (Engberg/ Heller 2008). In the EU's directives, as we will see, what is required is subjective interpretation of utterances on the part of each Member State on issues related to common immigration policy. In the EU's directives, communicative negotiation of the exact meaning of a word/expression results in the EU allowing the Member States a wide margin of freedom in implementing measures on issues of immigration and asylum.

Extra-European immigration has become an EU concern only lately, namely after the political and supranational role of the EU was strengthened and its action in matters of transnational migration was perceived to be necessary. Since the entry into force of the Treaty of Amsterdam (May 1999) and the European Council of Tampere (October 1999), the EU has committed itself to developing a common policy on immigration and asylum to ensure more effective management of migration flows to EU countries.

A number of directives were introduced by the EU between 2001 and 2005 in order to grant refugees and displaced persons civil and human rights and promote "a balance of efforts between Member States" (Council Directive 2001/55/EC) in receiving such people, thus improving the process of harmonisation. These directives are aimed at laying the foundations for a Common European Asylum System, to establish the EU as a single asylum space and ensure that EU citizens have a system that gives protection to asylum seekers and deals fairly and efficiently with applications.

Nevertheless, the EU's policy and legislation have not been so effective as expected, as shown by the vagueness of lexis and legal concepts encoded in its formal pronouncements. For this purpose, we have investigated EU directives on immigration and asylum with a view to identifying the ideological implications of vagueness and its role in the discursive organisation of such texts.

We will start with the background to the study. Next, after defining the corpus and intra- and extra-textual features of EU directives we will concentrate on the analysis of vagueness carriers (adjectives, definitions and time expressions) in relation to migrants and the granting of migrants' rights. A binary definition of vagueness (strong vs. weak) will serve to highlight issues of power and control on the part of the EU in negotiating meaning in the directives with reference to acceptance of migrants and granting human rights to them. We will conclude by pointing at ideological implications underlying a certain use of vagueness which may make harmonisation complex and create problems in coping with such delicate matters as immigration and asylum.

2. Vagueness

Vagueness has been described as “a central technique of normative texts: it is needed to pursue the purposes of formulating such texts” (Endicott 2005: 28). The type of vagueness encountered in normative texts does not include hedging devices (e.g. *approximately*, *more or less*) or crystallized expressions (e.g. *without undue delay*) but “extravagantly vague language” such as the adjective *reasonable* (Endicott 2005: 28).

Following Pinkal (1985), adjectives may be classified according to their precisification qualities into ‘restrictive’ and ‘non-restrictive’ adjectives. The latter (e.g. *possible*, *former*) have little or no clarifying force: they do not specify an entity but only its epistemological status. The former can be either precise or indefinite: in the case of precise adjectives (e.g. *square*, *married*), vagueness is dependent on context, whether these are used as technical terms or in informal conversation; indefinite adjectives are also vague, due to their referential relativism (as in the case of *heavy* and *big*) or fuzzy boundaries (e.g. *green*). Indefinite adjectives confer a positive/negative connotation on nouns that is gradable and relies on interpretation as they have no inherent value in themselves.

Since indefinite adjectives are gradable, interpretation needs to take into account both the noun that they modify and a class of comparison, However, gradability acts differently in dimensional, as compared to evaluative adjectives (Bierwisch 1987). Whereas interpretation of dimensional adjectives is dependent on the external properties of the referent of the noun and a scale of comparison based on conventional standards, interpretation of evaluative adjectives depends on a subjective scale of measurement, as in the case of *small* and *fast*, and relies on conventional ideals, as in the case of *good* and *nice*. A semantic shift from objective measurement to subjective assessment occurs when nouns denoting measurable dimensions are modified by evaluative adjectives. In normative texts, adjectives are used as "signs of interpretation according to juridical assessment when applying the law in a particular case" (Fjeld 2005: 162).

However, with dimensional adjectives (which refer to size, time, distance, quantity, weight and age) the scale may be explicit or the class of comparison may be found in a standardised or conventional norm, or in the culture of a language; instead, when no class of comparison can be found, the adjective can be said to have a high degree of vagueness. Thus, interpretation of evaluative adjectives like *adequate*, *necessary* or *proper* "is dependent not only on contextual parameters, but also on the total situation of interpretation" (Fjeld 2005: 166), for which precisification, which regulates natural language interpretation relying on contextual clues, should leave no space for alternative interpretations.

3. Ideological implications

Being "fairly general and abstract mental representations which govern the shared mental representations (knowledge and attitudes) of social groups" (van Dijk 2000: 93), ideologies are socially and discursively formed, reproduced and changed (Fairclough 1989, 1995) in a variety of ways which include institutional forms of discourse among their most prestigious varieties (van Dijk 2000). The notion of language as a form of action which is socially shaped and socially constitutive allows us to think of any text as constitutive of social identity, social relations and systems of knowledge and beliefs (Fairclough 1992). Directives as legal texts can be described as linguistic products expressing a stance with regard to reality, as forms of discourse which reflect cognitive attitudes and power roles in society, accounts of practice and beliefs operating across cultures and jurisdictions.

The procedures enacting agreed legal principles (cf. Catenaccio 2007) reflect the ideological implications of EU discourse, which in turn influence the EU's social practices within the harmonisation process. Thus, the granting of legal rights to migrants is dependent on interpretations of the directives which have to be understood within the communicative and social context in which they were produced (cf. Gavazzi 1956). Providing vs. non-providing definitions may reveal the adoption of a system of values, a representation of the world and cultural assumptions that are time-specific (cf. Lantella 1979; Tiersma 1993; Antelmi 2007) or related to the broad social context. Linguistic choices can thus be viewed as the result of a preliminary selection which depends on given world view:

> When a definition is given, the selection of what is defined, i.e. the *definiendum*, has an ideological value, it implies that the arguer wants to give special relevance to the concept.
>
> (Antelmi 2007: 106)

Definitions, alongside with adjectives and adverbials, are functional to the expression of evaluations of reality.

4. Corpus and method

The corpus for the present study consists of five texts:

- Council Directive 2001/55/EC on minimum standards for giving temporary protection in the event of a mass influx of displaced persons and on measures promoting a balance of efforts between Member States in receiving such persons and bearing the consequences thereof.

- Council Directive 2003/9/EC laying down minimum standards for the reception of asylum seekers.
- Council Directive 2003/86/EC on the right to family reunification.
- Council Directive 2004/83/EC on minimum standards for the qualification and status of third country nationals or stateless persons as refugees or as persons who otherwise need international protection and the content of the protection granted.
- Council Directive 2005/85/EC on minimum standards on procedures in Member States for granting and withdrawing refugee status.

Our focus is not on crystallized vague lexis or formulaic expressions but on vagueness carriers which call for negotiation of meaning and may reveal ideological implications. The methodological framework is mainly provided by various studies on vagueness in normative texts (Endicott 2001; Bhatia *et al.* 2005; Engberg/Heller 2008), on the semantics of adjectives (Pinkal 1995; Fjeld 2005) and on legal discourse and ideology (Fairclough 1989, 1992, 1995; Tiersma 1993; van Dijk 2003; Antelmi 2007). Since vagueness is commonly found to be strategic to all-inclusiveness, we will investigate if and to what extent the normative message in the EU directives on immigration and asylum is unambiguously and all-inclusively constructed in an unbiased way that ensures clarity of interpretation and effectiveness of application while showing respect for migrants as being entitled to civil and human rights.

5. The Common Policy on immigration and asylum

Since the Treaty of Amsterdam (1997) and the Tampere European Council (1999), immigration and asylum policy has become the 1st pillar of EU action. Measures targeting refugees and displaced persons were first provided by the Treaty of Amsterdam, through minimum standards for granting temporary protection to displaced persons and refugees and for promoting harmonised efforts by Member States in receiving such persons and bearing the consequences. After the Tampere European Council, the European Union committed itself to a common policy on immigration and asylum to ensure fair treatment of third country nationals, partnership with countries of origin, a balanced approach to migration management and the development of a common European asylum system. The two further steps, the Laeken European Council (2001) and the Thessaloniki European Council (2003), were more concerned with establishing a system for exchanging information on asylum, migration and countries of origin and setting up a European Migration Monitoring Centre, which suggests that the EU is much more involved in controlling and monitoring migrants than in granting rights to them.

Even the titles of the directives listed above reflect a change in attitude on the EU's part, from a positive approach favouring the recognition of migrants' civil rights to a more cautious attitude to migration, which is qualified as a 'multidimensional', slippery phenomenon, viewed as something that is hard to manage. In fact, these directives show the adoption of different policies: first the setting of minimum standards for giving temporary protection to displaced persons and measures promoting common efforts between Member States in accepting migrants (2001/55/EC); then minimum standards for the protection of asylum seekers and for granting rights to them (2003/9/EC and 2003/86/EC), which means identifying and accepting displaced persons as asylum 'seekers'; further, a move to issues more closely related to the identity and status of 'third country nationals' or 'stateless persons' and to the type of protection they should receive (2004/83/EC); and finally the minimum standards on procedures in Member States for granting and withdrawing refugee status (2005/85/EC), thus allocating Member States the power to decide for exclusion.

6. EU directives and legal responsibility

Directives are the result of a binary process. The EU act is not able to achieve its goal by itself and relies on the conjoined action by the Member States. As prescriptive rules, directives aim at a final goal to be performed within a given deadline; they convey a normative message which requires national implementation, allowing the Member State to choose the legal instrument (Polese 2006). Directives belong to the family of normative texts (cf. Williams 2007) and, like Regulations, are totally binding, meaning that the Member States cannot decide to apply them only in part. Unlike regulations, directives are legally binding as to the objectives to be achieved within a given deadline but allow freedom of choice to Member States. However, what type of freedom is this? Member States are directly concerned with:

- applying directives in national territories;
- implementing directives by adapting the national legislation;
- enacting directives within a given deadline: in so doing they have to respect the hierarchical legislative framework of the State's territory.

Thus the choice of forms and means is not totally free, in that the legal instruments chosen by a national legislator must be able to produce adaptations of national legislation in the direction required by the directive. This means that such measures as circulars, letters or forms of instructions employed in administrative offices are not reliable because they can be subject to modifications and have no adequate systematic application (Adam/Tizzano 2008).

Drawing a boundary between the result and forms/means may therefore be arduous, and it is not easy to find an area of competence reserved to Member States in which EU directives cannot intervene. Intervention by the EU and Member States is a result of political evaluations made by the States to comply with the directives (Daniele 2008).

7. Classification of vague adjectives

In the following sections, vagueness will be mainly analysed as far as concerns adjectives with reference to definitions and expressions of time. Vague adjectives will be investigated as co-occurring in phrases concerning the definition of the status of 'migrant' and of the conditions under which certain rights should be granted to them.

In order to analyse vagueness of adjectives in our corpus, two main theoretical perspectives were taken into consideration. Pinkal argues that adjectives can be classified according to their precisification quality, as "Possible precisifications provide internal structure to the meanings of indefinite expressions" (1995: 52). Thus, a first distinction can be made between referential and non-referential adjectives. The former include adjectives such as *rectangular* and *married*, which have stable domains of definite applicability. Conversely, the latter include adjectives such as *large* and *fast*, which can be 'specified' through precisification; these adjectives are also known as degree adjectives. The other category is that of borderline indefinite adjectives such as *healthy*, *sick* and *sweet*, whose main features are fuzzy boundaries. Thus the adjectives we investigated could be classified as borderline indefinite adjectives, as it is not possible to control their interpretation.

Adjectives commonly employed in normative texts can also be classified according to their main semantic properties (Fjeld 2005) into: general qualities / modal / relational / ethic / consequence / evidence / frequency adjectives. All of these are also defined 'multi-dimensional', as they have no stable dimension. Of these, modal (*necessary*), relational (*sufficient*, *suitable*, *appropriate*), general qualities (*well-founded*, *particular*) and consequence (*serious*, *significant*, *special*) adjectives have resulted with a higher frequency in the directives investigated. Their use affects the value of the utterance in which they occur as expressions of linguistic and conceptual/legal vagueness which require subjective interpretation.

8. Strong vs. weak vagueness

In these sections a distinction will be assumed between 'weak' and 'strong' vagueness. More specifically, between a kind of vagueness mainly depending on the text type and socio-pragmatic context linked to the means that each Member State is allowed to implement ('weak' vagueness), and another type of vagueness, mainly related to the actual legal effects of defining migrants' status and granting them specific rights ('strong' vagueness).

8.1. Strong vagueness

Strong vagueness can be conceived as a form of indeterminacy with ideological implications in the legal definitions of migrants and the granting of migrants' rights. It is mainly conveyed through borderline indefinite adjectives with a strong evaluative meaning, which affects the legal efficacy of the norms aiming at granting rights to migrants.

8.1.1. Vagueness in definitions

The words *immigrant* and *migrant* are both commonly employed in everyday language but have not been defined in legal discourse. Thus, apart from these two words, our attention will focus on other phrases/words denoting people with a precise legal status.

Refugees. A definition of 'refugee' first appeared in the Geneva Convention on Refugees (1951, Art. 2):

(1) any person who […] owing to *well founded* fear of being persecuted for reasons of race, religion, nationality, membership of a *particular* social group or political opinion, is outside the country of his nationality and is unable or, owing to such fear, is unwilling to avail himself of the protection of that country; or who, not having a nationality and being outside the country of his former habitual residence as a result of such events, is unable or, to such fear, is unwilling to avail himself of the protection of that country; or who, not having a nationality and being outside the country of his former habitual

residence as a result of such events, is unable or, owing to such fear, is unwilling to return to it. [my italics here and below]

What is interesting here is the type of vagueness of the adjectives *well-founded* and *particular* co-occurring with the noun *fear* and the phrase *social group* respectively. Following Pinkal (1995), the adjective *particular* could be classified as a 'borderline indefinite adjective', for it has, as its main feature, fuzzy boundaries. Thus, it is impossible to define this social group exactly, as the qualifying adjective *particular* has a strong evaluative meaning.

The concept of 'refugee' was further specified in Directive 2004/83/EC, Art. 10:

(2) The concept of race shall in particular include considerations of colour, descent, or membership of a *particular* ethnic group; [...] a group shall be considered to form a *particular* social group where in particular: members of that group share an innate characteristic, or a common background that cannot be changed, or share a characteristic or belief that is so *fundamental* to identity or conscience that a person should not be forced to renounce [...]

As can be deduced from the example above, adjectives with an indefinite, strongly evaluative meaning are used. While *particular* refers to an ethnic group and is used to clarify what is meant by the concept of race, *fundamental* refers to conditions for establishing that a person belongs to a social group. Both of these are indefinite and characterized by a very strong evaluative meaning. Thus, despite the EU's attempt to better specify membership of a particular social group, vagueness seems to be persistent. The story of Seyed Mehdi Kazemi (http://www.everyonegroup.com) is an example of what can be originated by freedom of interpretation originating from vagueness.

Displaced person. Displaced persons are defined in Council Directive 2001/55/EC (Art. 2) in the following terms:

(3) persons who have fled areas of armed conflict or endemic violence; persons at *serious* risk of, or who have been the victims of, systematic or generalised violations of their human rights.

As mentioned earlier, *serious* belongs to the category of 'consequence adjectives' (Fjeld 2005). Because of its strongly evaluative meaning, it can be classified as an indefinite adjective with no common scale of comparison.

8.1.2. Vagueness in granting rights

Indefinite adjectives are also employed when granting specific rights to immigrants, as in the following instances from Council Directive 2004/83/EC (Art. 8.1):

(4) As part of the assessment of the application for international protection, Member States may determine that an applicant is not in need of international protection if in a part of the country of origin there is no *well-founded* fear of being persecuted or no real risk of suffering serious harm and the applicant can reasonably be expected to stay in that part of the country.

This article refers to conditions for determining that an applicant is not in need of international protection. The adjective *well-founded* co-occurring with the word *fear* makes it very arduous to know when the condition of being persecuted can be established.

In the following article (Council Directive 2004/83/EC, Art. 12.2) the conditions for exclusion from refugee status are defined:

(5) A third country national or stateless person is excluded from being a refugee where there are serious reasons for considering that:
(a) he or she has committed a crime against peace, a war crime, or a crime against humanity, as defined in the international instruments drawn up to make provision in respect of such crimes;
(b) he or she has committed a *serious* non-political crime outside the country of refuge prior to his or her admission as a refugee, which means the time of issuing a residence permit based on the granting of refugee status; particularly *cruel* actions, even if committed with an allegedly political objective, may be classified as *serious* non-political crimes.

Also in these instances, indefinite adjectives with a strongly evaluative meaning have been employed. The same type of adjectives can be found in Council Directive 2004/83/EC (Art. 16.2):

(6) Cessation
A third country national or a stateless person shall cease to be eligible for subsidiary protection when the circumstances which led to the granting of subsidiary protection status have ceased to exist or have changed to such a degree that protection is no longer required.
In applying paragraph 1, Member States shall have regard to whether the change of circumstances is of such a *significant* and non-temporary nature that the person eligible for subsidiary protection no longer faces a real risk of *serious* harm.

This Article refers to a change of circumstances that causes non-eligibility for subsidiary protection. It is extremely difficult to establish, however, when these are *significant.*

Adjectives with the same value can be found in some Articles aimed at granting specific rights, making it impossible to measure them on a common scale of comparison:

(7) The Member States shall ensure that persons enjoying temporary protection have access to *suitable* accommodation or, if necessary, receive the means to obtain housing. (Council Directive 2001/55/EC, Art. 13.1)

(8) The Member States shall provide necessary medical or other assistance to persons enjoying temporary protection who have *special* needs, such as unaccompanied minors or persons who have undergone torture, rape or other *serious* forms of psychological, physical or sexual violence. (Council Directive 2001/55/EC, Art. 13.4)

(9) Member States may decide on the residence of the asylum seeker for reasons of public interest, public order, or, when necessary, for the swift processing and effective monitoring of his or her application. When it proves necessary, for example for legal reasons or reasons of public order, Member States may confine an applicant to a *particular* place in accordance with their national law. (Council Directive 2003/9/EC, Art. 7.3)

8.2. Weak vagueness

'Weak' vagueness is mainly due to the text type and its pragmatic dimension (e.g. Member States' freedom to choose how to implement directives).

8.2.1. Determining 'time' in the granting of rights

'Time' may be included in the free choice conceded to Member States, as they seem to have enough freedom to decide when to implement specific rights within the time span provided. In our corpus, reference to time shows degrees of vagueness. In particular, prepositional phrases, with a time-adverbial function seem to be vague, as in the following examples:

(10) The Member States shall *as soon as possible* take measures to ensure the necessary representation of unaccompanied minors enjoying temporary protection by legal guardianship, or, where necessary, representation by an organization which is responsible for the care and well-being of minors, or by any other appropriate representation. (Council Directive 2001/55/EC, Art. 16)

(11) Member States, protecting the unaccompanied minor' s best interests, shall endeavour to trace the members of his or her family *as soon as possible.* (Council Directive 2003/9/EC, Art. 19)

In (10) and (11) the phrase *as soon as possible* mainly refers to the time required to ensure certain rights (e.g. representation of unaccompanied minors by legal guardianship and tracing members of an unaccompanied minor's family). The same phrase or a variant is also employed in a different context:

(12) The Member States shall, regularly and *as quickly as possible*, communicate data concerning the number of persons enjoying temporary protection and full information on the national laws, regulations and administrative provisions relating to the implementation of temporary protection. (Council Directive 2001/55/EC, Art. 27)

(13) Member States shall require applicants to inform the competent authorities of their current address and notify any change of address to such authorities as *soon as possible.* (Council Directive 2003/9/EC, Art. 7)

(14) Member States may consider it the duty of the applicant to submit *as soon as possible* all elements needed to substantiate the application for international protection. (Council Directive 2004 /83/EC, Art.4)

In (12-14), *as soon as possible* signals the time within which Member States are bound to carry out a specific action. However, in (14) timing is decisive when applying for international protection. Thus, although apparently 'weak', vagueness seems to seriously compromise the acquisition of a right (international protection).

Vagueness could be defined as embracing two main categories: incommensurability and immensurability. The former is "a relation that holds between X and Y, if and only if it is impossible to measure both X and Y on some common scale" (Endicott 2000: 41). Immensurability is very similar but is used to "describe criteria of application that do not correspond to a scale", it is "the property that something has if and only if it can be assessed in some respect in which it cannot be measured" (Endicott 2001: 46). Thus, the prepositional phrases *as soon as possible/as quickly as possible* are vague because they cannot be measured along a common scale of comparison. Both belong to the category of immensurability.

In other instances, the phrase *as soon as possible* is followed by a time clause based on the structure 'after + N+ VP/PP', but although more restrictively specified, it remains still vague:

(15) Member States shall provide persons recognised as being in need of international protection, *as soon as possible after the respective protection status has been granted*, with access to information, in a language likely to be understood by them, on the rights and obligations relating to that status. (Council Directive 2004/83/EC, Art. 22)

(16) *As soon as possible after their status has been granted*, Member States shall issue to beneficiaries of subsidiary protection status a residence permit which must be valid for at least one year and renewable, unless compelling reasons of national security or public order otherwise require. (Council Directive 2004/83/EC, Art. 24)

(17) *As soon as possible after the granting* of refugee or subsidiary protection status, Member States shall take the necessary measures, to ensure the representation of unaccompanied minors by legal guardianship or, where necessary, by an organisation responsible for the care and well-being minors. (Council Directive 2004/83/EC, Art. 30)

Something similar can be observed in the structure 'immediately + N + VP':

(18) Member States shall authorise beneficiaries of refugee status to engage in employed or self-employed activities subject to rules generally applicable to the profession and to public service, *immediately after the refugee status has been granted.* (Council Directive 2004/83/EC, Art. 26)

(19) Member States shall authorise beneficiaries of subsidiary protection status to engage in employed or self-employed activities subject to rules generally applicable to the profession and to the public service *immediately after the subsidiary protection status has been granted.* (Council Directive 2004/83/EC, Art. 26.3)

More precision is found in the following instances since vagueness is somehow reduced by phrases expressing a time-span which make interpretation easier:

(20) Member States shall inform asylum seekers, *within a reasonable time not exceeding fifteen days* after they have lodged their application for asylum with the competent authority, of at least any established benefits and of the obligations with which they must comply relating to reception conditions. (Council Directive 2003/9/EC, Art. 5)

(21) The competent authorities of the Member State shall give the person, who has submitted the application, written notification of the decision *as soon as possible* and, in any event, *no later than nine months from the date on which the application was lodged.* (Council Directive 2003/86/EC, Art. 5)

In (20) the vague phrase *within a reasonable time* is made more precise by *not exceeding fifteen days*. In (21) the phrase *as soon as possible* is followed by the more precise phrase *no later than nine months from the date on which the application was lodged*. In both cases the vague phrase is disambiguated by a more specific reference to time.

At times vagueness is strengthened by a sequence of vague prepositional phrases:

(24) Member States may exceptionally set modalities for material reception conditions different from those provided for in this Article, *for a reasonable*

period which shall be as short as possible. (Council Directive 2003/9/EC, Art. 14).

8.2.2. The legal concept of 'necessary/appropriate measures'

Before investigating vagueness in noun phrases, it is necessary to establish when a phrase ranks as vague. Referring to vagueness of sentences, Pinkal (1995: 40), claims that "an expression is semantically indefinite if it is responsible for the semantic indefiniteness of sentences in which it occurs as a subexpression". In the texts examined here, two adjectives mainly co-occur with the word measures (*appropriate, necessary*), as in the following clusters:

1	11	measures to
2	5	adopt measures
3	5	measures promoting
4	4	and measures
5	4	appropriate measures
6	4	measures, in
7	4	measures, they
8	4	necessary measures
9	4	of measures
10	4	take measures
11	4	the measures
12	3	measures in
13	3	measures necessary
14	3	on measures
15	3	these measures
16	2	integration measures
17	2	measures relating
18	2	measures shall
19	1	adequate measures
20	1	all measures
21	1	by measures
22	1	flanking measures
23	1	implementing measures
24	1	judicial measures

Figure 1. Clusters involving the noun *measures*.

In the following examples, *measures* can be found to occur with the adjectives *necessary* and *appropriate*:

(25) Member States shall adopt the *necessary* measures to provide asylum seekers with the document referred to in paragraph 1. (Council Directive 2003/9/EC, Art. 6.4)

(26) Member States shall take *appropriate* measures to ensure that authorities and organizations implementing this Directive have received the necessary basic training with respect to the needs of both male and female applicants. (Council Directive 2003/9/EC, Art. 24.1)

(27) The Member States shall adopt the *necessary* measures to provide persons enjoying temporary protection with residence permits for the entire duration of the protection. (Council Directive 2001/55/EC, Art. 8.1)

(28) The Member States shall take the *necessary* measures concerning the condition of residence of persons who have enjoyed temporary protection and who cannot, in view of their state of health, reasonably be expected to travel. (Council Directive 2001/55/EC, Art. 23)

Two main reasons could be highlighted here to assert the vagueness of such expressions. Firstly, particular attention has to be paid to the adjectives employed. According to Fjeld (2005), *appropriate* can be classified as relational adjective and is used to convey indisputable standards or requirements. Conversely, *necessary* belongs to the modal category, as evaluative adjectives can be classified according to their modal force and "The modal adjective with the highest modal strength is *necessary;* there are more requirements needed to qualify something as necessary than as advisable (Fjeld 2005: 167). Notwithstanding this, it is not always easy to understand why or when something is 'necessary'.

Another perspective concerning the vagueness of the phrases investigated is strongly related to their pragmatic context. Particularly, a distinction has to be made between the speaker's and the hearer's perspective. A speaker is usually sure of what s/he means, as s/he is clear about the assumptions that s/he makes. Conversely, the hearer's perspective is wider (Pinkal 1995: 67-68):

> the hearer's state of information ranges from 'fully informed' to 'fully uninformed', thus the hearer's contexts include the speaker's contexts to a certain extent as a special case.

In the directives, the 'speaker' is the EU, which requires Member States to pursue certain aims, such as ensuring the necessary representation of unaccompanied minors by legal guardianship, ensuring that authorities and other organizations implementing this directive receive basic training with respect to the needs of applicants, etc. But in so doing Member States are assigned, through lexical and legal vagueness, a wide margin of freedom. The following press release (11 March 2008, from <http://www.everyonegroup.com>) illustrates a situation where lack of precision and of a common policy turned into lack of legal efficacy:

> Medhi is the 19-year old Iranian, member of EveryOne Group who faces the death sentence in Iran for his homosexuality. The boy, who is being held in the detention centre at Rotterdam Airport was judged by the Dutch Supreme Court today. Mehdi had fled to Holland after the United Kingdom had turned down his request for asylum [...]. It seems unbelievable, and yet – while people all over the world discuss human rights and spend millions of euros organising conferences on the subject of asylum rights – once again an innocent young man like Mehdi is running a serious risk of dying with a rope around his neck because some European governments prefer to get round the laws that protect refugees rather than carry out their duties towards them.

Freedom of interpretation conceded to Member States resulted into an iterated rejection of Medhi's asylum application with a serious risk for his own life, as reported above in the press release. This urged the leaders of EveryOne Group, the Group for International Cooperation on Human Rights Culture, to stress that "we have to make sure Europe identifies and formalizes a common policy, without any loopholes, to solve the refugee problem in a humane way". In order to find a solution, the European Parliament approved with 60 votes (46 in favour, 2 against and 12 abstentions) an urgent resolution (13 March 2008) on the case of Seyed Mehdi Kazemi who was about to be extradited from Holland to the United Kingdom and risked immediate deportation from London to Teheran, where a death sentence would be awaiting him because of his homosexuality.

9. Concluding remarks

The discursive organisation of the EU directives under scrutiny harmonising protection for refugees and displaced persons reveals more than a cautious attitude on the part of the EU when dealing with immigration and asylum. Although the discourse of human rights is by its definition inclusive, the EU attitude towards granting rights to migrants appears to allow for exclusion (cf. Catenaccio 2007). By conceding freedom to Member States through forms of lexical and conceptual/legal vagueness, the EU appears to operationalise an ideologically based discourse which creates opportunities for reducing and controlling rather than granting acceptance of migrants and recognition of human rights to them. Although the final authority stays with Member States, these are bound to act in compliance with the normative force of EU directives. In this process, the effect of vagueness is to delegate power to Member States.

Vagueness in time expressions characterises the actions of Member States when granting forms of protection to beneficiaries of refugee status. In some cases, precisification relies on vague modifiers, while the adjectives *necessary* and *appropriate* in utterances which are binding for Member States, have fuzzy boundaries: they can be classified as 'borderline indefinite adjectives' (Pinkal 1995) or modal/relational adjective (Fjeld 2005) with no stable dimension calling for evaluation and interpretation. In fact, the adjectives which have proved to be frequent in the directives examined include *necessary*, *appropriate*, *suitable*, *sufficient*, *particular*, *well-founded*, *serious*, *significant* and *special*, often used as 'deprecisification tools'. Interpretations of their normative value largely depend on understanding their meaning with reference to the legislative context.

Thus, although vagueness can be said to be "a useful, non arbitrary technique for allocating power to officials [...] or for leaving decisions to private actors" (Endicott 2005: 28), it leaves wide discretionary powers to Member States on such matters as identity and acceptance of migrants, which ultimately means adhering to the EU's ideological positioning stated in the structural component of the directives known as the Recital.

To conclude, the urgent resolution approved by the European Parliament in the case of Seyed Mehdi Kazemi recognised persecution for sexual orientation as a ground for granting asylum. It was stated that the EU and its Member States "cannot apply European and national laws and procedures in a way which results in the expulsion of persons to a third country where they would risk persecution, torture and death, as this would amount to a violation of European and international human rights obligations (Art. 3). Art. 5 of the above-mentioned resolution requires EU institutions and Member States "to take action to prevent similar situations, in the future, through cooperation and EU guidelines to find solutions in similar cases" .

A further development of this study will concentrate on the investigation of vagueness in the Recital where the ideological framework is laid down and as the site for the EU to claim power and knowledge in a dialogic relationship with the Member States which nevertheless does not seem so far to have resulted in harmonising policies in respect for migrants and the granting of human rights to them.

References

Adam, Roberto / Tizzano, Antonio 2008. *Lineamenti di Diritto dell'Unione Europea.* Torino: G. Giappichelli.

Antelmi, Donatella 2007. Manifest Ideology and Hidden Ideology in Legal Language. Definitions and Terms. In Garzone, Giulana / Sarangi, Srikant (eds) *Discourse, Ideology and Specialized Communication*. Bern: Peter Lang, 101-117.

Bhatia, Vijay K. / Engberg, Jan / Gotti, Maurizio / Heller, Dorothee (eds) 2005. *Vagueness in Normative Texts*. Bern: Peter Lang.

Bierwisch, Manfred 1987. Dimensionadjektive als strukturierender Ausschnitt des Sprachverhaltens. In Bierwisch, M. / Lang, E.

(eds) *Grammatische und konzeptuelle Aspekte von Dimensions-adjectiven*. Studia Grammatica. Berlin: Akademie-Verlag.

Caliendo, Giuditta 2003. The Multilingual Voices of Europe: The European Commission Translation Service. In Lima, Maria (ed.) *Language, Culture and Politics: Issues and Debates in Political Science*. Naples: CUEN, 11-20.

Caliendo, Giuditta 2004a. Modality and Communicative Interaction in EU Law. In Gotti, Maurizio / Candlin, Christopher N. (eds) *Intercultural Aspects of Specialized Communication*. Bern: Peter Lang, 241-259.

Caliendo, Giuditta 2004b. EU Language in Cross-Boundary Communication. *Textus* 17/10, 121-140.

Catenaccio, Paola 2007. De-humanizing the 'Alien': The Construction of Migrants' Rights in EU Legislation. In Garzone, Giuliana / Sarangi, Srikant (eds) *Discourse, Ideology and Specialized Communication*. Bern: Peter Lang, 355-377.

Daniele, Luigi 2008. *Diritto dell'Unione Europea*. Milan: Giuffrè.

van Dijk, Teun A. 2000. Ideologies, Racism, Discourse: Debates on Immigration and Ethnic Issues. In Ter Wal, Jessica / Verkuyten, Maykel (eds) *Comparative Perspectives on Racism*. Aldershot: Ashgate, 91-116.

van Dijk, Teun A. 2003. The Discourse-Knowledge Interface. In Weiss, Gilbert / Wodak, Ruth (eds) *Critical Discourse Analysis. Theory and interdisciplinarity*. New York: Palgrave Macmillan, 85-109.

Endicott, Thomas. 2001. *Vagueness in Law*. Oxford: Oxford University Press.

Endicott, Thomas 2005. The Value of Vagueness. In Bhatia, Vijay K. / Engberg, Jan / Gotti, Maurizio / Heller, Dorothee (eds) *Vagueness in Normative Texts*. Bern: Peter Lang, 27-48.

Engberg, Jan / Heller, Dorothee 2008. Vagueness and Indeterminacy in Law. In Bhatia, Vijay K. / Candin, Christopher N. / Engberg, Jan (eds) *Legal Discourse across Cultures and Systems*. Hong Kong: Hong Kong University Press, 145-168.

Fairclough, Norman 1989. *Language and Power*. London: Longman.

Fairclough, Norman 1992. *Discourse and Social Change*. Cambridge: Polity Press.

Fairclough, Norman 1995. *Critical Discourse Analysis*. Harlow: Longman.
Fairclough, Norman 2003. *Analysing Discourse.* London: Routledge.
Fjeld, Ruth V. 2005. The Lexical Semantics of Vague Adjectives in Normative Texts. In Bhatia, Vijay K. / Engberg, Jan / Gotti, Maurizio / Heller, Dorothee (eds) *Vagueness in Normative Texts*. Bern: Peter Lang: 157-172.
Gavazzi, Giacomo 1956/1994. Legislazione e linguaggio perfetto. In Scarpelli, Uberto / Di Lucia, Paolo (eds) *Il linguaggio del diritto*. Milano: LED, 305-310.
Gotti, Maurizio. 2005. Vagueness in the Model Law on International Commercial Arbitration. In Bhatia, Vijay K. / Engberg, Jan / Gotti, Maurizio / Heller, Dorothee (eds) *Vagueness in Normative Texts*. Bern: Peter Lang, 227-253.
Hunston, Susan / Thompson, Geoff (eds) 2000. *Evaluation in Text. Authorial Stance and the Construction of Discourse.* Oxford: Oxford University Press.
Lantella, Lelio 1979. Pratiche definitorie e proiezioni ideologiche nel discorso giuridico. In Belvedere, Andrea / Jori, Mario / Lantella, Lelio (eds) *Definizioni giuridiche e ideologie*. Milan: Giuffrè.
Orsello, Gian Piero 2003. *L'Unione Europea.* Rome: Newton Compton.
Pinkal, Manfred 1995. *Logic and Lexicon.* The Hague: Kluwer.
Polese, Vanda 2006. Patterning, Regularity and Variation in the EUSLEX Corpus On line. *Linguistica e Filologia* 23, 91-111.
Tiersma, Peter M. 1993. Linguistic Issues in Law. *Language* 69/1, 113-135.
Weiss, Gilbert / Wodak, Ruth 2003. *Critical Discourse Analysis. Theory and Interdisciplinarity*. New York: Palgrave Macmillan.
Williams, Christopher ²2007. *Tradition and Change in Legal English.* Bern: Peter Lang.

ROSS CHARNOCK

Traces of Orality in Common Law Judgments

1. Introduction

The law is often assumed to be lexically and syntactically complex. However, at least as far as common law judgments are concerned, this reputation is to some extent undeserved. In England, where the majority of legal judgments are still given orally, the available reports retain many of the characteristics of oral discourse, including elements of both conversation and story-telling. The apparent simplicity of expression has the effect of making the judicial analysis more persuasive, and may thus affect the result of the case. Judicial expression should not therefore be considered independently of the content, as it may influence the historical development of the law.

The persistent assumption regarding the complexity of law leads to frequent over-generalisations concerning legal language. It is often taken for granted that legal judgments, originally given orally in open court, are today essentially written documents with all the characteristics of written style. In a related idea it is often affirmed that the law is therefore terminologically and syntactically complex and obscure. A closer look at the situation shows that, in English law, the complexity of the discourse is much exaggerated (Charnock 2006). Although modern law reports are longer than in the past, they are often less complex, sometimes to the point of being conversational. The significance of this lies in the fact that the style cannot be divorced from the content.

The law has admittedly developed certain specialised linguistic features, some of which are associated with statutes and copperplate contractual texts. However, such texts were never intended to be read from beginning to end as a continuous discourse. Like dictionaries, they are used mainly for reference.[1] Although they clearly remain a valid source of law, they can only be applied as interpreted by the judges. Judgments, on the other hand, are fully structured arguments intended to be read in their entirety. They are also more numerous than statutes. In this sense they have a better claim to be representative of the law than statutes.

Tiersma (2007) reminds us of the generally accepted idea that for hundreds of years, English judges expressed their opinions orally, their judgments "only later being summarised in writing". This appears to be an over-simplification. Even when given orally, judgments form part of an extensive written record, going back at least to the year 1220. The reports have always had a dual function, not just that of communicating the result of the trial to those present, but also that of creating precedents for future use. This explains why solicitors insist on reading aloud to their clients certain stereotypical written texts, including wills, oaths and promises of sale, even where purely verbal comprehension is to all intents and purposes impossible.[2]

Most cases are explicitly stated to be published as transcribed by the various official shorthand writers to the court, including Wordwave International, Smith Bernal Reporting Ltd, and Communications Co. of 190 Fleet Street. To the extent that the reports are indeed transcriptions, they have a claim to be classed as oral discourse. This explains why they are commonly included in large, commercially available corpora of oral English, including for example the Oslo corpus.

The aim of this chapter is simply to show, through readily available examples of judicial discourse, that, contrary to received ideas, many older cases show more characteristics of written language

---

1 The idea of reference and consultation is present in the very nature of a legal code. A Roman codex consisted originally of a set of pages which could be turned and consulted separately, as opposed to a scroll, designed to be read continuously.

2 Cases from as early as 1220 are collected in the *English Reports* (1932). Where there is no definitive written report, as for example in the judgments of Solomon (briefly discussed in the Bible), the cases cannot function as precedents and may therefore be considered examples of arbitration rather than true litigation.

than more recent ones, which preserve on the contrary many of the features of oral discourse. The recognition of the authenticity of legal discourse is a prerequisite for understanding how the law can contribute to the study of language, not just as a corpus to be analysed, but also through the judicial analysis of problems of meaning and interpretation.

2. Characteristics of English common law judgments

Common law, being based primarily on precedent rather than statute, is often referred to as 'unwritten law' (*lex non scripta*). But, as has often been remarked,[3] this does not mean that the law is not actually written. Indeed, without a written record,[4] no judgment could function as an authoritative precedent.

Nowadays, almost all modern judgments are available in print, for example in the *All England Law Reports*, the *Law Reports* or the *Weekly Law Reports*. Today, they are also available online.[5] However, in the majority of English courts, they are first given orally. The principal exception is the House of Lords, which abandoned oral delivery of judgments in 1963. However, the *Practice Directive* (1963) makes it clear that "it will always be open to a Lord of Appeal, should he wish to do so, to deliver his opinion orally in the House". Indeed, for historical reasons, these judgments are still known as 'speeches'. It is therefore not surprising that English judgments should display many of the essential characteristics of both oral and written language. Contrary to American practice, where judicial 'opinions' are

---

3 This point was made by former Chief Justice Hale as early as the 16th century (Hale 1971).

4 Judges do occasionally refer to unreported cases, which can help them to form an opinion. Perhaps the most famous of these is *High Trees* (1947), in which Denning J, still a junior judge, introduced the notion of equitable estoppel, now a fundamental part of contract law.

5 Cases since 1997 may be found at <http://www.bailii.org>.

nowadays communicated almost exclusively in writing, English reports are still reported *seriatim*, rather than as the definitive judgment of the whole court.

It is easy to show that older judgments are more likely to display the characteristics of written language. Indeed, many old cases make use of strange, esoteric language, and include not just Latin but also Legal French (sometimes known as Law French), of which thousands of pages may be found in the *English Reports*. In spite of its historical importance, Law French appears to be essentially macaronic, and cannot be considered a natural language. It follows that the judgments concerned must have been prepared in writing. They cannot even be convincingly read aloud, as the following extract shows:[6]

> Bromage sue en lea marches de Gales vers Genning, pur non fesant d'un leas solonque son bargaine, & sur ceo un prohibition fuit praie per Bridgeman pur ceo que il poet aver un action sur le case al comen ley, Ser. Harris le suite la eat solment a compeller le partie d'executor le possession, scilicet a faire le leas solonque son bargaine & nemy a recover damages & ceo est usualment fit en Chancerie. [...] Ser. Harris confesse que ll move ceo encontre son conscience, pur cause del'use, & un prohibition fuit graunt accordant.
>
> (*Bromage versus Genning* 1675)

Even when originally given in English, until at least the middle of the 18th century, most judgments were drafted in advance before being read aloud in court. Indeed, Mansfield CJ attracted attention in 1756 by announcing in his first case as Lord Chief Justice that he would henceforth give judgment *ex tempore*:[7]

> Where we have no doubt, we ought not to put the parties to the delay and expence [sic] of a farther [sic] argument; nor leave other persons who may be

6 Even where the court proceedings may be assumed to have been in English, the reports, including those by Lord Coke himself, were often published in Law French. *Bromage v Genning* is historically significant, as it introduced the idea of damages for breach of contract, as an alternative to obligatory performance.

7 This meant a substantial loss of fees for the lawyers, as they no longer needed to attend court again the following week to hear the decision.

> interested in the determination of a point so general, unnecessarily under the anxiety of suspense.
>
> (*Raynard v Chase* 1756, *per* Mansfield CJ)

However, although Mansfield's style as reported is often somewhat laconic, his language normally has little in common with oral discourse, as may be seen from the following paragraph in the same case:

> The defendant is to share the profits with Coxe in moieties, and is liable to the debts of the partnership: but it is positively and expressly found, 'that during all the time charged he never acted in or exercised the trade.' He was not, by the terms of his agreement, to act in the trade: the other partner was to do the whole, and had a particular salary on that account. It is not found that either Coxe or any servant under him was set to work by Chase; nor that Chase did any act whatever of exercising the trade : he was only concerned in the profit.
>
> (*Raynard v Chase* 1756, *per* Mansfield CJ)

Today, English judges almost invariably read from a written text. Before giving a concurring judgment, the judge will commonly state, according to the time-honoured phrase, that he has "had the advantage of reading in draft" a judgment prepared by a colleague on the bench. Other judgments, even in celebrated cases, are explicitly stated to be 'read' in the absence of the author. In other cases, senior judges, who are normally expected to speak first, may invite a junior colleague to 'read' the judgment he/she has prepared. Nevertheless, the written text preserves many of the characteristics of oral language.

3. Judgments as written discourse

Consideration of the stylistic features of legal judgments requires an acceptable distinction between oral and written discourse. Written language tends to include long sentences, often with numerous subordinate clauses. The written style may also include an explicit rhetorical structure, possibly using subtitles and footnotes. It will certainly involve explicit cohesion, in which repetition is systematically preferred to pronouns or other forms of substitution. Certain abbreviations are also specific to written language. All these characteristics may be observed in the older cases.

In *Mirehouse v Rennel* (1833), for example, Parke J used a single, complex sentence to state a rule which is often cited in modern discussions of the rule of precedent:

> Our common law system consists in the applying to new combinations of circumstances those rules of law which we derive from legal principles and judicial precedents; and for the sake of attaining uniformity, consistency, and certainty, we must apply those rules, where they are not plainly unreasonable and inconvenient, to all cases which arise; and we are not at liberty to reject them, and to abandon all analogy to them, in those to which they have not yet been judicially applied, because we think that the rules are not as convenient and reasonable as we ourselves could have devised.

Such long sentences are unlikely to be produced in oral conversation. Even longer sentences, going beyond what would even be conceivable today, are often found in the statements of the facts in cases of this period. The following example is from *Davies v Mann* (1842):

> The declaration stated, that the plaintiff theretofore, and at the time of the committing of the grievance thereinafter mentioned, to wit, on &c., was lawfully possessed of a certain donkey, which said donkey of the plaintiff was then lawfully in a certain highway, and the defendant was then possessed of a certain waggon and certain horses drawing the same, which said waggon and horses of the defendant were then under the care, government, and direction of a certain then servant of the defendant, in and along the said highway; nevertheless the defendant, by his said servant, so carelessly, negligently, unskilfully, and improperly governed and directed his said waggon and horses, that by and through the carelessness, negligence, unskilfulness, and improper conduct of the defendant, by his said servant, the said waggon and horses of the defendant then ran and struck with great violence against the said donkey of the plaintiff, and thereby then wounded, crushed, and killed the same, &c.

Numerous instances may be found in which single sentences fill more than a full page, often using a colon to replace modern full stops. It may occasionally be possible to produce an effect of breathless oral production by interpreting these colons as dashes. However, the explicit cohesion of these texts makes this stenographical device implausible.

In order to take account of as many possible states of affairs as possible, the published text often makes use of multiple synonyms. The statement of the facts in *R v Howell* (1864) provides an almost Rabelaisian example ("conspire, combine, confederate and agree together [...] designedly to solicit, persuade and procure"):

> The fourth count alleged that they being evil-disposed persons, and having no regard for good morals or for public decency, did unlawfully conspire, combine, confederate and agree together wickedly, knowingly and designedly to solicit, persuade and procure, and in pursuance of the said conspiracy did unlawfully and wickedly solicit and incite and endeavour to procure the said Louisa Mackett, then being an unmarried girl within the age of eighteen years, to wit, of the age of seventeen years, to become and be a common prostitute and to commit whoredom and fornication for lucre and gain with men, to wit, with all such men as should be willing to concur with her in the commission thereof.

3.1. Cohesion

Explicit cohesion, used to reduce to a minimum the need for pragmatic inference (Charnock 1995), is an essential characteristic of written, technical language. It is easy to find examples in older cases, in which co-reference is reinforced through the use of cohesive devices like 'the said' or 'the aforesaid'. In the example given above from *Davies v Mann*, we find repetitions of 'the waggon', 'the highway' or 'the donkey' where pronouns would normally suffice. These repetitions are frequently combined with 'the said' even though the meaning is already clear. Such devices now appear purely stylistic.

The statement of the facts in *R v Sharpe* (1857) includes three consecutive occurrences of 'the said':

> The indictment in the first count charged that the defendant [...] unlawfully and wilfully did break and enter a certain grave there, in which the body of one Louisa Sharpe had before then been interred, [...] and the said body of the said Louisa Sharpe out of the said grave unlawfully, wilfully, and indecently did take and carry away.

However, the co-reference is already clear, and would still be clear even if pronouns were used instead of nouns ('body', 'grave'), and proper names ('Louisa Sharpe'). The repeated use of the expression 'the said' appears here simply as an old-fashioned stylistic device, inevitably associated with written expression.

3.2. Abbreviations and subtitles

While written sentences tend to be longer than many spoken utterances, this does not preclude the use of abbreviations, some of which are almost exclusively limited to written discourse. One particularly productive example is '&c.', which allows the writer to avoid frequent recopying. In this context, it rarely has its modern function as a synonym of 'and so on', with its implicit invitation to supply other examples not mentioned explicitly in the text.[8]

The statement of facts in *R v Joseph Webb* (1834) speaks of "taking &c, and swallowing &c the said noxious &c substances." In *R v Woodrow* (1846), a dealer is said to have supplied adulterated tobacco to one William Hedges, "unknown, contrary, &c; whereby, &c".

Such abbreviations are common even in the most celebrated cases. In *Pinnel's case* (1602), for example, Lord Coke gave examples of three objects other than money which may serve to make a contractual transaction good. Contrary to the examples given above of '&c.', Lord Cokes' use of 'etc.' implies that his list is not exclusive. It is stylistically significant that the entire phrase is repeated in toto in the same sentence:

> It was resolved by the whole court that payment of a lesser sum on the day in satisfaction of a greater, cannot be any satisfaction for the whole, because it appears to the judges that by no possibility a lesser sum can be a satisfaction to the plaintiff for a greater sum; but the gift of a horse, hawk or robe, etc., in satisfaction is good, for it shall be intended that a horse, hawk or robe, etc,

8 This common abbreviation is less likely to be found in statutes – although it may occasionally figure in the titles. Although Parliament recently discussed an *Apprenticeships etc. Bill*, this now seems more likely to become law as an *Apprenticeships and Skills Act.*

> might be more beneficial to the plaintiff than the money, in respect of some circumstance, or otherwise the plaintiff would not have accepted of it in satisfaction. But when the whole sum is due, by no intendment the acceptance of parcel can be a satisfaction to the plaintiff.
>
> (*Pinnel's case* 1602, *per* Coke CJ)

Modern judgments also include subtitles which serve to clarify their rhetorical structure (American cases also frequently include substantive footnotes.) In *George Mitchell v Finney Lock Seeds* (1982), for example, Lord Denning, Master of the Rolls, includes an 'Outline' which functions as a kind of abstract, even though his language is largely conversational in tone:

> In outline
> Many of you know Lewis Carroll's Through the Looking-Glass. In it there are these words (ch 4): 'The time has come, "the Walrus said, To talk of many things: Of shoes – and ships – and sealing wax, Of cabbages – and kings [...]' Today it is not 'of cabbages and kings', but of cabbages and whatnots.
> In detail [...]
>
> (*George Mitchell v Finney Lock Seeds* 1982, *per* Denning MR)

Denning's genius for presenting the facts as a simple, almost conversational narrative frequently allows him to obtain the desired result whilst seeming to allow the facts to speak for themselves. This goes some way to explaining his influence on the development of the English law in the second half of the 20th century.

Examples taken from more recent cases show on the contrary that, even though most modern judgments are available in written form, the language used preserves many traces of orality.

4. Judgments as oral discourse

In the lower courts today, judgments are occasionally given extempore, immediately after argument. The judgment of Laws LJ in *R ex. p Ofcom v Information Commissioners* (2008) is stated in the report of the appeal case to have been extempore. However, as reported, it appears indistinguishable from written discourse:

> This is an appeal brought under Section 59 of the Freedom of Information Act 2000 ('the 2000 Act') against a decision of the Information Tribunal ('the tribunal') promulgated on 4 September 2007 by which the tribunal dismissed the appeal of the Office of Communications ("Ofcom") brought pursuant to Section 57 (1) of the 2000 Act against a decision notice issued by the Information Commissioner on 11 September 2006 which required Ofcom to disclose certain information held by it concerning the location, ownership and technical attributes of mobile phone cellular-based stations.
> (*R ex. p Ofcom v Information Commissioners HC 2008, per Laws LJ*)

Naturally, most examples of hesitation or repetition will be 'edited out' of the final, published version of the report. Nevertheless, the written versions of many modern judgments include other elements of oral discourse. Many make use of short sentences, sometimes with exaggeratedly simple syntax. There are many examples of conversational connectives and deictic references relating both to the discourse situation and to the interlocutor, as well as indications of emotion and dramatic effect. The judgments invariably include speech acts, and often involve storytelling.

Lord Denning's judgments were celebrated for their short sentences, sometimes consisting of only three words. The immediate effect is to eliminate all syntactic complexity:

> Introduction
> Abortion is a subject on which many people feel strongly. In both directions. Many are for it. Many against it. Some object to it as the destruction of life. Others favour it as the right of the woman. Emotions run so high on both sides that I feel that we as judges must go by the very words of the statute – without stretching it one way or the other – and writing nothing in which is not there.
> (*College of Nursing v DHSS* 1980, *per* Denning MR)

The rhetorical simplicity of his approach is sometimes found to be convincing in itself.

4.1. Conversational connectives and interjections

Although judges normally attempt to adjudicate objectively, without reference to personal opinion, they often use connectives like 'Well...' or 'Well then...', both of which are found in *Dickinson v Dodds* (1874) in paragraph initial position:

> Well, that being the state of things, it is said that [...] (*per* James LJ)
>
> Well, then, this being only an offer, the law says – and it is a perfectly clear rule of law – that, although it is said that the offer is to be left open until Friday morning at 9 o'clock, that did not bind Dodds. (*per* Mellish LJ)

Interjections without propositional content, but conveying a direct reaction to the immediate circumstances, are less common. However, it is possible to find examples which convey a certain dramatic effect. In *Sommerset v Stewart* (1772), Lord Mansfield found it necessary severely to limit the rights of slave owners in England. He may have inadvertently betrayed his personal feelings by referring to the plaintiff at the very end of his judgment not by name, but simply as 'the black':

> Whatever inconveniences, therefore, may follow from the decision, I cannot say this case is allowed or approved by the law of England; and therefore the black must be discharged.

More recently, in a case depending to a large extent on Roman law, Lord Rodger began his speech in Latin, thus: "My Lords, Dominus membrorum suorum nemo videtur" (*Regina v Bentham* HL, 2005).[9]

---

9 The accused had pushed his fingers out against his zipped-up jacket, so as to give the impression that he had a gun. The applicable text referred to an offence carried out by a person in possession either of a firearm or an imitation firearm. Lord Rodger was citing Ulpian D 9.2.13.pr to the effect that no one could be said to be in possession of their own limbs.

4.2. Deixis

Deixis involves reference to elements directly related to the context of utterance, usually along the dimensions of time, space, or persons present at the time of utterance. It is therefore a reliable indicator of oral discourse. We find deictic references to the immediate discourse situation in *Mitchell v Finney Lock Seeds* (1982) referred to above:

> There is only one case in the books so far on this point. [...] Our present case is very much on the borderline. (*per* Denning MR)

Self-reference may be observed in *Fisher v Bell* (1960), where Parker CJ refers to 'I myself':

> I confess that I think most lay people and, indeed, I myself when I first read the papers, would be inclined to the view that to say that if a knife was displayed in a window like that with a price attached to it was not offering it for sale was just nonsense. In ordinary language it is there inviting people to buy it, and it is for sale. (*per* Parker CJ)

In discussing medieval wills, Del Lungo Camiciotti (2001) proposes a reading of the surviving texts in which the testator appears to be addressing himself directly to his executors. The first person plural in *Jackson v Horizon Holidays* (1974) seems to refer in the same way to the legal representatives present in court during the judgment, as well as the judges on the bench:

> We have had an interesting discussion as to the legal position when one person makes a contract for the benefit of a party. (*per* Denning MR)

A similar example is found in *Mitchell v Finney Lock Seeds* (1982):

> There was much discussion before us as to the construction of that condition. (*per* Denning MR)

In the following examples from the same case, Lord Denning seems to be addressing himself not just to the parties or their legal representatives, but also to the young lawyers present in the courtroom:

> Many of you know Lewis Carroll's Through the Looking-Glass. (*per* Denning MR)
>
> None of you nowadays will remember the trouble we had, when I was called to the Bar, with exemption clauses. (*per* Denning MR)

Occasionally, a participant in the proceedings is referred to in the third person, even where that person seems to be present:

> The appellant, Thorsten Nordenfelt, a Swedish gentleman, a person of much intelligence, as his able address to your Lordships proved, and of great skill in certain branches of mechanical science, had established in England and Sweden a valuable business in connection with the manufacture of quick-firing guns. His customers were comparatively few in number, but his trade was world-wide in extent.
>
> (*Nordenfelt v Maxim Nordenfelt Ltd* 1894, *per* Lord MacNaghten)
>
> At the outset I must point out that we are here concerned with a suit by a foreign state to enforce its laws. I hope our New Zealand friends will forgive me calling them a 'foreign state'. I only use the term so as to bring home the fact that we are concerned with an independent sovereign government which exercises sovereign authority over its own territory, and which, by international law, has no right to exercise sovereign authority beyond its own territorial limits.
>
> (*AG New Zealand v Ortiz* CA 1983, *per* Denning MR)

Clearly, although the legal rules are generally applicable, and the judges' decisions in particular cases are assumed to have general effect, the discourse situation remains an important element in the judgments handed down. This is not the case in other forms of technical discourse, including accounts of research in physics, for example, in which only minimal reference is made to the specific situation in which the experiment was carried out.

4.3. Performative effect

In their classic presentation (Austin 1962), speech acts occur predominantly in the present tense and in the first-person singular, and are normally effective only in the immediate context of discourse.

They may therefore be taken as an indicator of orality.[10] Judicial statements inevitably have performative effects, involving most obviously the status of the accused as guilty or not guilty, or, more commonly, the ownership of property. The effects of these legal acts often go beyond the immediate case. Indeed, they may also have the institutional effect of modifying the law itself by introducing new rules or guidelines or by declaring earlier decisions overruled (Charnock 2009).

Regarding this function of speech acts, it should be noted that American judges are more willing than their English counterparts to state explicitly that a precedent has been overruled, sometimes to the extent of using the adverb *hereby* as an explicit performative marker ("*Bowers* was not correct when it was decided, is not correct today, and is hereby overruled", *Lawrence v Texas,* 2003).

Judicial speech acts are normally performed through the use of verbs like *hold* or *declare*, which have performative effect when used to signal authoritative decisions. The same verbs may conveniently be used in the past tense to refer to the speech acts accomplished in earlier cases. However, because American opinions are now rarely given orally, such acts are often referred to with the verb *write*, as observed in *Furman v Georgia* 1972:

> Emphasizing the flexibility inherent in the words 'cruel and unusual', the Chief Justice wrote that [t]he Amendment must draw its meaning from the evolving standards of decency that mark the progress of a maturing society.
>
> (*per* Justice Marshall, concurring)

> Mr. Justice Story wrote that the Eighth Amendment's limitation on punishment 'would seem to be wholly unnecessary in a free government, since it is scarcely possible that any department of such a government should authorize or justify such atrocious conduct.'
>
> (*per* Justice Marshall, concurring)

As the verb *write* cannot itself be used in discourse to accomplish an explicit performative act, Justice Marshall must here be referring to

10 In the legal context, performatives frequently occur in the passive ('objection overruled'), the conditional ('I would reject the appeal'), or in the third person ('this court rejects...').

rules and presumptions introduced by a (written) declaration in earlier cases.

4.4. Dialogues and story-telling

The reports of cases heard in the lower courts often include dialogues between the judges and counsel, usually relating to costs or matters of procedure. However, the transcriptions of these dialogues are not particularly realistic. The effect is rather stilted, as seen in the following transcription, taken from *R ex parte Haw v Sec Home Department*, HC 2005.[11]

> 113 LADY JUSTICE SMITH: I think we had better retire to consider that. Do any of you want to say anything about it?
> 114 MR CLEMENS: My Lady, no.
> 115 LADY JUSTICE SMITH: Mr Drabble?
> 116 MR DRABBLE: My Lady, no, we resist it on the basis that if permission is given at all, it should be given by the Court of Appeal, and we would only repeat our submissions that the construction is in place.
> 117 LADY JUSTICE SMITH: We will retire for a moment.
> (Brief adjournment)

The importance of story-telling in the law was pointed out by Llewellyn (1952), who considered that one of the main functions of legal procedure was to allow different viewpoints to emerge through dialogue during the trial. Because the judge will naturally evaluate particular claims in accordance with his/her overall understanding, his judgment will depend on which story is accepted:

> Here are our plaintiff and defendant, with their divergent stories, and the judge has settled that the outcome will be different according to whose tale he believes.

---

11 Judgment was given for a lone demonstrator on Parliament Square, against the wishes of the Home Secretary, and in spite of the clear intention of Parliament. As a result, the demonstrator is still there, five years later.

As Dean of the Harvard Law School, Llewellyn was primarily addressing himself here to prospective lawyers. However, the point also applies to judges. Indeed, the statement of the facts with which most judgments begin is an exercise which often approximates to story-telling. Because of its apparent simplicity, it is arguably the most effective form of narration. It sometimes influences the results of cases by bringing out details which had previously seemed irrelevant. Lord Denning's mastery of the story-telling genre, complete with conversational style and homely points of detail, not doubt helped him to convince his colleagues on the bench of his point of view, and thereby to obtain the majority. This approach may be observed in some of his most celebrated opening lines:

> Old Peter Beswick was a coal merchant in Eccles, Lancashire. He had no business premises. All he had was a lorry, scales and weights. He used to take the lorry to the yard of the National Coal Board, where he bagged coal and took it round to his customers in the neighbourhood.
>
> (*Beswick v Beswick* CA 1966, *per* Denning LJ)

> It happened on April 19, 1964. It was bluebell time in Kent. Mr. and Mrs. Hinz had been married some 10 years, and they had four children, all aged nine and under. The youngest was one. Mrs. Hinz was a remarkable woman. In addition to her own four, she was foster-mother to four other children. To add to it, she was two months pregnant with her fifth child.
>
> (*Hinz v Berry* 1970, *per* Denning LJ)

> Broadchalke is one of the most pleasing villages in England. Old Herbert Bundy, the defendant, was a farmer there. His home was at Yew Tree Farm. It went back for 300 years. His family had been there for generations. It was his only asset. But he did a very foolish thing. He mortgaged it to the bank. Up to the very hilt. Not to borrow money for himself, but for the sake of his son. Now the bank have come down on him. They have foreclosed. They want to get him out of Yew Tree Farm and to sell it.
>
> (*Lloyds Bank v Bundy* CA 1974, *per* Denning LJ)

> This is the case of the barmaid who was badly bitten by a big dog. It was a guard dog, an Alsatian about two years old. It kept guard over a yard next to the Maypole public house in East London.
>
> (*Cummings v Granger* CA 1976, *per* Denning LJ)

> In summertime village cricket is the delight of everyone. Nearly every village has its own cricket field where the young men play and the old men watch. In the village of Lintz in County Durham they have their own ground, where they have played these last 70 years. They tend it well. The wicket area is well rolled and mown. The outfield is kept short. It has a good club house for the players and seats for the onlookers. The village team play there on Saturdays and Sundays.
>
> (*Miller v Jackson* CA 1977, *per* Denning MR)

These cases are celebrated principally because of the important legal questions raised and presented with admirable clarity. Few authors share Lord Denning's ability to communicate personally with the reader.[12]

The importance of narration in adjudication is now accepted not just by specialists in 'law and literature' but also by the judges themselves. However, although persuasive, it is not necessarily determinative.

In the Court of Appeal, in *Jain v Trent Strategic Health Authority* (2007), for example, Wilson LJ admitted the extent to which he had been influenced by Jacob LJ's earlier presentation of the facts, while regretting that on a purely technical level, he was unable to provide an adequate legal solution: "In the light of the facts so vividly – yet accurately – summarised by Jacob L.J., my conclusion gives me no pleasure". Similar points were later made in the House of Lords. In the words of Baroness Hale: "We shared his view that there was indeed a serious injustice here which deserved a remedy" (*Trent SHA v Jain* HL 2009, *per* Baroness Hale).

However, the story of the case preserves an importance which goes beyond adjudication in individual cases to affect the development of the law itself. Indeed, in the common law system, decisions made in particular cases are likely to create precedents which are generally applicable. In this context, it is significant that a reinterpretation of

---

12 Justice Cardozo had similar success in America in the first half of the 20th century. Although expressing himself in a very different style (many of his most celebrated opinions read like concentrated prose poems), he also seems to be communicating directly with the reader.

precedent will usually involve a retelling of the earlier case in order to derive a different rule.

Invented examples are commonly used to clarify the salient points in legal argument, and these also involve story-telling. Numerous examples may be found in the leading case of *Haughton v Smith* (1973), concerning the question of how far someone can be guilty of an attempt to commit a crime, where what was attempted turns out to have been either legally or physically impossible. In his judgment in this case, Lord Morris envisaged a fictitious case of attempted murder where the victim was already dead. Lord Hailsham referred to episodes from fiction, including 'The day of the jackal' and stories from Sherlock Holmes. References are also made to 19th century discussions of similar problems.

5. Conclusion

English judgments are still normally prepared individually and given seriatim. This means that where judges differ on points of detail, their apparent inconsistency sometimes makes it difficult to find a coherent rule common to the different concurring judgments. In the American system, by contrast, the official judgment of the court is always clearly marked, and the rules adopted are stated explicitly. According to Tiersma (2007), American judges, knowing that their opinions are readily available (in electronic form) and likely to be cited in argument,[13] have tended to adopt a standard, written form of expression. This situation, combined with the fact that American judgments are usually given in writing, has led to the adoption of a more complex style. In a book review, Schauer (1995: 1455) goes so far as to suggest that American judicial opinions, because of their precedential function, tend more and more to 'read like statutes'. This may apply more to the lower courts than to the higher courts. It is in

13 The fact that the reports are available online means that it is now possible to locate relevant quotations without reading the whole judgment.

any case a comparatively recent development. Indeed, many of the most significant Supreme Court cases, as late as the second half of the twentieth century are relatively short and expressed in simple terms.[14]

In a recent pronouncement on this subject, the English Lord Chief Justice pointed out a similar change of approach which he suggested was an inevitable consequence of online publication. However, his reproach is aimed not at judges but at lawyers, who now tend to multiply citations beyond reason:

> Every single judgment of this court is now available to the advocate [...]. Understandably, the advocate doing his duty by his client seeks to identify each and every case which even remotely appears to bear on the principle under consideration or which has some passing factual similarity to the one with which he is immediately concerned. The development of legal argument [...] is therefore, we venture to suggest, more rebarbative and less focussed than it used to be. [...] And so, like Topsy, the process has grown, and lengthened, and continues to grow and lengthen without the slightest discernible improvement in the doing of justice [...].
>
> (*R v Erskine* CA 2009, *per* Judge CJ)

However, Lord Judge's own style, which here includes a literary reference (to 'Topsy'), cannot itself be said to "read like statutes". As the Chief Justice himself demonstrates, English judges still often make use of an idiosyncratic, sometimes conversational style, and usually attempt – with varying degrees of success – to provide clear analysis, in easily understandable terms. Lord Judge's complaint is precisely that the encyclopedic approach of the lawyers is making this task more difficult.

From the legal point of view, it should be accepted that the style adopted may affect the results of cases and thereby influence the historical development of the law. The 'narrative' element may indeed provide what is sometimes the most plausible explanation of surprising or historically inconsistent results, not only regarding the question of 'attempting the impossible' but also of 'appropriation' in theft, or 'mistake as to person' in the law of contract, mentioned by

14 See for example the opinions of Warren CJ in *Brown v Board of Education* (1954) or *Miranda v Arizona* (1966). Although the consequences of these decisions were incalculable, the language used is both simple and direct.

Jackson (1988: 105). In all of these fields, as predicted by Llewellyn (1952), the reasoning depends on the point of view rather than on pure facts. It may therefore be seen as a source of legal indeterminacy.

From a linguistic point of view, especially regarding the needs of those studying language for law, it is important to distinguish between the language of judgments and the language of statutes. While the language of English judges is explicit where necessary, it is nevertheless relatively clear and sometimes actually conversational, to the point of exhibiting many of the basic characteristics of oral language. Their language, as observed in common law judgments, is neither syntactically complex nor particularly obscure. Indeed, far from indulging in linguistic obscurity, the judges are the first to complain when the drafting of statutes makes judicial interpretation difficult. The recognition of this fact is a prerequisite for understanding the importance of the law in linguistic research.

On a more theoretical level, seen as a corpus of authentic language, legal judgments provide valuable material for the study of rhetoric and argumentation, as well as the history of the language, or for example clarity, discourse analysis and speech acts. The fact that the meanings of technical terms, like *consideration* or *remoteness*, is not fixed, as in most technical disciplines, but is frequently a matter of debate, raises obvious problems in the field of terminology.

As expert witnesses, linguists can sometimes make a useful contribution to legal procedure, where it is necessary to provide a forensic analysis of the linguistic evidence. However, the judges are often confronted with problems of interpretation and analysis to which linguists are unable to provide answers. These concern most obviously the meaning of general terms in statutes, questions of reference (in contracts or wills), or questions of deontic modality. Such problems frequently involve a theoretical distinction between literal and intentional meaning. Judicial reasoning on these subjects is both explicit and coherent. Helpful bibliographies on various relevant aspects of legal theory will be found in Patterson (1996). As the judicial analysis is founded on authentic examples, which often raise interesting theoretical problems, it should be taken seriously by linguists. Acknowledgement of the problems common to the different disciplines may then lead to reciprocal illumination.

References

Austin, John L. 1962. *How to Do Things with Words*. Oxford: Oxford University Press.

Charnock, Ross 2002. L'Argumentation Rhétorique et l'Enseignement de la Langue de Spécialité: L'Exemple du Discours Juridique. *ASp/Geras* 35-36, 121-136.

Charnock, Ross 2006. Clear Ambiguity. In Wagner, Anne / Cacciaguidi-Fahi, Sophie (eds) *Legal Language and the Search for Clarity*. Bern: Peter Lang, 65-103.

Charnock, Ross 2009. Overruling as a Speech Act: Performativity and Normative Discourse. *Journal of Pragmatics* 41/3, 401-426.

Del Lungo Camiciotti, Gabriella 2001. The Expression of Volition in Late Medieval English Wills. In Gotti, Maurizio / Dossena, Marina (eds) *Modality in Specialized Texts*. Bern: Peter Lang, 71-88.

Hale, Matthew 1971 [1736]. *The History of the Common Law of England*. Chicago: University of Chicago Press.

Jackson, Bernard 1988. *Law, Fact and Narrative Coherence*. Merseyside: Deborah Charles.

Llewellyn, Karl 1952 [1930]. *The Bramble Bush: On Our Law and Its Study*. New York: Oceania Publications.

Patterson, Dennis (ed) 1996. *A Companion to Philosophy of Law and Legal Theory*. Oxford: Blackwell.

Schauer, Frederick 1995. Opinions as Rules [book review]. *University of Chicago Law Review* 62, 1455-1475.

Tiersma, Peter 2007. The Textualization of Precedent. *Notre Dame Law Review* 82, 1187.

Appendix

Sources

English Reports 1220-1865. Published 1900-1932. Edinburgh: W. Green & Son.
The Law Reports (1865-present). London: ICLR.

Cases

AG New Zealand v Ortiz CA [1983] 2 WLR 809 (CA); [1884] AC 1 (HL)
Beswick v Beswick CA [1966] 3 WLR 396 (CA)
Brown v Board of Education 347 US 483 (1954)
Central London Property v High Trees House [1947] KB 130
College of Nursing v DHSS [1981] 2 WLR 297 (CA); [1981] 1 AC 800 (HL)
Cummings v Granger [1976] 3 W.L.R. 842 (CA)
Davies v Mann (1842) 153 ER 588
Dickinson v Dodds [1876] 2 ChD 463
Fisher v Bell CA [1960] 3 All ER 731 (CA)
Foakes v Beer [1884] 9 AC 605 (HL)
Jackson v Horizon Holidays CA [1975] 1 WLR 1468
Foakes v Beare [1884] 9 AC 605 (HL)
Furman v Georgia 408 US 238 (1972)
Haughton v Smith HL [1973] 3 All ER 1109
Hinz v Berry [1970] 2 WLR 684 (CA)
Jain v Trent Strategic Health Authority [2008] 2 WLR 456 (CA)
Lawrence v Texas 539 US 558 (2003)
Lloyds Bank v Bundy [1974] 3 W.L.R. 501 (CA)
Miller v Jackson [1977] 3 W.L.R. 20 (CA),
Miranda v Arizona 384 US 436 (1966)
Mirehouse v Rennel (1833) 6 ER 1015
George Mitchell v Finney Lock Seeds (1982) 3 WLR 1036 (CA)
Nordenfelt v Maxim Nordenfelt Ltd [1894] AC 535 (HL)
Practice Directive 1 WLR 1382 [1963] (HL)
Raynard v Chase (1756) 97 ER 155
Ofcom v Information Commissioners [2009] CA Civ 90
Pinnel's case (1602) 77 ER 237
R ex parte Haw v Sec Home Department, [2005] 2061 (HC Admin)
R ex parte Ofcom v Information Commissioners [2008] QB 1445
Regina v Bentham HL [2005] 2 CrApp R 11 (HL)
R v Erskine CA [2009] EWCA Crim 1425
R v Howell and Bentley (1864) 176 ER 513
R v Sharpe (1857) CCR, Dearsly & Bell 160
R v Joseph Webb (1834) 174 ER 140
Sommerset v Stewart (1772) 98 ER 499
Trent SHA v Jain [2009] 2 WLR 248 (HL)

JUDITH TURNBULL

Harmonisation of the Law and Legal Cultures in the EU: A Linguistic Approach

1. Introduction

Harmonisation in the European Union (EU) aims to create common standards across its internal market and achieve uniformity in the laws of Member States. It is built on the consensus between all interested parties and seeks to co-ordinate different legal systems by "eliminating major differences and creating minimum requirements or standards" (Kamba 1974: 501). In the words of an American jurist (Boodman 1991) harmonisation is "the combination or adaptation of parts, elements or related things, so as to form a consonant and orderly whole". Boodman draws on the origins of the term in music to give some insight into its meaning: harmonisation presupposes and preserves the diversity of the objects harmonised; its components, while retaining their individuality, form a new and more complex musical sound; and it produces consonance, that is, an agreeable combination of sounds. The words *diversity*, *individuality* and *consonance* seem particularly relevant, as they call to mind the EU motto 'United in Diversity'.

The Court of Justice of the European Union plays an important role in the harmonisation process, as it has the ultimate say on matters of EU law in order to ensure its equal application across all EU Member States. The Court is itself a product of harmonisation, since it is composed of 27 judges and eight Advocates General appointed by all the Member States. The aim of this chapter is to assess whether the language, style and rhetoric of the Court of Justice (in their judicial opinions delivered at the Court) reflect the ongoing process of harmonisation in European law.

For this purpose I analysed the Opinions of the Advocates General, which are an independent and impartial analysis of each case, as presented to the Court after an Advocate General (henceforth AG) has taken part in the preliminary meeting and hearing, but before the judges deliberate and deliver their judgment. The AG's Opinion is advisory and does not bind the Court, but is nevertheless very influential and is followed in the majority of cases. Since each Opinion is the work of a single author and is almost always written in his/her native language, it provides an opportunity to make a comparative analysis of the language, style and rhetoric of judges from different legal cultures and to assess to what extent they remain faithful to, or deviate from, the conventions of their own legal culture.

Judgments have been the subject of several juridical analyses, especially in English-speaking common law countries where there is a strong interest in the rhetoric and argumentation strategies of judges (Posner 1995; Wald 1995). Within the context of the European Court, Salmi-Tolonen (2005) has investigated persuasive argumentative strategies in AG Opinions, but focused entirely on British AGs. This chapter will make a comparative analysis of the Opinions of British and Italian AGs and will therefore draw on studies which have adopted a cross-cultural approach (Rega 1997; Scarpa/Riley 2000; Kurzon 2001). In order to assess the degree of harmonisation that has taken place, a brief description of judgments in the English and Italian legal systems will be given first in section 1.1.

1.1. English and Italian judgments

Historically speaking, the role of the judge in the civil law and common law systems is based on two opposite principles. In the Roman-Germanic system of the kind in Italy, the judge applies the law that is entirely written in the codes and acts as an official of the law. In contrast, in a common law system a judge interprets and, at times, even creates the law, as judgments of the higher courts create precedents and represent one of its main sources.

This basic difference is reflected in the style and approach adopted in the writing of judgments. Italian judges veil their personal contributions and subordinate their opinion to a panel decision, since Italian judgments "are conceived and written as bureaucratic documents [...] the formal explanation of an impersonal decision" (Taruffo 1988: 207). Instead, English judges sit in court alone (except in appeal courts) and argue their own point of view about the facts of the case and the law individually and personally. As a consequence, their style can be either "conversational, combative or rhetorical" (Hope of Craighead 2005: 1) and, at times, even allow the use of humour (Hobbs 2007).

The two national judgments have been described according to their morpho-syntactic and lexical characteristics (Rega 1997; Scarpa/Riley 2000). Italian judgments use an impersonal and technical type of language, presenting unusual features such as adjectives or past participles positioned before the noun as pre-modifiers, a frequent use of the passive, often together with the gerund, systematic inversion of subject-verb into verb-subject, the use of Latin expressions, formulaic language and redundant stereotypical phrases. In contrast, English judgments do not deviate very noticeably from everyday language and have a relatively simple sentence structure, frequent use of hypothetic propositions, extensive use of pronouns and personal adjectives (especially 1st person), a frequent use of modality expressions and emotionally intensive lexis.

Given the (im)personal nature of judgments in the two systems, the analysis of the AG Opinions will focus on those elements of the language in which the person of the judge is visible, namely: the explicitly direct and personal expressions that indicate the judge's attitude and position towards the message; and expressions of politeness. It will also investigate to what extent Opinions incorporate features typical of impersonal and bureaucratic language, such as nominalization, passives and impersonal forms.

2. Corpus and methodology

The corpus consists of 40 Opinions delivered by British and Italian AGs, 20 for each group, as a sample representing two very different legal systems. The United Kingdom and Italy are among the countries which have a permanent AG at the European Court, Germany, France and Spain being the others; the remaining three positions are held by the other Member States on a rotation basis. The Opinions, which were selected at random, cover a variety of issues and different types of cases dating from 1998 to 2008. They are of varying length (2,500-21,000 words), for a total of 310,162 words. Their great range in length depends on the complexity of the cases and on how many legal issues are raised.

AGs are appointed by common accord by the governments of Member States for a renewable term of six years. This means that there is not a frequent turnover and indeed, in the case of British AGs, only two judges held office in the period covered by the corpus. As a consequence, some allowance must be given for possible, if not probable, idiolectal usage and personal preferences of expression. There were four Italian AGs, however, which gives a broader, though still limited, sample.

My analysis of the Opinions of AGs is both quantitative and qualitative. The former was limited because of the type of analysis undertaken and the difficulties arising from the use of a bilingual comparable corpus made up of texts written independently in their respective languages and put together on the basis of similarity of content and domain. The grammatical tagging to identify Italian 1st person verb forms was carried out with TalTac2, while concordance lines for both subcorpora were obtained using ConcApp. The politeness analysis, however, was performed only qualitatively in order to capture the pragmatic meaning of a possibly very wide range of expressions, since "politeness is implicated by the semantic structure of the whole utterance, not communicated by 'markers' or 'mitigators' in a simple signalling fashion" (Brown/Levinson 1987: 22).

3. Results

3.1. Explicitly personal expressions

The most overtly marked expressions involve personal pronouns and adjectives *I*, *me* and *my* in English and their equivalents in Italian. As subject pronouns are usually omitted (zero pronoun) in Italian, the figure for 'I' includes all 1st person verb forms. Contrary to expectations, there is an extensive use of first-person expressions in Italian, though clearly less than in British Opinions. The higher figure for the plural probably results from the use of *noi* [we/us] in the formal discourse of authority in Italian.

	British		*Italian*	
	Occurrences	*Normalized*	*Occurrences*	*Normalized*
I	337	260	375	208
my	103	79	125	69
me	84	65	156	86
we	1	1	25	14
our	2	2	20	11
us	4	3	26	14

Table 1. First-person pronouns and adjectives (normalized per 100,000 words).

The next table shows the 15 most frequently occurring verbs used in the 1st person (all tenses):

British		*Italian*	
consider	42	ritengo	120
am (the view)	34	ricordo	36
agree	32	osservo	29
conclude	15	propongo	29
think	12	credo	26
feel	10	dico	18
see	9	rilevo	12
refer	9	suggerisco	9
add	9	concludo	8
note	8	convengo	8

explain	7	passo	8
accept	5	aggiungo	7
set out	5	ripeto	6
propose	4	premetto	4
understand	4	vedo	4

Table 2. Most frequent verbs used in the first person (occurrences).

Top of the list are *consider* and *ritengo*, which have the same meaning but the difference in the number of occurrences is quite striking, with 42 as opposed to 120. In the Italian list there are five other verbs which have a high number of occurrences, whereas in the British list there are only another two which occur frequently.

The total number of verbs used in the first person were similar in the two languages: 65 in English, 67 in Italian. However, given the larger size of the Italian corpus and the greater lexical variation favoured in Italian, this may suggest a more formulaic, standardised use of language by Italian AGs, in keeping with their legal culture. The types of verbs in both lists indicate a metadiscursive use of 1st person expressions to make explicit reference either to the Advocate's stance (*agree*, *think*, *feel*, *see* and *ritengo*, *convengo*, *credo*) or to the organisation of the text (*add*, *set out* and *ricordo*, *passo*, *aggiungo*).

Table 3 shows all the items collocating with 1st person singular possessives in the two corpora. The first in each list (*view*/*avviso*) has the same meaning but this time with a similar number of occurrences. There is, however, a greater variety in the English list, some of them being even very personal, such as *forty years of teaching and practising IP law*.

British		*Italian*	
(in my) view	66	(a mio) avviso	70
(to my) mind	10	corsivo	25
analysis	2	parere	9
conclusion	2	(da/per) parte	9
example	2	giudizio	4
part	2	modo di vedere	3
understanding	2	conclusioni	2
concern	1	convinzione	1
forty years of	1	intenzione	1

teaching	1	perplessità	1
interpretation	1		
knowledge	1		
reading	1		
remarks	1		
rendering	1		
translation	1		

Table 3. Items collocating with 1st person singular possessive adjectives.

This could suggest that British AGs, even within the European legal context, take advantage of the greater personal freedom of expression granted by their own legal culture, as can be seen below (my italics), whilst Italian AGs rely on a more 'formulaic' use of the language, to limit the projection of their personality on the Opinion.

(1) *I am not,* however, persuaded by either of the above arguments that *my understanding* of the Directive is misconceived. It is settled case-law that Community legislation must be interpreted not solely on the basis of its wording, but also in the light of the overall scheme and objectives of the system of which it is a part. *I have explained* above *what I consider* to be the scheme and objectives of the Directive and why *my interpretation* of its provisions is consistent therewith. The concepts of a 'holding [...] in the capital' of a company and a parent company's 'association with its subsidiary' must be understood in that context, which is – again – not primarily a company law context. (C 48/07)

The following rather long extract (2) shows how personal expressions, which appear in initial position in the sentence and paragraph, are used simply to 'signpost' the points in the argumentation, rather than express the involvement and commitment of the author in the argument.

(2) *Devo tuttavia notare che* in nessuna fase della procedura, né di fronte al giudice nazionale né di fronte alla Corte, è mai stato messo in dubbio che la piccola Catherine possegga effettivamente la cittadinanza irlandese [...]
Mi limito a ricordare che, per quanto attiene all'ordinamento comunitario, la Corte ha affermato nelle sentenze Micheletti e Kaur che «la determinazione dei modi di acquisto e di perdita della cittadinanza rientra, in conformità al diritto internazionale, nella competenza di ciascuno Stato membro» [...]
Mi sembra pertanto di poter concludere che, in considerazione della cittadinanza irlandese della piccola Catherine, la controversia pendente

davanti all'Immigration Authority rientra in linea di principio nell'ambito di applicazione del Trattato e che l'eccezione di irricevibilità sollevata dal governo del Regno Unito deve quindi essere respinta. (C 200/02)

The use of personal expressions, however, is not sufficient to indicate a more personal style. The next example, from a British Opinion, has a number of evaluative elements which explicitly convey the author's stance, even though there is only one explicit personal reference (*it seems to me*).

(3) In so saying, the national court made two *correct* statements and one *significant error*. The Community arrangements for market support in the agricultural sector do *indeed all* depend, *correctly*, upon making sure that those claiming support comply with the *necessary* conditions laid down by the Community regulations. The wine and grape producers were *indeed* the 'intended ultimate recipients of the aid'. However, *it seems to me* that, on a *proper* construction of Regulation No 2499/82, the distillers (DAI) were not, in any true sense, the 'intended recipients of the aid' in so far as concerns the minimum buying-in price. (C 51/05 P)

Bearing in mind the general characteristics of judgments in the two countries, the Opinions of British and Italian AGs show that some of these are maintained, such as the personal approach in (1) above and the technical 'bureaucratic' style typical of Italian judgments in (4):

(4) Più in generale, emerge dalla giurisprudenza che la *sussistenza del requisito di selettività* deve fare l'oggetto di una valutazione caso per caso, mirata a verificare se la misura di cui trattasi, *conto tenuto* della sua natura, del suo ambito di applicazione, delle sue modalità di attuazione e dei suoi effetti, comporti o no vantaggi a esclusivo profitto di talune imprese o di taluni settori di attività. Ove sia accertata la sussistenza di un *siffatto vantaggio*, anche la non imposizione di un nuovo tributo a determinati operatori economici può costituire un aiuto ai sensi dell'art. 87, n. 1, CE. (C 487/06)

On the other hand, some adaptation has also taken place, as can be seen in (5), which reads as natural modern Italian, and in (6), which is characterised by the use of impersonal forms, passives and nominalization.

(5) La cittadinanza irlandese di Catherine, dunque, è elemento sufficiente a escludere che la controversia che la oppone, assieme alla madre, al Secretary of State sia puramente interna all'ordinamento britannico [...]
Devo tuttavia notare che in nessuna fase della procedura, né di fronte al giudice nazionale né di fronte alla Corte, è mai stato messo in dubbio che la piccola Catherine possegga effettivamente la cittadinanza irlandese, come del resto non è stata contestata dal governo del Regno Unito la legittimità, dal punto di vista del diritto internazionale o comunitario, dell'attribuzione di quella cittadinanza da parte dello Stato irlandese. (C 200/02)

(6) *This aspect has not been discussed* before the Court in great detail, and it would not be appropriate to express a definitive view which should be based on a full appreciation of national circumstances. However, *the contested amendment appears to mean* that the rule precluding reimbursement where the burden of the tax has been passed on applies to all categories of claimant but one [...]
If it is the case that entitlement to benefit from *Anlaßfallwirkung* is confined to those bringing challenges under national constitutional law, then the rules governing reimbursement of taxes found incompatible with national law might be more favourable, in that regard, than in the case of taxes found incompatible with Community law.
For the amendment to comply with the principle of equivalence, *it would be necessary* either for the benefit of the exception to be extended to all those who have challenged a tax found to be incompatible with Community law or for the exception to be abolished entirely. (C 147/01)

3.2. Expressions of politeness

Politeness is a device by which social interactions can be managed and social relationships maintained. Fundamental in Brown and Levinson's politeness theory (1987) is the concept of face, the public self-image that every person tries to project. Negative face is the want to be unimpeded by others and positive face the want to be approved of. Intrinsically verbal or non-verbal acts threaten face, so the addresser may choose one of a variety of politeness strategies to minimise the threat or, alternatively, do the act baldly without redress.

Kurzon (2001) correctly points out that the use of politeness in the context of law courts may seem strange, given that their purpose is to resolve disputes between litigants. Nevertheless, he goes on to show

how American and English judges express more or less harshly their agreement/disagreement with arguments presented before the court (and previous decisions delivered in other courts) through a number of strategies that range from face-saving to face-threatening acts.

While the basic hierarchy of politeness strategies may be universal, as Brown and Levinson (1987) argue, the actual expression of politeness may vary enormously from one culture to another. The function of judgments in the English and Italian systems (persuasive and personal in the former, impersonal and logical in the latter) is likely to determine a different approach to politeness. Therefore the different cultural backgrounds of AGs may also influence the way they discuss the issues raised by the parties in their Opinions. Furthermore, the purely advisory role of an AG's Opinion may affect the level of politeness adopted. In fact, the addressees include, first and foremost, the panel of judges who will hear the Opinion before deciding on their own judgment. It will be useful therefore to consider what Lakoff (1989: 103) refers to as 'non-politeness', i.e. forms involving neutral expressions, especially where the communicative function of the text is primarily informative as in the case of judgments and Opinions. Other addressees are the litigants (the applicants), national courts, the European Commission, the governments who submit written observations, those who presented oral arguments at the hearing and the European Court of Justice (for case law and as the receiver of the Opinion), institutions which are of high standing and whose status may again influence the level of politeness.

3.2.1. Agreement in Opinions

Agreement relates to the addressee's positive face in that it creates common ground, creating solidarity between writer and reader. However, within the context of a court and given the AGs' institutional role of authority, this classical convention of politeness does not hold. Both British and Italian AGs adopt neutral non-polite wordings appropriate to the impartial and informative nature of the message, without any 'element of exaggeration' that distinguishes positive politeness (Brown/Levinson 1987: 101). At times agreement is expressed in an explicit, personal way:

(7) *I* agree with the Commission

(8) *I* am also of the view

(9) *I* am of the opinion

(10) *I* accept

(11) *I* share the analysis

(12) *I* consider the Commission's action well founded

(13) *Convengo* infatti con la Commissione

(14) *Ritengo* pertanto che il Tribunale abbia correttamente potuto affermare

In other cases agreement is conveyed indirectly, through an adverb:

(15) As the Commission *correctly* observes

(16) Come *giustamente* ha osservato il Tribunale

Italian often prefers impersonal or less direct forms, which is perhaps more in fitting with the less 'individualistic' approach of Italian legal culture:

(17) Quanto al primo aspetto, *è a mio parere indubbio* che

(18) Ugualmente *fondate mi sembrano* le censure della Commissione.

Claims may be intensified by the use of adverbs:

(19) I *fully* endorse

(20) I agree *entirely*

(21) Da parte mia condivido *appieno* tali osservazioni

(22) Tale qualificazione mi trova senz'alto d'accordo

or weakened through lexical choices:

(23) I *am inclined* to share the institution's view

(24) I find it *plausible*

(25) *Inclino* a condividere l'assunto della Commissione

(26) A mio modo di vedere, la prima delle tesi dianzi esposte merita di essere *preferita*.

There is a surprising correspondence at times between the two languages, as for example *I am inclined/Inclino* (23, 25) and *founded* in (12) and (18) in the sense of *justified.*

It is also interesting to note that there are no examples in the corpus of deference in addressing the judges or courts, as occurs in the English legal system with, for example, the expression 'The learned judge'. However, on a few rare occasions compliments are paid to colleagues in the European Court by the Italian AGs.

(27) Così ha *perspicuamente* rilevato l'avvocato generale Mischo nelle sue conclusioni del 12 marzo 1998. (C 392/96)

(28) L'avvocato generale Darmon ha *efficacemente* sottolineato nelle sue conclusioni l'opportunità di tener conto di tutte le possibili conseguenze di una tale causa di licenziamento. (C 12/08)

By comparison, English compliments tend to be much weaker:

(29) After *detailed* discussion Advocate General Jacobs concluded the judgment under appeal should be quashed. (C 128/05)

At times, however, agreement is expressed in a less direct way, which can become almost obscure.

(30) For my part, I am *most reluctant* to *presume against* them that they should *never* have appealed. (C 51/05 P)

(31) Il ragionamento seguito dal Tribunale per dichiarare l'argomento *irricevibile non mi sembra* possa essere oggetto di critica. (C 71/07P)

(32) *Non mi sembra* che la giurisprudenza della Corte relativa alla nota 5 E *sia contrastante* con l'interpretazione che intendo proporre. (C 362/07 and C 363/07)

In these examples the presence of two negatives, expressed either grammatically through the negative particle and through a negative meaning or connotation of a word, makes the sentence positive in meaning, though very indirect.

3.2.2. Disagreement in Opinions

There is a much greater variety of expressions used to modify the force of a disagreement according to the writer's intentions. However, this is frequently expressed in a non-polite manner, as in the following examples which simply inform the addressees of the AG's view of the issue at hand:

(33) I do not find that argument persuasive

(34) I am not convinced, however, that those factors are relevant

(35) I do not accept those arguments

(36) I do not see how

(37) I do not think that

(38) Non condivido l'interpretazione che il ricorrente dà al passaggio appena citato

(39) Non ritengo si possa desumere

(40) Più in generale, non vedo poi come si possa rimproverare al Tribunale

It is interesting to note how both languages use negative forms, which are less assertive and face-threatening than *disagree* or *reject* (one occurrence each) or *sono in disaccordo* (no occurrences). Furthermore, many of the negative Italian expressions of disagreement use a variant of *mi sembra(no)* for a total of 143 occurrences as opposed to 41 of *it seems to me* (no negative forms). In this way the AG is able to present an argument as his/her own view of the question.

Similarly, personal attribution may be expressed by phrases such as *a mio avviso*, *a mio parere* and *in my view* that may also tone down the disagreement. Salmi-Tolonen (2005: 90) argues that expressions of this kind do not act as hedges by mitigating the statements of AGs, but rather "stress the authority and expertise and thorough work of the writer". Their use, however, may also reflect the respect they have for their colleagues in the Court who will receive the Opinion. Such expressions may appear at the head of a sentence or in the middle, as in the following examples:

(41) *In my view*, however, the fact the national law *does not transpose* the Directive in identical terms *does not necessarily mean* that a request by a national court for an interpretation of the underlying directive should be regarded as *inadmissible*. (C 48/07)

(42) It would *in my view* be *wholly wrong* for the prescription defence to succeed in the exceptional circumstances of the present case. (C 51/05 P)

(43) *A mio avviso*, la ricorrente *non erra* nel ritenere che il principio «chi inquina paga» non rientri nella descrizione degli obiettivi dell'AGL... (C 487/06)

(44) Gli argomenti avanzati dalla ricorrente nel quadro del quinto e del sesto motivo d'impugnazione sono, *a mio avviso*, *manifestamente inadeguati* a dimostrare l'esistenza dei vizi contestati. (C 487/06)

When in initial position, such expressions firmly assert the writer as the source of the statement (Hyland 2002), whereas in the middle of the sentence they seem to mitigate the force of the utterance, as in *wholly wrong* (42) and *manifestamente inadeguati* (44).

Another way of hedging criticism, adopted by both the British and Italian AGs, is to address the views and arguments of the addressees, rather than the institutions or individuals themselves.

(45) That *argument* however is based on a misconception as to the nature and objective of the public lending right. (C 36/05)

(46) Those *arguments* however appear to me to disregard the more general provisions of the Regulation. (C 341/04)

(47) Gli *argomenti* sviluppati dal Tribunale in aggiunta alla predetta fondamentale constatazione, in particolare ai punti 124 e 125, mi sembrano, per quanto in linea di principio corretti, superflui ai fini della decisione sul motivo addotto dal ricorrente. (C 71/07P9)

(48) Si deve in effetti ammettere che il *procedimento logico* seguito dal giudice del rinvio per rivolgersi alla Corte non è privo di difetti. (C 12/08)

A further strategy adopted by both is the use of an apology to minimise the face-threatening act of disagreement. In (49) the writer takes some responsibility for failing to understand the matter fully and uses brackets in an attempt to further reduce the challenge.

(49) Adams is, of course, and as Commission implicitly argues, distinguishable in various respects from the present case *(although I confess to some puzzlement over the Commission's argument that it concerns not the determination of when time starts to run but rather when the limitation period expires, since the one surely depends on the other)*. (C 51/05 P)

A comparison with Italian examples once again reveals a surprising similarity in the choice of lexical items, as shown by the verb *confesso* [I confess].

(50) *Confesso* che mi sembra difficile attribuire all'espressione «secondary aggregates» impiegata in tale 'considerando' un significato diverso da quello che deriva dalla definizione che precede tale espressione: «aggregati estratti come sottoprodotti o scarti di un diverso processo». (C 487/06)

There are also a number of criticisms which involve superficially neutral adjectives, but can be interpreted as harsh and hence impolite, as they are challenging the legal expertise of the addressees.

(51) The order for reference is likewise extremely *laconic* as to the factual context. [...] It is certainly true that the order for reference is *succinct* in the extreme and that the Court has ruled that the need to provide an interpretation of Community law which will be of use to the national court makes it necessary that that court define the factual and legislative context of the questions it is asking. References which do not satisfy that requirement may indeed be dismissed as inadmissible. (C 48/07)

In the first paragraph, the order for reference presented by the national court is criticized as *laconic*. Eleven paragraphs later the AG quotes a general rule on the standards required and indirectly refers to the same inadequacy but with a synonym, thus reiterating implicitly the criticism in a less threatening manner.

In the following example, the expression *deeply innovative* may not appear immediately to be offensive, but it becomes evident that it is used in an ironic sense as the AG goes on to suggest that the approach adopted by the Court did not take into due consideration Community case law.

(52) L'approccio seguito dal Tribunale, quale emerge dall'esame dei punti della sentenza impugnata sintetizzati sopra, si rivela *profondamente innovativo* rispetto alla giurisprudenza comunitaria sull'applicazione del requisito di selettività e, più in generale, della nozione di aiuto ai sensi dell'art. 87, n. 1, CE. (C 487/06)

In (53) there are no lexical items with negative meanings, so it appears to be superficially polite:

(53) Fermo restando che *non è compito della Corte* interpretare il diritto nazionale, *devo confessare* che *fatico a comprendere* come il giudice nazionale possa preferire l'interpretazione più rigida dell'art. 67. (C 12/08)

This example sounds almost apologetic [it isn't the Court's responsibility... I have to confess] but becomes highly critical when it mentions the extreme difficulty of understanding the rationale behind the judge's decision.

So far it would appear that British and Italian AGs adopt similar expressions of agreement and disagreement with appropriate mitigating strategies. However, when they want to convey an outright expression of disagreement or criticism, some differences emerge. Italian AGs can be more direct and display elements of 'bald on record' impoliteness (Brown/Levinson 1987: 69).

(54) La questione posta dal giudice del rinvio non dovrebbe dunque neppure ricevere una risposta. (C 12/08)

(55) Il richiamo di tali decisioni è, però, privo di pregio ai fini dell'odierno giudizio. (C 212/97)

Examples of harsh criticism occur also in the British subcorpus, but they are usually accompanied by some form of mitigation:

(56) *Intellectually, it is difficult* to reconcile this with the claim that 'only a framework law will do'. (C 32/05)

(57) It therefore *seems both inappropriate and arbitrary* to limit the concept of 'extraction' to a process... (C 304/07)

In (56) the force of the adverb *intellectually* is mitigated to some extent by the phrase *it is difficult*, whilst in (57) *seems* weakens the criticism expressed by two adjectives and emphasized by the use of *both*.

4. Concluding remarks

Although previous studies of British and Italian judgments have emphasized the differences between the two legal cultures, the analysis of the British and Italian Opinions in the EU Court of Justice indicates many similarities that suggest an accommodation of the judges to a new legal context. Rhetorical changes have taken place on both sides. There is a notable use of personalized forms by Italian AGs, which will certainly have been favoured by the single authorship of the texts, but it still marks a radical change, as indeed the less 'technical' language adopted. On the other side, British AGs can be seen at times to use a more impersonal bureaucratic style which is unusual in their legal culture. Nevertheless, beyond these very evident signs of accommodation, some features of the Opinions 'betray' the origins of the AG. Personal expressions in Italian Opinions perform a purely signposting function to guide the reader through the AG's argumentation, whereas in British Opinions they convey the writer's involvement in and commitment to the message.

As far as politeness is concerned, non-polite forms are used extensively by both British and Italian AGs, but, more importantly, they adopt the same strategies to mitigate criticism and disagreement, with striking similarities in the actual wording of expressions. It is perhaps surprising that Italian Opinions show more face-threatening forms of politeness with overt compliments and bald-on-record impoliteness, while British AGs tend to be more restrained. This may indicate an adaptation by Italian AGs towards the greater freedom allowed in Opinions and by their British counterparts towards a more constrained style of continental judicial opinions.

It would seem therefore that the Opinions of Advocates General can be considered as hybrid texts, in so far as they are produced in a multilingual, multicultural context in which "specific linguistic and cultural conventions get mixed up and infiltrate each other" (McAuliffe 2009: 5). In terms of harmonisation, it can be said that the degree of adaptation that has taken place creates a consonant whole, but the diversity and individuality of the AGs' legal cultures still filter through and characterise their Opinions.

References

Boodman, Martin 1991. The Myth of Harmonization of Laws. *American Journal of Comparative Law* 39/Fall, 699-724.

Brown, Penelope / Levinson, Stephen C. 1987. *Politeness. Some Universals in Language Usage.* Cambridge: Cambridge University Press.

Hobbs, Patricia 2007. Judges' Use of Humour as a Social Corrective. *Journal of Pragmatics* 39/1, 50-68.

Hope of Craighead, Lord 2005. Writing Judgments. London: Judicial Studies Board. Retrieved from <http://jsboard.co.uk/downloads/annuallecture-2005-proof-220305.pdf> on 2 February 2009.

Hyland, Ken 2002. Authority and Invisibility: Authorial Identity in Academic Writing. *Journal of Pragmatics* 34/8, 1091-1112.

Kamba, Walter 1974. Comparative Law. A Theoretical Framework. *International Comparative Law Quarterly* 23/3, 485-519.

Kurzon, Dennis 2001. The Politeness of Judges: American and English Judicial Behaviour. *Journal of Pragmatics* 33/1, 61-85.

Lakoff, Robin 1989. The Limits of Politeness: Therapeutic and Courtroom Discourse. *Multilingua* 8/2-3, 101-129.

McAuliffe, Karen 2009. Hybrid Texts and Uniform Law? The Production of a Multilingual Jurisprudence by the Court of Justice of the European Communities. Paper presented at the Annual Meeting of The Law and Society Association, Montreal, 27 May 2008. Retrieved from <http://www. allacademic.com> on 10 September 2009.

Myers, Greg 1989. The Pragmatics of Politeness in Scientific Articles. *Applied Linguistics* 10/1, 1-35.

Posner, Richard 1995. Judges' Writing Styles (And Do They Matter?). *Chicago Law Review* 62/Fall, 1421-1449.

Rega, Lorenza 1997. La sentenza italiana e tedesca nell'ottica della traduzione. In Schena, Leandro (ed.) *La lingua del diritto. Difficoltà traduttive. Applicazioni didattiche.* Rome: CISU, 117-126.

Salmi-Tolonen, Tarja 2005. Persuasion in Judicial Argumentation. The Opinions of the Advocates General at the European Court of Justice. In Halmari, Helena / Virtanen, Tuija (eds) *Persuasion across Genres*. Amsterdam: John Benjamins, 59-61.

Salvi, Rita / Turnbull, Judith 2008. Literary Traces and Rhetorical Language in Legal Texts. *Textus* 21/3, 439-465.

Scarpa, Federica / Riley, Alison 2000. La fisionomia della sentenza in Inghilterra e in Italia: un'analisi orientata alla traduzione. In Schena, Leandro / Snel Trampus, Rita D. (eds) *Traduttori e giuristi a confronto. Interpretazione traducente e comparazione del discorso giuridico.* Vol. 1. Bologna: CLUEB, 227-291.

Schena, Leandro / Snel Trampus, Rita D. (eds) 2000. *Traduttori e giuristi a confronto. Interpretazione traducente e comparazione del discorso giuridico.* Vol. 1. Bologna: CLUEB.

Taruffo, Michele 1988. La fisionomia della sentenza in Italia. In *La sentenza in Europa. Metodo, tecnica e stile*. Padua: CEDAM, 180-214.

Wald, Patricia 1995. The Rhetoric of Results and the Results of Rhetoric. *Chicago Law Review* 62/Fall, 1371-1419.

Issues in Translation and Interpreting

PATRICK LEROYER / KIRSTEN WØLCH RASMUSSEN

Accessing Discursive Data Types in Legal Translation Dictionaries: The Case of *Sans Préjudice de*

1. Introduction

Legal translation as a textual activity is to a large extent a reconstruction of the constitutive discourses of the law across culturally-bound national legal systems. Thus, legal translators need intercultural knowledge of the textual conventions shaping legal discourse and of matching translation strategies (Kjær 1997; Sørensen 1999; Nielsen 2000; Acuyo-Verdejo 2004; Wagner 2004; Grass 2009). Bilingual legal dictionaries should help the translator by providing fast and easy access to this type of discursive information. Tarp (1999) claims that dictionaries are most useful at word level and, to a lesser extent, at the level of phraseological units. In his view, at sentence level the usefulness of dictionaries is strongly limited, while it is almost inexistent at text level.

In this chapter, we will refute this claim, which seems to rely on a lexicographic approach restricted to printed dictionaries or to e-dictionaries that reproduce printed dictionaries. Building on the methodology introduced in Leroyer/Rasmussen (2004), we will analyse legal translation issues at text level within the framework of a case study. Our evidence comes from a corpus of legal texts in French and from a translational corpus of aligned legal texts in Danish and French. It also draws on a selection of mono- and bilingual specialized dictionaries, including the EU's multilingual term base. We will make the case for a contrastive methodology aiming at the integration of discursive resources in online legal dictionaries designed for legal translation as their primary function.

A new category of contrastive textual data types will be selected and presented; using a neologism, these could be referred to as *textonyms*. The solution is to relate selected textonyms to contextually-dependent equivalents, adding translation instructions and links to a database of translated texts illustrating such equivalents and translation instructions. Some e-dictionaries actually include collections of texts, as in the French-Danish legal dictionary (JOFD) included in this study, but unfortunately these texts are not integrated to the lexicographic data, no references being made from and to the word list. Therefore, they do not provide textual assistance to legal translators.

To illustrate these features, we present the findings of a contrastive study of textual problems encountered in connection with the translation of the French phrase *sans préjudice de* in French>Danish legal dictionaries, and in the EU's multilingual term base (IATE) and EUR-Lex bases. The study also involves a corpus of texts extracted from the French Légifrance (LEGI) document base for benchmarking purposes. We conclude with new proposals for improving accessibility to discursive data types in two different user situations: translating L2>L1 legal texts[1] on the one hand, and learning about strategies and tactics for L2>L1 legal translation on the other.

2. Looking for lexicographic assistance

When translating a legal text into Danish (her mother tongue), our hypothetical translator Jette, who works as a freelance for the European Commission, is confronted with the following sentence (our emphasis):

> *Sans préjudice des* dispositions prévues aux articles 7 et 11, si, à l'expiration du délai prévu à l'article 5, la marchandise n'a pas reçu la destination

1 Where L1 is the translator's mother tongue.

> prescrite, le montant des droits non perçus doit être payé, *sans préjudice des* intérêts moratoires éventuellement exigibles, aux autorités compétentes de l'État membre dans lequel la marchandise a été déclarée pour la mise en libre pratique ou, en cas d'application de l'article 9, a été prise en charge en dernier lieu.

The complex prepositional phrase *sans préjudice de* is used in two contexts: *sans préjudice des dispositions prévues aux articles 7 et 11*, and *sans préjudice des intérêts moratoires éventuellement exigibles.* Jette feels uncertain about the right translation. She needs assistance and decides to consult three specialized reference works immediately available to her: JOFD, IATE and the most comprehensive bilingual dictionary for French and Danish (B&H). The results of her efforts are described below.

2.1. JOFD – Incomplete lexicographic data

Looking up the lemma *préjudice* as an entry word, Jette accesses the following data:

> **sans préjudice de** (*lovtekn*) jf. dog (hvis i slutningen af sætning), med forbehold af (hvis i starten af sætning), uden at det dog berører/for så vidt andet ikke er bestemt i. • Ex: *sans ~ préjudice des dispositions de l'article sus-mentionné.* Med forbehold af ovennævnte artikel.
> [**sans préjudice de** (*legislative drafting*) jf. dog (if at the end of the sentence), med forbehold af (if at the beginning of the sentence), uden at det dog berører/for så vidt andet ikke er bestemt i. • Ex: *sans ~ des dispositions de l'article sus-mentionné.* Med forbehold af ovennævnte artikel.]

The sub-lemma *sans prejudice de* is followed by the diatopic restriction label *lovtekn*, which is an abbreviation of *lovteknik* [legislative drafting]. The label seems to indicate that the phrase is exclusively used when referring to legal provisions. JOFD offers four equivalents. The first two – *jf. dog* [see however] and *med forbehold af* [subject to] – are followed by comments explaining that choice of equivalent depends on word order in the sentence *hvis i slutningen af sætningen* [if at the end of the sentence], *hvis i starten af sætningen* [if at the beginning of the sentence]. The dictionary entry, however, does not specify whether this information concerns the position of the lemma in the French source text (ST) or of its equivalent in the Danish target text (TT). The dictionary example (*sans préjudice des dispositions de l'article sus-mentionné* = med forbehold af ovennævnte artikel) does not help at all. It translates the phrase, but does not say anything about word order. Although the equivalents provided by the dictionary entry deal with uses of *sans préjudice de* reflecting the first occurrence in Jette's text, their context is not sufficiently explicit to help her make the right choice. For the second occurrence there is no information at all. Jette is back to square one and still feeling uncertain.

2.2. IATE – Misleading lexicographic data

Jette keeps searching and consults IATE, which provides the following equivalents:

> med forbehold af, jf. endvidere, for så vidt... ikke, jf. dog, uden at dette berører, jf., for så vidt andet ikke er fastsat i.
> [subject to, see furthermore, as far as it is not... see however, without this affecting, see, as far as not stated otherwise in.]

Jette then clicks on *Entrée entière* [full entry] and gains access to the following explanation:

> Expression couramment employée dans les textes de loi pour indiquer que la règle posée laisse intégralement subsister telle autre disposition.
> [A phrase used in legal texts with the meaning that what is being enacted or provided is not to affect the provision referred to.]

As in the case of JOFD mentioned earlier, the explanation only deals with contexts where the phrase is used to make a reference to a provision or a legal act in order to establish a reservation. Jette also accesses the following translating instructions:

> 'Sans préjudice de' oversættes som hovedregel til dansk med 'jf. dog', når der henvises til en præcis bestemmelse, gruppe af bestemmelser eller en retsakt,

> eller 'med forbehold af', jf. Formularsamlingen 4. udg. s. 142. Udtrykkene 'jf.', 'jf. dog' og 'jf. endvidere' vil ofte være at foretrække; de kan ikke stå først i sætningen.
> [As a general rule 'sans préjudice de' is translated into Danish by 'jf. dog' [see however] when reference is being made to a specific provision, a group of provisions, or a legislative act, or by 'med forbehold af' [subject to], see Collection of forms 4th edition p. 142. The expressions 'jf.', 'jf. dog' og 'jf. endvidere' [see, see however, see furthermore] are often to be preferred; they cannot be placed at the beginning of the sentence.]

This clearly states that the Danish expression *jf.* cannot be placed in initial position in a sentence. Jette will conclude that she can translate the first occurrence of *sans préjudice de* by either *med forbehold af* or by *jf.* in non-initial position. If she chooses *jf.*, she will have to select one of the three listed Danish equivalents (*jf., jf. dog* or *jf. endvidere*). Yet no help is available to make the right choice.

Furthermore, the presentation of *jf.* [see] and of *jf. endvidere* [see furthermore] as synonyms of *jf. dog* [see however] is misleading, since *jf.* only makes reference to a provision, whereas *jf. dog* also denotes a potential source of conflict. *Jf. endvidere* [see furthermore] is used in the same sense as *jf.*, but in cases where a number of parallel references are being made.

Besides the equivalents *uden at dette berører* [without this affecting] and *for så vidt andet ikke er fastsat i* [as far as not stated otherwise in], IATE also includes alternative candidates. The following variants are included for the first equivalent: *uden at dette anfægter* [without this challenging], *uden at gribe ind i* [without intervening in], *uden at indskrænke* [without restricting]; while the second equivalent has: *for så vidt andet ikke er bestemt i* [as far as no other provisions have been made in], *for så vidt andet ikke følger af* [unless this does not entail something else], *medmindre andet gælder ifølge* [unless something else prevails in accordance with]. Unfortunately, IATE omits to include the collocates of such variants, e.g. *anfægte et princip* [to challenge a principle] and *indskrænke en ret/en beføjelse* [to restrict a right/powers].

In accordance with the definition given in the entry, the examples should illustrate contexts of legal provisions. However, IATE includes four examples (*sans préjudice de ces dispositions, sans préjudice des décisions antérieures, sans préjudice à l'égard de la responsabilité, sans préjudice de l'article 4 dudit protocole*) where the second and third examples clearly indicate that *sans préjudice de* is also used in other contexts. Thus IATE does not provide any help with the translation of the second occurrence in Jette's text.

2.3. B&H – Misleading data

Jette now consults B&H, which, according to its publishers, covers "not only the vocabulary of the language for general purposes" (LGP), but also "the main terms and expression variants in languages for special purposes" (NNF). Jette accesses the following data:

> ***sans*** *~ de a)* uden skade for, uden at tage noget fra, uden at give afkald på; *b)* uden hensyn til, uden at dermed noget præjudiceres med hensyn til; uden at foregribe *(n.)*; *c)* med forbehold af; *sans préjudice des dispositions de l'article 3 (drt.)* uden at bestemmelserne i paragraf 3 foregribes; *sans ~ de mes droits* uden at min ret trædes for nær; *sans ~ du droit* (el. *de la faculté*) *de* uden at retten til… afskæres (*el.* fortabes); *sans ~ du fait que* uden hensyn til den omstændighed at.

The entry is divided into three subfields. Under (a) the article includes the equivalent *uden skade for* [without prejudice to], and in (b) *uden hensyn til* [regardless of]. The problem here is that the two equivalents are antonyms. The article also mixes up data belonging to different registers of language: (a) *uden at tage noget fra* (LGP register [without taking something away from]), and (b) *uden at dermed noget præjudiceres med hensyn til* [without this being prejudicial as far as... is concerned] which belongs to an archaic legal register. In (c) the equivalent *med forbehold af* [subject to] is followed by an example illustrating a reference made to a provision (*sans préjudice des dispositions de l'article 3*), but a different equivalent is used in the translation of the example itself: *uden at... foregribes* [without anticipating]. The translation is also misleading, as the verb *foregribe* can normally only be used in connection with forthcoming events and cannot refer to an existing article. The three subsequent examples – *sans p. de mes droits, sans p. du droit (el. de la faculté)* and *sans p. du fait que* – do not refer to legal provisions and do not give any information on the different uses of *med forbehold af.* Again, legal registers – *uden at retten til... afskæres (el. fortabes)* [without losing the right to], and LGP – *uden at min ret trædes for nær* [without my right being trampled underfoot] – are presented without sense distinctions.

The lexicographic function of the dictionary entry – to provide efficient solutions to translation problems encountered by the translator – is jeopardized by the presentation of misleading data types. Furthermore, the *jf. dog* equivalent, which in JOFD and IATE is the first equivalent being provided, is not even mentioned. At the end of her lexicographic quest, Jette is still in doubt about the translation of *sans préjudice des dispositions.* As far as the translation of *sans préjudice des intérêts moratoires* is concerned, no assistance has been found and her problem remains unsolved.

2.4. Establishing equivalence: lexicographic shortcomings

All the dictionaries we have analysed above employ multiple candidates to establish equivalence, but unfortunately they also include misleading data. Furthermore, they omit important information and fail to include sense divisions or necessary comments and explanations for choosing the right equivalent among listed candidates. It appears that the following four criteria for selection were used in the lexicographic presentation of candidates.

2.4.1. Referents

Equivalent selection is determined by the nature of referents. Although this is not explicitly stated, it appears that JOFD restricts selection exclusively to referents belonging to the lexical frames of legislative drafting. Much in the same way, IATE has a strong focus on the same types of equivalent, both in its definition field and in instructions to the legal translator. JOFD and IATE remain silent as to other uses. B&H includes one example of legislative drafting and three of alternative uses, but fails to provide explicit information on meaning discrimination, which would help the user select the right candidate.

2.4.2. Position

Equivalent selection is determined by the position of the prepositional phrase in the sentence. In this regard, the comments of JOFD (*si en tête de phrase* and *si en fin de phrase*) are unclear. Does this apply to the lemma or to the equivalent? IATE on the other hand clearly states that the restriction applies to the Danish equivalent *jf. dog* which, unlike the French preposition, cannot be used at the beginning of a sentence. What JOFD and IATE do not say, however, is that in such cases the translator can still use *jf. dog* as an equivalent by simply moving it to the end of the TT sentence.

2.4.3. Language registers

Equivalent selection is determined by registers. B&H provides a list of equivalents from different registers, but fails to specify what register they belong to (LGP or LSP).

2.4.4. Collocates

Equivalent selection is determined by collocates, but none of the analysed works provides a systematic presentation of collocations for the legal translator.

In short, the solutions provided by these lexicographic reference works do not fulfil their primary function: to provide efficient solutions to problems encountered by the translator. Assistance is inadequate for the first translation of *sans préjudice de*, and non-existent for the second. This is how Jette's text could be rendered (our translation): the first occurrence is translated by *jf. dog* [see however] in middle position; the second one (*sans préjudice des intérêts moratoires éventuellement exigibles*) is translated by the coordinating conjunction *og* [*and* possible late payment interests]:

> Hvis varerne efter udløbet af den i artikel 5 fastsatte frist ikke er blevet anvendt i overensstemmelse med det foreskrevne formål, skal det ikke opkrævede afgiftsbeløb *og* eventuelt forfaldne morarenter, *jf. dog* bestemmelserne i artikel 7 og 11, betales til de kompetente myndigheder i den medlems-

stat, hvor varerne er angivet til fri omsætning, eller i tilfælde af anvendelse af artikel 9, senest er undergivet toldkontrol.

In order to avoid the lexicographic *mine fields* mentioned by Lind (2004), translation dictionaries for legal language must be designed so as to provide access to accurate, relevant data types adapted to the needs of the legal translator; in particular data at text level, and also specific instructions for translation. This is the concern of the next part of our case study.

3. *Sans préjudice de*: meaning, use and context

The aim of this section is to clarify the meanings and uses of the prepositional phrase, as well as the contextual factors governing its choice of equivalent. It is supported by an analysis of French general and specialized monolingual dictionaries and by a corpus of 277 examples extracted from French statutes in LEGI.

3.1. Meaning and directionality: a potential source of confusion

The complex phrase *sans préjudice de* is constructed on a PREP + N + PREP pattern. In this pattern, *préjudice* is synonymous with *perte* [loss], *tort* [fault] and *dommage* [harm]. The phrase should be distinguished from related phrases incorporating the preposition *à*, such as *porter préjudice à, préjudicier à, préjudiciable à.* French monolingual, specialized legal dictionaries (LTJ, VJ, DJ and DEJ)[2] and French comprehensive LGP dictionaries (NPR and LAR) only give *sans préjudice* followed by the preposition *de.* A search of *sans préjudice* in seven codes accessible on LEGI gave 277 instances, all with the preposition *de.* This is the 'lightest' of all French prepositions. In most cases, it has the mere function of establishing

2 All the dictionaries consulted are listed below at the end of the References.

dependence relations between the base and the complements it governs. Thus, the *de* of the complex preposition *sans préjudice de* is to a certain degree ambiguous. In legal contexts, interpretation is submitted to a directional reading, as 'sans porter préjudice à' [without bringing prejudice *to*] (BDL), whereas *de* tends to favour the opposite reading 'sans subir de préjudice provenant de' [without suffering prejudice *from*]. We have found a number of cases of confusion in EU texts, where translations into Danish make use of the equivalent *uanset* [notwithstanding]; the semantics of *uanset* goes in the opposite direction, and encodes the opposite meaning.

The following example is from the Council's draft regulation on the status of the Société Privée Européenne (25 June 2008). In the French text, decisions on matters stated in section 1 (a-p) and submitted to a vote are passed with a majority as defined in the statutes. However, provisions made in section 1 give way to (i.e. are without prejudice to) provisions made in section 2, which hold that resolutions mentioned in section 1 (a-c, i-p) are passed with a qualified majority.

Article 27 Résolutions des actionnaires 1. *Sans préjudice du* paragraphe 2, les matières suivantes au moins font l'objet d'une résolution des actionnaires adoptée à une majorité définie dans les statuts du SPE: (a) modification des droits attachés aux actions; [...] (m) transformation de la SPE; (n) fusions et scissions; (o) liquidation; (p) modification des statuts, à l'exclusion des matières figurant aux points (a) à (o). 2. Les résolutions sur les matières figurant au paragraphe 1, points (a), (b), (c), (i), (l), (m) (n), (o) et (p), sont adoptées à la majorité qualifiée.	Artikel 27 Selskabsdeltagerbeslutninger 1. *Uanset* bestemmelserne i stk. 2 skal mindst følgende anliggender afgøres ved selskabsdeltagerbeslutning med et flertal i henhold til SPE-selskabets vedtægter: 50. variation i de rettigheder, der knytter sig til andele [...] 62. omdannelse af SPE-selskabet 63. fusioner og spaltninger 64. afvikling 65. ændringer i vedtægterne, der ikke vedrører anliggender, som er nævnt i litra a) til o). 2. Beslutninger om de anliggender, der er nævnt i stk. 1, litra a), b), c), i), l), m), n), o) og p), vedtages med kvalificeret flertal.

In other words, the provisions in section 1 are subordinated to those in section 2. The French text holds that decisions on the transformation of the company's statutes are passed with a qualified majority. In the Danish text, it is the other way around: provisions made in section 1 hold notwithstanding section 2, and decisions submitted to a vote are passed with a majority (whether absolute or qualified) defined in the statutes.

3.2. Definitions of meaning in monolingual legal dictionaries

In order to clarify the semantics of the prepositional phrase, we consulted a number of reference works, including legal dictionaries. However, none of these provided definitions of all meanings. VJ and LTJ only deal with meaning in contexts where *sans préjudice de* is followed by a legal provision, meaning that what is being enacted or provided is not to affect the provision referred to. This use is illustrated by the following example, where *sans préjudice de* establishes that the provision being made gives way, in a case of conflict, to the legislative act:

> *Sans préjudice de* la directive 89/552/CEE, toute forme de publicité ou de parrainage est interdite dans la Communauté.
> [Without prejudice to Directive 89/552/EEC, all forms of advertising and sponsorship shall be banned in the Community.]

In contrast, DEJ only deals with meanings in other types of contexts. DEJ first defines the general meaning using glosses: *sans préjuger* [without prejudice]; and *réserve faite* [with reservation]. It then makes a distinction between two different meanings depending on context: *sans attenter à/sans faire disparaître* [without violating/without making disappear]; and *sans exclure la possibilité de* [without excluding the possibility of]. It specifies that *sans exclure la possibilité* is mainly used in the context of sanctions, in particular in the fixed expression *sans préjudice des dommages-intérêts* [without prejudice to damages]. The same distinctions are made in specialized dictionaries, and in the general monolingual dictionaries NPR and LAR.

3.3. Checking referents: multiple categories and denominations

The analysis of examples from LEGI reveals that the referents of complements governed by the preposition belong to a large number of semantic fields. In legislative acts these can be:

(a) strictly legislative terms: *disposition, article, loi, directive* [provision, article, law, directive];

(b) legal terms associated to legislative terms, in particular denominations of possibility, rights, powers and competences: *possibilité, faculté, droit, pouvoir, attributions, mission, compétence* [possibility, faculty, right, power, attributions, mission, competence];

(c) terms denoting sanctions: *dommages et intérêts, indemnité, sanction disciplinaire, poursuite pénale, peine, pénalité* [compensation, claims paid, disciplinary sanction, criminal court proceedings, sentence, penalty];

(d) various types of referent: *principe, propriété, vaccination, recherches, notification, tarif* [principle, property, vaccination, research, notification, tariff].

4. Equivalents and translation instructions

The presentation of equivalents and translation instructions was evaluated through a contrastive analysis of Danish equivalents extracted from the multilingual EUR-Lex document base. Our priority was to highlight all factors governing the selection and use of equivalents, drawing only on authentic examples.

4.1. The phrase is followed by a provision, group of provisions or legislative act

Sans préjudice de is normally translated as *jf. dog* [see however] in contexts of legislative drafting:

La Commission peut [...] modifier la liste et les dates fixées au paragraphe 1, les délais fixés ne pouvant en aucune façon être prolongés, *sans préjudice des* dérogations prévues au paragraphe 7.	Kommissionen kan [...] ændre listen og tidsfristerne i stk. 1, men må under ingen omstændigheder forlænge de deri nævnte frister, *jf. dog* undtagelserne i stk. 7.

Unlike *sans préjudice de*, the *jf. dog* phrase cannot be placed at the beginning of a sentence. The translation of initial *sans préjudice de* phrase can be rendered by a *jf. dog* phrase in non-initial position, normally at end of a sentence:

Sans préjudice de la directive 89/552/CEE, toute forme de publicité ou de parrainage est interdite dans la Communauté.	Enhver form for reklame og sponsorering forbydes inden for Fællesskabet, *jf. dog* direktiv 89/552/EØF.

It is also possible to use the phrase *med forbehold af* [subject to]. *Med forbehold af* belongs to a more formal register but its use is not restricted to contexts of legislative drafting. As a general rule, the phrase is placed at the beginning of a sentence:

Sans préjudice de l'article 42, le capital de la SPE est exprimé en euros.	*Med forbehold af* artikel 42 skal SPE-selskabets kapital udtrykkes i euro.

In the above example, a *jf. dog* phrase in final position would also be possible, i.e. *SPE-selskabets kapital skal udtrykkes i euro, jf. dog artikel 42* [The capital of the SPE will be expressed in euros, see however article 42].

In certain contexts, a *jf. dog* phrase at the end of the sentence would cause ambiguity and should be avoided. This is particularly true of syntactic constructions featuring several subordinate clauses, which lead to competing readings and meanings. In the following example, a *jf. dog* phrase at the end of the sentence would be ambiguous, as the reservation could refer to *giver ret til* clause [only entitle right] as well as *har en specifik tilladelse* clause [have a specific licence]:

Sans préjudice de l'article 3, les Etats membres n'admettent l'acquisition et la détention d'armes à feu que par des personnes qui se sont vu délivrer une licence ou, en ce qui concerne les catégories C ou D, à qui il est spécifiquement permis de les acquérir ou de les détenir conformément à la législation nationale.	*Med forbehold af* artikel 3 giver medlemsstaterne kun ret til erhvervelse og besiddelse af skydevåben til personer, som har licens, eller, med hensyn til våben i kategori C eller D, personer, som har en specifik tilladelse hertil i henhold til national ret.

Finally it is possible to translate using a subordinate clause of the type *for så vidt... ikke* [as far as... not] or variants:

- *For så vidt andet ikke er fastsat i/fastsættes i* [as far as other provisions have not been made in]
- *Medmindre andet er bestemt i/bestemmes i* [unless other provisions have been made in]
- *Hvis ikke andet gælder ifølge/følger af* [if nothing else applies, as far as this does not entail something else].

3. *Sans préjudice de* l'article 7, les États membres peuvent exclure des mesures qu'ils arrêtent en vue de la mise en œuvre de la présente directive les conducteurs de train opérant exclusivement sur: a) les métros, les tramways et les autres systèmes ferroviaires légers; b) les réseaux qui sont séparés sur le plan fonctionnel du reste du système ferroviaire...	3. *For så vidt andet ikke er fastsat i* artikel 7, kan medlemsstaterne undtage lokomotivførere fra de foranstaltninger, de vedtager til gennemførelse af dette direktiv, hvis de udelukkende kører på: a) metroer, sporvogne og andre letbanesystemer b) net, der funktionsmæssigt er adskilt fra resten af jernbanesystemet...

In the above example, translation of *sans préjudice de l'article 7* into *med forbehold af artikel 7* [with reservation of article 7] at the beginning of the sentence would also be possible. On the other hand, *jf. dog artikel 7* [see however article 7] at the end of the sentence might cause ambiguity, as the reservation could refer to the *kan undtage* clause [can exclude] as well as the *kører på* clause [operating on]:

4.2. The phrase is not followed by a provision, group of provisions or legislative act

It will often be possible to translate using a subordinate clause of the type:

- *uden at det (dog/i øvrigt) berører (tilsidesætter/skader) ngt* [without this affecting/harming]
- *idet det (dog/i øvrigt) ikke berører ngt* [provided this does not affect]
- *uden at ngt. (derved) berøres* [without this being hereby affected]

La directive 95/31/CE, telle que modifiée par les directives visées à l'annexe II, partie A, est abrogée, *sans préjudice des* obligations des États membres en ce qui concerne les délais de transposition en droit national des directives indiqués à l'annexe II, partie B.	Direktiv 95/31/EF, som ændret ved de direktiver, der er nævnt i bilag II, del A, ophæves, *uden at dette berører* medlemsstaternes forpligtelser med hensyn til de i bilag II, del B, angivne frister for gennemførelse i national ret af direktiverne.

Verb selection in subordinate clauses is governed by collocates, e.g.:

- *sans préjudice des intérêts de l'entreprise* = uden at skade/uden at tilsidesætte virksomhedens interesser [without prejudice to/ without damaging the interests of the company]
- *sans préjudice du principe* = uden at anfægte/tilsidesætte princippet [without contesting the principle]

Sans préjudice du principe de la formation à plein temps énoncé à l'article 2 paragraphe 1 point b), les Etats membres peuvent autoriser une formation spécifique en médicine générale à temps partiel...	*Uden at* princippet om heltids-uddannelse, jf. artikel 2, stk. 1, litra b) *derved anfægtes*, kan medlemsstaterne give tilladelse til, at den særlige uddannelse til alment praktiserende finder sted...

If the logical subject of the verb is animate, it can be translated as *uden at give afkald på* [without waiving]:

Il ne faut pas oublier que les états et les régions ont à plusieurs reprises manifesté le souhait de conserver leurs compétences en matière de tourisme, *sans préjudice de* l'exercice par l'Union de la fonction de catalyseur et de coordination...	Man må ikke glemme, at medlemsstaterne og regionerne ved flere lejligheder har erklæret, at de ønsker at bevare beføjelserne på turismeområdet *uden at give afkald på* muligheden for, at EU spiller en igangsættende og koordinerende rolle...

It is also possible to translate using the more formal preposition *med forbehold af* [without reservation/subject to]:

Sans préjudice des cas de force majeure cette caution reste totalement ou partiellement acquise:...	*Med forbehold af* force majeure tilfælde fortabes denne sikkerhed helt eller delvis:...

When *sans préjudice de* is used to establish relations with future sanctions, the prepositional phrase may be translated by a subordinate clause of the following type:

- *uden at det(te) (dog/i øvrigt) begrænser/udelukker muligheden for* [without this restricting/exluding the possibility of]
- *idet dette dog ikke begrænser/udelukker muligheden for* [in so far as this does not restrict/exclude the possibility of]
- *uden at dette hindrer/er til hindring for* [without this being in opposition to/an obstacle to]

4. Le montant de la contribution financière n'est définitivement arrêté qu'après que l'institution a accepté les rapports et les comptes finaux, *sans préjudice de* tout contrôle ultérieur.	4. Det finansielle bidrag bliver først endeligt, når institutionen har godkendt de endelige rapporter og regnskaber, *uden at dette dog begrænser* institutionens *mulighed* for senere at gennemføre kontrol.

Sans préjudice de is finally used in fixed expressions such as *sans préjudice de la preuve du contraire*, normally translated by *medmindre det modsatte bevises* [unless the contrary can be proven]:

Le fait de pouvoir exercer une influence dominante est présumé établi, *sans préjudice de la preuve du contraire*, lorsqu'une entreprise, directement ou indirectement, à l'égard d'une autre entreprise: a) détient la majorité du capital souscrit de l'entreprise...	2. *Medmindre det modsatte bevises*, formodes bestemmende indflydelse godtgjort, når en virksomhed, direkte eller indirekte, i relation til en anden virksomhed: a) ejer størstedelen af virksomhedens tegnede kapital...

The fixed expression *sans préjudice des intérêts* is to be translated by *og/med tillæg af/samt renter* [and/with interests].

Lorsque l'aide à la production a déjà été payée, l'État membre récupère les montants payés qui dépassent la compensation financière due réduite comme indiqué ci-avant, *sans préjudice des* intérêts mentionnés à l'article 16 paragraphe 5.	Hvis producentstøtten allerede er udbetalt, inddriver medlemsstaten det beløb, der overstiger det ovenfor anførte nedsatte beløb *med tillæg af* renter i overensstemmelse med artikel 16, stk. 5.

5. Towards the design of an integrated lexical text base

The last part of our study is devoted to the formulation of theoretical proposals for extended accessibility to lexicographic data types. As argued above, data types should include the presentation and explanation of competing equivalents, specific translation examples and aligned textual examples illustrating both translation instructions and uses of equivalents in context. In all cases, access should be adapted to the needs of the legal translator. As Nielsen (1994) aptly claims, legal translation dictionaries must not be seen as containers of linguistic and conceptual knowledge, but as functional tools that (should) be designed to solve the lexicographically relevant problems of legal translators. Wiegand (1988) stresses that a dictionary is a utility object (what he calls a 'Gebrauchsgegenstand'). The efficiency of the tool is entirely dependent on access to lexicographic data types suited to specific user situations. In the case of problems caused by the translation of *sans préjudice de*, access to data is determined by the two following lexicographic functions:

5.1. Function 1: knowledge of L2>L1 legal translation

Knowledge of L2>L1 legal translation is a cognitive user situation governed by the need to acquire or verify knowledge of translation strategies and tactics through sporadic consultation in the case of a specific translation problem, or through more systematic consultation in the case of a systematic learning process. Consultation is thus of the direct kind (cf. Bergenholtz 2005) *legal translator* → *dictionary* → *legal translator* and the user needs access to the following data sets:

- introduction to the legal domain
- comparative review of legal systems
- generic translation instructions

5.2. Function 2: L2>L1 legal translation

Legal L2>L1 translation is a communicative user situation governed by the translational activity itself, which is made up of recurrent translation phases: reception of ST, transfer of ST to TT (the 'translation' itself), production and revision of TT. Consultation here is of the indirect type *legal translator* → *textual string*$_x$ → *legal translator* → *dictionary* → *legal translator* → *textual string*$_x$.

By entering *sans préjudice de* in the search field, and specifying the referent and the position of the phrase (initial/middle/final), the legal translator would gain access to the following data sets:

- equivalents
- textual examples illustrating uses of equivalent in context
- specific translation instructions

5.3. Functional gateway between Functions 1 and 2

By linking the combined resources of a text base and a lexical base, it should be possible to access discursive data types supporting two different lexicographic functions. These can be fulfilled alone or can be combined, creating functional synergy: learning how to translate (Function 1), and learning how to translate while translating (Function 2).

The legal translator should gain access to such data through a search interface that can be customized in line with the user situation (translating/learning to translate). The translator could then change access modes by moving from one data set in the corpus (CORP) to another: (i) from introduction to subject field to subject field terms and their translation in context; (ii) from a comparative review of legal systems to textual examples highlighting differences in context; (iii) and from generic translation instructions to specific translation instructions in context.

(i) legal introductions	← CORP →	equivalents
(ii) comparative reviews	← CORP →	examples
(iii) generic instructions	← CORP →	specific instructions

The bilingual L2>L1 lexical text base corpus would thus serve as a functional gateway in situations where dictionary consultation provides combined assistance at a conceptual level (help to understand terms and pick their right equivalent) and discursive level (instructional help to use such terms in the right legal discourse when producing a TT) – in other words, a learning of translation while translating.

6. Conclusion

Legal translators translate texts, they do not translate isolated terms or expressions. This combined study of translational data associated with *sans préjudice de* in lexicographic reference works, and of textual data in mono- and bilingual corpora, has shown that lexicographic information available to legal translators is incomplete and misleading. It is limited to lists of equivalent candidates at word level but is often incomplete at clause and sentence level. Textonyms, i.e. text-level discursive data types providing authentic translated examples from legal documents, are entirely missing. Thus, the equivalent lexicographic presentation may impair the translation process and its results in complex settings.

As a case in point, we have shown that the translation of *sans préjudice de* phrases in various settings has a direct impact on the TT information-structuring process at sentence level, as well as on translation tactics. The solution is to incorporate new types of contextual data into legal dictionaries, primarily in the form of translational textual examples (cf. Leroyer 2002).

But it is possible to go further by using translational corpora as functional elements. We have outlined the design of a lexical text base which allows for a functional synergy through the combination of different types of access. This is instrumental to the genuine purpose of legal dictionaries – assisting the legal translator in solving problems linked to the practice, training and learning of legal translation. To be truly operational, such assistance should extend to the discursive level and combine access to equivalences, instructions and contextual information in an interactive, integrated manner.

References

Acuyo-Verdejo, Maria del Carmen 2004. Textual Knowledge in Legal Translation. *Hermes* 3, 167-184.

Bergenholtz, Henning 2005. Den usynlige elektroniske produktions- og korrekturordbog. *LexicoNordica* 12, 19-38.

Grass, Thierry 2009. Jurilinguistique, terminologie et lexicographie juridiques au Canada. *Lebende Sprachen* 1/2009, 11-17.

Kjær, Anne Lise 1997. Thi kendes for ret. Om lemmata og eksempler i juridisk fagleksikografi. *Hermes* 18, 157-175.

Leroyer, Patrick 2002. *Les exemples textuels unificateurs*. Aarhus: Aarhus School of Business.

Leroyer, Patrick / Rasmussen, Kirsten Wølch 2004. [Review of] Juridisk Ordbog fransk-dansk. *Sprint* 2, 93-103.

Lind, Åge 2004. Navigation through the Minefields. On the Making of an English-Norwegian Dictionary of Law. In Geoffrey Williams and Sandra Vesssier (eds) *Proceedings of the 11th Euralex International Congress*. Lorient: Université de Bretagne-sud, 595-602.

Nielsen, Sandro 1994. *The Bilingual LSP Dictionary. Principles and Practice for Legal Language*. Tübingen: Günter Narr.

Nielsen, Sandro 2000. Translation Strategies for Culture-Specific Textual Conventions in Bilingual Dictionaries. *Lexicographica* 16, 152-168.

Sørensen, Rita 1999. *Principper for integration af kulturelle forskelle i leksikografiske værker med særligt henblik på dansk/spansk arveret*. Aalborg: Aalborg University.

Tarp, Sven 1999. Lørnerordbøger for indvandrere og andet godtfolk. *LexicoNordica* 6, 107-132.

Wagner, Anne 2004. Les marques de lisibilité comme éléments de planification du discours juridique. *Cahiers du C.I.E.L.* 2004, 85-103.

Wiegand, Herbert Ernst 1988. Was eigentlich ist Fachlexikographie? Mit Hinweisen zum Verhältnis von sprachlichem und enzyklopädischem Wissen. In Munske, Horst Haider / Polenz, Peter von / Reichmann, Oskar / Hildebrandt, Reiner (Hrsg.) *Deutscher Wortschatz. Lexikologische Studien*. Berlin: de Gruyter, 729-790.

Dictionaries and other reference works:

[B&H] Blinkenberg, Andreas / Høybye, Poul 1999: *Fransk-dansk ordbog*. Copenhagen: Nyt Nordisk Forlag Arnold Busck.

[BDL] Office québécois de la langue française. *Banque de dépannage linguistique*. Retrieved from <http://www.olf.gouv.qc.ca/ressources/bdl.html> on 20 September 2009.

[DEJ] Roland, Henri 1983. *Dictionnaire des expressions juridiques*. Lyon: Éditions L'Hermes.

[DJ] Guiho, Pierre 1996. *Dictionnaire juridique*. Lyon: Hermès.

[EUR-Lex] *EUR-Lex, Adgang til EU-Lovgivningen*. Retrieved from <http://eur-lex.europa.eu/da/index.htm> on 12 May 2009.

[IATE] *InterActive Terminology for Europe*. Retrieved from <http://iate.europa.eu/iatediff/SearchByQuery Load.do?method=load> on 12 May 2009.

[JOFD] Christensen, Dorthe / Fich, Thomas 2003. *Juridisk Ordbog fransk-dansk*. Copenhagen: Gads Forlag.

[LAR] Dubois, Jean 2000. *Dictionnaire du français d'aujourd'hui*. Paris: Larousse.

[LEGI] Lavisgne, Serge (Dir.). *Legifrance. Le service public de la diffusion du droit*. Paris: Secrétariat général du Gouvernement. Retrieved from <http://www.legifrance.gouv.fr. on 19 July 2008>.

[LTJ] Guillien, Raimond /Vincent, Jean 2007. *Lexique des termes juridiques*. Paris: Dalloz.

[NNF] Blinkenberg, Andreas / Høybye, Poul 1991. *Dansk-fransk ordbog*. Nyt Nordisk Forlag Arnold Busk. Retrieved from <http://www.nytnordiskforlag.dk/shop/ordboeger/100-fransk-dansk-ordbog.htm> on 23 September 2009.

[NPR] Robert, Paul 2009. *Le nouveau petit Robert. Dictionnaire alphabétique et analogique de la langue française*. Paris: Le Robert.

[VJ] Cornu, Gérard 2007. *Vocabulaire juridique*. Paris: Presses Universitaires de France.

ÁNGEL M. FELICES LAGO

Axiological Analysis of Entries in a Spanish Law Dictionary and their English Equivalents

1. Introduction

In this study we present the results of applying an axiological analysis approach to Spanish terms and expressions included in *Diccionario Básico Jurídico* (Del Arco Torres 2004). The initial corpus, consisting of over 4,500 entries, was reduced to a target group of entries (approximately 15%) which proves how a small but relevant group of legal terms and idioms are formulated in terms of well-established values in our society, particularly those related to human behaviour (qualities and faults). Consequently, concepts such as loyalty, cooperation, trustworthiness, guiltiness or punishment are also represented by a substantial number of entries in the dictionary above. The provision of equivalent terms in English will offer a complementary perspective: the extent to which the axiological load of the terms selected is mirrored within other cultural boundaries. However, this approach might also help to answer other questions:

- To what extent is legal terminology sensitive to the most common scales of values?
- If legal terms and axiology can be linked, which values can be classified as relevant and in which order?
- What conclusions can be drawn from such associations?

Krzeszowski (1997) contributed decisively to the debate when he rightly claimed that, for many years, linguistic semantics was dominated by logic, or, more strictly, by the aspect of logic which deals with truth values. In his opinion, the most central opposition in linguistic semantics should not be 'true-false', but rather 'positive-negative'. Evidence of this can be found in Osgood *et al.*'s (1957) research and in the concept of 'semantic differential' (Osgood 1980), which was designed to measure the connotative meaning of concepts. A respondent is asked to choose where his/her position lies on a scale between two bipolar adjectives (for example 'adequate-inadequate', 'good-evil' or 'valuable-worthless'). Semantic differentials may be used to describe not only people, but also the connotative meaning of concepts – an ability used extensively in affect control theory. Leading pedagogues and anthropologists (cf. Malinowski 1923; Piaget 1946) have also claimed that the first categorisations a baby makes are evaluative in that they involve the division of all things into good and bad in the most primitive, sensory meaning of these terms.

2. Theoretical background

Humanisation is evident in valuation, as our emotions are connected with certain values. To appreciate their presence, we need to recognize a system of values. Krzeszowski (1997) lists many previous references that allowed him to conclude that valuation constitutes an aspect of all categorisations which, in turn, directly manifest themselves in language. This establishes a direct link between values and language. The Saussurean and Chomskyan traditions in linguistics are usually silent about axiological distinctions between 'good' and 'bad' or 'ugly' and 'beautiful', which are also relevant to the semantics of natural languages. This dimension has been widely dealt with by linguists and philosophers working outside the structuralist-generative tradition, usually only in connection with connotation, and is often referred to as an 'emotive' aspect of meaning. However, Lakoffian semantics, a cognitive linguistic theory on the centrality of metaphor in human thinking, political behaviour and society, has been intensely interested in the comprehension of this key aspect of meaning. For instance, Langacker (1988), following Lakoff (1987), distinguishes four types of perspective that are relevant to valuation: orientation, vantage point, directionality, and subjectivity.

The *orientations* RIGHT-LEFT, UP-DOWN, and FRONT-BACK can be metaphorically extended to valuation, with a resulting difference in the axiological construal of various concepts. The SCALE schema is more or less explicitly present in every valuation, as it can be understood in terms of the UP-DOWN or FRONT-BACK orientation. What makes SCALE different is the PLUS-MINUS polarity imposed on other schemata: UP/FRONT is PLUS and DOWN/BACK is MINUS. *Vantage point* is closely connected with orientation. A particular scene may be construed positively or negatively, depending on the vantage point of the valuator. As a default-case option, the speaker is the valuator. Different construals in valuation may also be due to contrasts in *directionality*. For example, given entities of different size, one can compare them by relating the size of entity A to the size of entity B or by relating the size of entity B to the size of entity A. *Subjectivity* is particularly relevant in all valuations. As Langacker (1988) rightly observes, subjectivity is graded and varies on a scale from very subjective to very objective.

In this functional paradigm, the axiological feature (positive or negative) is a permanent component of the definitional structure of many lexical entries (in lexeme-level predicate schemas) and should be described systematically (Felices Lago 1998). It is my purpose to maintain that axiologically-loaded terms result from intersubjectively uniform valuations made by language users rather than from objective measurements or individual intuitions. A higher degree of intersubjective agreement increases the likelihood that a given linguistic expression will become axiologically conventionalised. Following the lines of cognitive semantics, it was Krzeszowski (1990, 1993, 1997, 2004), among other contemporary researchers (Felices Lago 1991, 1992; Pauwels/Simon-Vandenbergen 1993, 1995; Simon-Vandenbergen 1995) who definitively laid the foundations of *axiomatics*. This is a new field of research that attempts to integrate into modern linguistics the best axiological insights of other disciplines (philosophy, psychology, pedagogy, etc.); its main goal is the analysis of the way in which leading or recurrent values are encoded in a given discourse. Other contributions have applied axioematic analysis to various areas of language for specific purposes (Felices Lago 1996, 1998, 1999, 2002, 2006, 2008a, 2008b; Felices Lago/Hewitt 2004;

Cortés de los Ríos 2001, 2007; Felices Lago/ Corral Hernández 2008). In business discourse, the topics covered so far are brand names, financial and investment terms, marketing terms, banks' advertisements, job offers, and ecological advertising in the business press.

The classification of axiological top-rank concepts adopted here is based on lexical items (see Figure 1). As the selection of data will show, however, a significant percentage of legal terms, phrases and collocations can be assigned to different subdivisions of the good-bad scale by readapting their distribution.

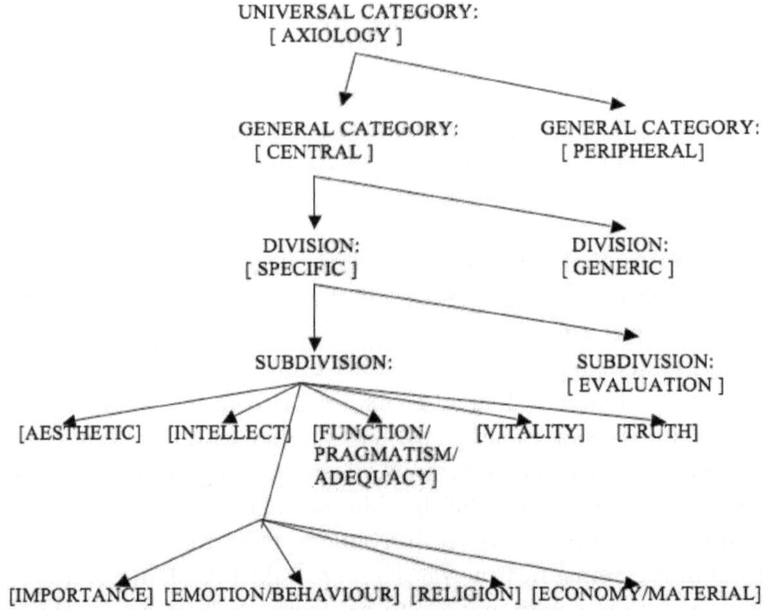

Figure 1. Axiological categories: top-rank concepts (cf. Felices Lago 1991: 408).

This classification is the result of an exhaustive functional-lexematic analysis, partly based on my onomasiological lexicon in preparation. However, it does not ignore the fundamental work of several philosophers, psychologists, educators and linguists (see Felices Lago 1991 for a summary of all these contributions). The most valuable non-philosophical contributions of the last two centuries can be found in the synoptic lists of classical references such as Roget (1852) and McArthur (1981). The *Longman Language Activator* (1993) also provides excellent insights for compiling more accurate axiological classifications. However, as far as I know, the most complete intuitive classification of the axiological component in modern linguistics has been the work of Sorin Stati (1979), despite its lack of a reliable model for analysing vocabulary.

3. Corpus analysis

The specific corpus used in this study is the law dictionary mentioned above (Del Arco Torres 2004), whose total number of entries is approximately 4,000, of which those sensitive to scales of value are 598 (approximately 15% of the total). I included entries (lemmas) that refer literally, metaphorically or symbolically to well-established axiological classifications based on Figure 1 and the Appendix. The decision does not exclude other possible associations of meaning, but reflects the belief that meanings and ideas associated with this corpus are axiologically prominent and justifiable as shown by axiologists (see Appendix), regardless of other interpretations. However, terms that refer to phenomena which are perceived as axiologically-loaded by a majority of specialists have also been included.

Around one in seven entries is axiologically loaded, which might not be a surprising result but is clear evidence of how a significant group of legal terms is formulated in terms of well-established scales of value. This evidence opposes an erroneous but widespread belief that terminology is not associated with subjective or emotional events in its creation. Intuitively, the legal domain can be regarded as dealing with units and expressions linked to the negative axis of the axiological scale, which accounts for 459 items (77%) compared to 139 items (23%) on the positive axis. However, the surprisingly high percentage of positive axiologically-loaded entries probably suggests that human rights and their protection also play an important role in the creation of legal terminology.

Regardless of the bias towards the positive or negative axis, the final output of the corpus analysis consists of 598 entries (lemmas) belonging to axiological divisions that refer literally, metaphorically or symbolically to well-established axiological classifications – as described in Felices Lago (1991) – and are given in the tables below, which list the values from more to less frequent (20 divisions in total).

Tables 1 and 2 show, respectively, the general and specific legal wrongs punished by law as part of deviant behaviour, which contributes to 32% of the total (189 items) and is ranked as Number 1 in the list of value divisions.

1. BEHAVIOUR [DEVIANT BEHAVIOUR] 1.1. LEGAL WRONGS [PUNISHED BY LAW] GENERAL (40 items) [GENERAL ACTIONS AND PEOPLE DOING THEM] (24 items). Antijurídico *Unlawful*, Antijuridicidad *Illegality*, Contravenciones *Infringement*, Contumaz *Contumacious*, Crimen (Criminal) *Crime (Criminal)*, Delito (Delincuente) *Crime/Felony (Delinquent)*, Delictivo *Delinquent*, Desafuero *Outrage*, Falta/Faltas *Misdemeanor*, Facineroso *Criminal*, Ilegalidad *Illegality*, Ilicitud *Unlawfulness*, Infracción/Infracciones *Infringement/Violation,* Iniuria *damage*, Injusticia (injusto) *Injustice (unfair)*, Malhechor *Malefactor*, Ofensas *Transgression*, Prófugo *Fugitive*, Provocación *Provocation*, Transgresión *Transgression*, Vejaciones *Humiliation.* [GENERAL AGGRAVATING CIRCUMSTANCES AND FACTS] (16 items). Agravio *Affront*, Alevosía *Premeditation*, Dolo *Deceit*, Ensañamiento *Viciousness*, Habitualidad penal *Habitual criminality*, Imprudencia *Recklessness*, Iter criminis *Iter criminis*, Lesa majestad *Lese-majesty*, Mala fe *Bad faith*, Malicia *Malice*, Males innecesarios para la ejecución del delito *Aggravated felony,* Nocturnidad (Noche) *Nocturnality*, Peligro *Danger*, Peligrosidad *Riskiness*, Temeridad *Recklessness*.

Table 1. Deviant behaviour values (general wrongs punished by law).

1. BEHAVIOUR [DEVIANT BEHAVIOUR]
1.2. LEGAL WRONGS [PUNISHED BY LAW]
SPECIFIC (149 items)
[DECEPTION] (7 items). Encubrimiento *Concelament*, Impo stura *Calumny*, Ocultación *Concealment*, Perjurio *Perjury*, Plagio *Plagiarism*, Simulación *Simulation*, Suposición de parto (delito de) *Supposition of birth.*
[DISCRIMINATION] (7 items). Antisemitismo *Antisemitism*, Apartheid *Apartheid*, Discriminación *Discrimination*, Racismo *Racism*, Sexismo *Sexism*, Xenofobia (Xenófobo) *Xenophobia (Xenophobe).*
[ECONOMY, TRADE AND MONEY MATTERS] (15 items).
Acaparamiento *Speculative hoarding*, Agiotaje (Agiotista) *Usury (Usurer)*, Apropiación indebida *Misappropriation*, Blanqueo de dinero *Money laundering*, Contrabando *Smuggling*, Depredación *Depredation*, Desfalco *Defalcation*, Falsificación *Falsification*, Fraude *Fraud*, Infractor tributario *Tax infringement*, Malversación *Malversation*, Manipulación/Manipulaciones *Manipulation/Manipulations*, Maquinación *Contrivance*, Rapiña *Pillage/Robbery.*
[FAMILY] (5 items). Bigamia *Bigamy,* Celebración de matrimonios ilegales *Celebrations of illegal weddings*, Crueldad mental *Mental cruelty*, Incesto *Incest*, Sevicia *Saevitia.*
[FREEDOM] (9 items). Acoso *Harassment*, Amenazas *Threats*, Coacción, *Coercion,* Esclavitud *Gripe*, Intimidación *Intimidation*, Matonismo *Bullying*, Rapto *Abduction*, Secuestro *Kidnapping*, Tortura (delito de) *Torture.*
[HONOUR] (4 items). Calumnia *Calumny*, Difamación *Defamation*, Infamia *Infamy*, Injurias (delito de) *Calumny.*
[INTIMACY] (2 items). Escuchas ilegales *Illegal phone-tapping*, Revelación de secretos *Violation and disclosure of secrets.*
[JUSTICE] (7 items). Falso testimonio *False testimony*, Negativas *Refusal*, Prevaricación (delito de) *Prevarication*, Prevaricador *Prevaricator*, Acusación y denuncias falsas, *Accusation and complaint*
Obstrucción a la justicia *Denial of justice*, Quebrantamiento *Evasión.*
[LIFE] (15 items). Aborto *Abortion*, Asesinato *Assassination*, Auxilio *Help*, Conyugicidio *Murder of spouse*, Eutanasia *Euthanasia*, Feticidio *Feticide*, Filicidio *Murder of son or daughter*, Genocidio *Genocide*, Homicidio (homicida) *Homicide*, Infanticidio (delito de) *Infanticide*, Lesión/lesiones *Injuries*, Regicidio *Regicide*, Uxoricidio (uxoricida) *Uxoricide (wife murderer).*
[MILITARY LAW, WAR, NATIONAL SECURITY] (15 items).
Complot *Conspiracy*, Derrotismo [War times] *Defeatism*, Deserción *Defection*, Espionaje militar *Espionage*, Espía *Spy*, Insumisión (Insumiso) *Insubordination (Insubordinate)*, Obediencia *Obedience* [+/-], Rebeldía *Mutiny*, Rebelión *Rebellion*, Sabotaje *Sabotage*, Sedición (Sedicioso) *Sedition (Seditionist)*, Traición *Treason*, Ultraje a la nación española *Outrage to the Spanish nation.*

[PROFESSIONAL ACTIVITY] (2 items). Deslealtad profesional *Professional disloyalty*, Intrusismo *Poaching.*
[PROPERTY] (20 items). Atraco (Atracador) *Robbery (Robber)*, Bandido *Bandit*, Bandolerismo (Bandolero) *Racketeering (Bandit)*, Cuatrería *Horse theft*, Daño/Daños *Damages*, Estafa (delito de) *Fraud*, Extorsión (Chantaje) *Extortion (Blackmailing)*, Hurto (delito de) *Theft*, Incendio (Indendiario) *Arson (Arsonist)*, Latrocinio *Larceny*, Monedero falso *Counterfeiter*, Mendicidad *Mendicity*, Piratería (delito de) *Piracy*, Robo (delito de) *Stealing*, Sustracción *Theft*, Usura (Usurero) *Usury (Usurer).*
[PUBLIC HEALTH] (5 items). Adulteración *Adulteration*, Curanderismo *Quackery*, Envenenamiento de aguas *Water poisoning*, Tráfico ilegal *Bootlegging*, Vertidos ilegales y tóxicos *Liquid waste.*
[PUBLIC ORDER AND ADMINISTRATION] (12 items). Arrogación *Arrogation*, Cohecho *Bribery*, Connivencia *Complicity*, Escándalo público *Public scandal*, Incitación al delito *Incitation to crime*, Conspiración *Conspiracy*, Nepotismo *Nepotism*, Usurpación *Usurpation*, Negligencia *Negligence*, Receptación (delito de) *Receiving*, Receptador *Receiver*, Soborno *Bribery.*
[SEXUALITY] (11 items). Estupro (Estuprador) *Rape without violence (Rapist*), Exhibicionismo *Exhibitionism*, Lenocinio *Procuring*, Pederastia *Pederasty*, Pedofilia *Pedophilia*, Pornografía infantil *Child pornography*, Proxenetismo *Procuring/Pimping*, Rufianismo (Rufián) *Pimping (Pimp)*, Violación *Rape.*
[VIOLENCE] (12 items). Agresión (Agresor) *Battery (aggressor),* Atentado/Atentados *Attempted murder*, Bandas armadas *Armed gang*, Desórdenes públicos *Public unrest*, Dirigente (Directivos) de banda terrorista *Terrorist group leader*, Estragos *Ravages*, Malos tratos *Physical abuse*, Riña *Quarrel*, Vandalismo *Vandalism*, Violencia *Violence.*

Table 2. Deviant behaviour values (specific wrongs punished by law).

Table 3 includes the vitality set of values (11.5% of the whole corpus), referring to disease or death and featuring second in the ranking. It is worth noting the high frequency of concepts connected with diseases and the extent to which certain illnesses are key factors in determining innocence or guiltiness. Divisions ranking 9 and 13 in the list have been added due to their close relationship with the vitality group.

2. VITALITY (70 items, 11.5%)
2.1. LIFE AND DEATH (19 items) Positive*:* Salvamento *Salvage.*
Negative: Agonía *Agony*, Ahogados *Drowning*, Ahorcadura *Hanging*, Decapitación *Decapitation*, Degollamiento *Throat Slitting*, Fratricida *Fratricide*, Fulguración

Fulguration, Guillotina *Guillotine*, Lapidación *Lapidation*, Muerte *Death*, Necrofagia *Necrophagy*, Occisión (Occiso) *Death* (*Deceased*), Parricida *Parricide*, Putrefacción *Putrefaction*, Suicidio *Suicide*, Tiranicidio *Tyrannicide*, Verdugo *Executioner*
2.2. HEALTH AND DISEASE (51 items) Positive: Analgesia *Analgesia*, Eugenesia *Eugenics*, Lucidez *Lucidity*, Salud *Health*. Negative: Alcoholismo *Alcoholism*, Algia *Algia*, Alucinaciones inducidas por droga *Drug hallucinogenic*, Alucinosis alcohólica *Alcoholic hallucinosis*, Alucinación *Hallucination*, Contaminación acústica *Noise pollution*, Contagiosidad *Contagiousness*, Deformación *Deformation*, Deformidad *Deformity*, Degeneración *Degeneration*, Delirio *Delirium*, Delirium tremens *Delirium tremens*, Demencia *Insanity*, Dolor *Pain*, Dorsalgia *Dorsalgia*, Ebriedad *Inebriation*, Embriaguez *Drunkenness*, Enfermedad *Disease*, Engendro *Deformed child*, Epidemia *Epidemic*, Epilepsia *Epilepsy*, Esquizofrenia *Schizophrenia*, Esterilidad *Infertility*, Fetopatía *Malformation*, Hebefrenia *Hebephrenia*, Hemofilia *Hemophilia*, Hiperalgia *Hyperalgesia*, Hiperestesia *Hyperaesthesia*, Hipertensión *Hypertension*, Impotencia *Impotence*, Incapacidad (Incapacitado) *Incapacity (Incapacitated)*, Incapacitación *disableness*, Incapaz *Incapable person*, Intoxicación *Intoxication*, Larga enfermedad *Long disease*, Locura *Insanity*, Maníaco *Maniac*, Megalomanía *Megalomania*, Paranoia *Paranoia*, Piromanía *Pyromania*, Sociopatía *Sociopathy*, Talalgia *talalgia*, Tóxico *Toxic*, Toxicomanía *Drug addiction*, Trastorno mental *Mental disorder*, Veneno *Poison*..

9. DAMAGES, INJURIES AND MISFURTUNE (23 items, 3.8%)
Negative: Accidente *Accident*, Agraviado *Offended*, Atropello *Running-over*, Automutilación *Self-mutilation*, Avería *Average*, Baratería (marítima) *Barratry (Admiralty law)*, Calamidad *Misfortune*, Contusión *Bruise*, Damnum *Damnum*, Destrucción *Destruction*, Inundación *Flood*, Molesto *Annoying*, Mutilación *Mutilation*, Naufragio *Shipwreck*, Nocivo *Harmful*, Ofendido por el delito *Offended*, Perjuicio (Perjudicado) *Injury (Injured party)*, Perturbación *Disturbance*, Quemaduras *Burnings*, Ruina *Ruin*, Siniestro *Loss or damage*, Vicio/Vicios *Defect/Fault*.

13. EMOTIONAL STATES (19 items, 3.2%)
Positive: Affectio *Affection*, Amor *Love*, Arrepentimiento espontáneo (Arrepentido) *Active repentance (Repentant)*, Gozar y gozar (a) *Enjoy*, Catarsis *Catharsis*. Negative: Abatimiento *Discouragement*, Alteración *Alteration*, Angustia *Anguish*, Ansiedad *Anxiety*, Depresión *Depression*, Histeria *Hysteria*, Ira *Wrath*, Iracundia *Rage*, Miedo *Fear*, Pasión *Passion*, Temor reverencial *Awe*. [Mitigating circumstances]: Arrebato u obcecación *Without malice aforethought*, Ofuscación *Obfuscation*.

Table 3. Vitality and emotion values.

Table 4 includes the third division in the ranking, where the bias towards the positive axis prevails, contrarily to most of the other divisions collected in the sample. The eighth division (innocence vs. guiltiness) has been added, although the positive-negative axis is more balanced here.

3. COMPLIANCE WITH MORAL/LEGAL NORMS (45 items, 7.5%) 3.1. COMPLIANCE WITH THE LAW (11 items) Positive: Bona fide *Bona fide*, Buena fe *Good faith*, Legal *Legal*, Legalidad *legality*, Legitimación *Legitimation*, Legitimidad *Legitimacy*, Legítimo *Legitimate*, Lícito *Lawful*, Pro reo *Giving the defendant the benefit of the doubt* , Respeto a la ley *Law abiding.* 3.2. COMPLIANCE WITH SOCIAL AND ETHICAL NORMS (34 items) Positive: Bioética *Bioethics*, Boni mores *Boni mores*, Buen padre de familia *Good father*, Buenas costumbres *Good customs*, Civilización *Civilization*, Decencia *Decency*, Decoro *Decorum*, Deontología médica *Medical ethics*, Derecho/Derechos *Equity/Rights*, Derechohabiente *Rightful claimant*, Equidad *Equity*, Equilibrio *Balance*, Honra *Honour/Good reputation*, Honestidad *Honesty*, Honor *Honour*, Imparcialidad *Impartiality*, Ius *Justice*, Iustitia *Justice*, Justa causa *Just cause*, Justicia *Justice*, Moral *Morality*, Pudor *Modesty*, Xenofilia *Xenophilia.* Negative: Corruptela *Illegal practice*, Darwinismo social *Social Darwinism*, Deshonesto *Dishonest*, Deshonra *Dishonor*, Desnaturalizado *Denaturalized*, Indignidad para suceder *Indignity of inheriting*, Ignominia *Ignominy*, Inmoralidad *Immorality*, Irresponsabilidad *Irresponsibility*, Maquiavelismo *Machiavellism*, Prejuicio *Prejudice.*
8. INNOCENCE vs GUILTINESS (24 items, 4%) Positive: Absolución *Acquittal*, Absuelto *Acquitted*, Atenuantes (circunstancias) *Mitigating circumstances*, Eximentes (circunstancias) *Grounds for acquittal*, Condonación *Condonation*, Descriminilización *Decriminalization*, Despenalización *Legalization*, Inculpabilidad *Inculpability*, Indulto *Pardon*, Inocencia *Innocence*, No exigibilidad *Non imputability* , Perdón *Pardon*, Redención *Redemption.* Negative: Agravantes (circunstancias) *Aggravating circumstances*, Coimputado *Codefendants*, Cómplices *Accomplices*, Convicto *Convict*, Culpa (Culpable) *Guilt (Culprit)*, Culpabilidad *Guiltiness*, Damnatus *Damnatus*, Reo *Accused*, Responsabilidad (responsable) *Criminal liability (liable)*, Tanto de culpa *Excerpt of the record,* Víctima *Victim.*

Table 4. Values related to compliance with legal norms.

Table 5 shows the divisions linked to economic activity, reward (vs. punishment), generosity, pragmatism and work-related attitudes, ranked as 4, 5, 11 and 14. Lexicographic sources prove that axiologically-loaded negative concepts prevail.

4. ECONOMY (MATERIAL) / FUNCTION / PRAGMATISM (33 items, 5.5%)
Positive: Adecuación *Adequacy*, Beneficiario *Beneficiary*, Beneficio *Benefice*, Bien/bienes *Goods*, Ganancia/Ganancias *Profit*, Interés/intereses *Interest*, Justiprecio *Fair price*, Lucrativo *Lucrative*, Lucro *Profit*, Óptimo de pareto *Pareto efficiency*, Rentabilidad *Profitability*, Solvencia (Solvente) *Solvency (Solvent)*, Superávit presupuestario *Budget surplus*, Útil *Useful*, Utilidad *Usefulness*.
Negative: Carestía *Scarcity*, Déficit *Deficit*, Deflación *Deflation*, Desheredación, Devaluación *Devaluation*, Dumping, Enriquecimiento injusto *Unjust enrichment*, Escasez *Scarcity*, Espiral inflacionista *Inflationary Spiral*, Insolvencia *Insolvency*, Laessio enormis *Unfair advantage*, Morosidad (Moroso) *Slowness in paying (Doubtful debtor)*, Oneroso *Onerous*, Pérdida *Loss*, Quiebra *Bankruptcy*, Sobreendeudamiento *Overindebtedness*.

5. REWARD VS. PUNISHMENT (27 items, 4.5%)
Positive: Bonificación *Bonus/Discount*, Compensación *Compensation*, Premio/Premios *Prize/Prizes*, Privilegio/Privilegios *Privilege/Privileges*.
(+/-): Recompensa *Reward*, Reparación/Reparaciones *Redress/Reparations*, Resarcimiento *Compensation*, Satisfacción *Settlement*. Negative: Alejamiento *Stay away*, Amonestación *Warning*, Apartamiento *Removal*, Azote *Lashing*, Boicot *Boycot*, Condena *Sentence*, Expulsion *Deportation*, Expropiación *Expropriation*, Impunidad *Impunity*, Inhabilitación *Incapacitation*, Multa *Fine*, Pena *Punishment*, Privación *Dispossession*, Punibilidad *Punibility*, Punitivo *Punitive*, Represalia/Represalias *Retaliation*, Sanción/Sanciones *Penalty*, Vindicación *Vindication*.

11. WORK-RELATED ATTITUDES AND COOPERATION (21 items, 3.5%)
Positive: Aptitud *Aptitude*, Buenos oficios *Good offices*, Cualificación profesional *Professional qualifications*, Diligencia (Diligente) *Dedication (Diligent)*, Eficacia (Eficiencia) *Efficacity (Efficiency)*, Promoción *Promotion*.
(+/-): Cooperador (necesario) *Accessory*. Negative: Absentismo *Absenteeism*, Abulia *Extreme apathy*, Antisocial *Delinquent*, Apatía (política) *Political indifference*, Burocratismo *Red tape*, Descuido *Carelessness*, Dilación procesal indebida *Undue delay*, Impericia *Lack of skill*, Indisciplina laboral *Labour indiscipline*, Ineficacia *Incompetence*, Ineptitud *Ineptitude*, Lata culpa *Gross fault*.

14. GENEROSITY / LACK OF GENEROSITY (12 items, 2%) Positive: Beneficiencia *Charity*, Dádiva *Donation*, Donación *Donation*, Favor *Favour*, Gracia *Grace*, Solidaridad *Solidarity*, Gratificación/Gratificaciones *Reward*. Negative: Favorecimiento *Favoritism*, Ingratitud *Ingratitude*, Prodigalidad (Pródigo) *Prodigality (Prodigal)*, Usurario *Usurer*.

Table 5. Economy/work-related values.

Table 6 includes divisions of values strictly associated to moral rules inspired in religious codes of conduct which can be found in most religions, such as sexual practices (ranked 7 in the top values list), respect for physical integrity and life (ranked 10), sincerity (ranked 12) and loyalty (ranked 16). A small number of entries directly linked to religious matters (ranked 17) have also been inserted.

7. SEX [TRADITIONAL PERSPECTIVE] (25 items, 4.2%) Positive: Virginidad *Virginity*. Negative: Androfobia *Androphobia*, Burdel *Brothel*, Buscona *Prostitute*, Coprofilia *Coprophilia*, Coprolalia *Coprolalia*, Desviación/Desviaciones *Deviation/Deviations*, Escopofilia *Scopophilia*, Fetichismo *Fetishism*, Frotteurismo (frotación) *Frotteurism*, Lascivia *Lasciviousness*, Lujuria *Lechery*, Masoquismo *Masochism*, Necrofilia *Necrophilia*, Obsceno *Obscene*, Parafilias *Paraphilia*, Sadismo (Sádico) *Sadism (Sadistic)*, Sadomasoquismo *Sadomasochism*, Sodomía *Sodomy*, Trata *White slavery*, Travestismo *Transvestism*, Voyeurismo *Voyeurism*, Zoofilia *Zoophilia*.
10. AGGRESSION (KILLING), ATTACK/PROTECTION OR DEFENCE (22 items, 3.6%) Positive: Acogimiento *Fosterage*, Autodefensa *Self-defense*, Coexistencia pacífica *Peaceful coexistence*, Custodia *Custody*, Defensa (Defensor) *Legal defence (Defence Lawyer)*, Defendido *Defendant*, Seguridad *Security (Legal)*, Tutela (Tutelado) *Tutelage (Ward)*, Tutor *Tutor*. Negative: Abandono *Abandonment*, Agresividad *Aggressiveness*, Beligerancia *Belligerency*, Coerción *Threat*, Desamparo *Abandonment*, Esbirro, Fuerza/fuerzas, Guerra *War*, Guerrilla *Guerrilla*, Hostilidad *Hostility*, Indefensión *Defenselessness*.
12. TRUTHFULNESS/CERTAINTY vs FALSEHOOD/UNCERTAINTY (21 items, 3.5%) Positive: Adveración *Certification*, Autenticidad ideaológica *Ideological*

Authenticity, Auténtico *Authentic*, Transparencia *Transparency*.
Negative: Astucia (fraude o disfraz) *Artful maneuvering*, Capcioso *Captious*, Consilium fraudis, Defraudación/Defraudaciones *Embezzlement*, Delincuencia oculta *Hidden delinquency*, Demagogia (Demagogo) *Demagogy* (*Demagogue*), Disfraz *disguise*, Engaño *Deceit*, Error *Error*, Falsedad *Falsity*, Incierto *False*, Insidia *Maliciousness*, Libelo *Libel*, Testaferro *Figurehead*, Yerro *Mistake*.

16. LOYALTY (8 items)
Positive: Fidelidad conyugal *Fidelity*, Fieles *The faithful*, Reconciliación conyugal *Reconciliation*. (+/-): Amistad *Friendship*. Negative: Enemistad *Enmity*, Enemistad manifiesta *Animosity*, Infidelidad *Adultery*, Infidencia *Disloyalty*.

17. RELIGION (7 items)
Positive: Sagrado *Holy*. Negative: Anomalías consensuales en el matrimonio canónico *Incapacity for valid matrimonial consent*, Escarnio *Ridicule*, Profanación *Desecration*, Proselitismo ilegal *Illegal proselytism*, Sacrilegio *Sacrilege*, Sacrílego *Sacrilegious*.

Table 6. Sets of moral values supported by religion.

Table 7 includes the remaining values in the ranking list. However, qualities and faults linked to political and social activities and conduct prevail. It is worth noting the low number of lemmas in the dictionary referring to positive generic evaluations or intellectual skills. No entry for negative generic evaluation could be found.

6. FREEDOM vs LACK OF FREEDOM / AUTHORITARISM (27 items, 4.5%)
Positive: Desbloqueo *Unblocking*, Democracia (Demócrata) *Democracy* (*Democrat*), Igualdad *Equality*, Independencia *Independence*, Libertad/Libertades (Libre) *Freedom* (*Free*). Negative: Arresto *Arrest*, Autoritarismo *Authoritarianism*, Bloqueo *Blockade*, Caciquismo *Caciquism*, Cooptación *Cooptation*, Despotismo *Despotism*, Detención *Arrest*, Dictadura (Dictador) *Dictatorship (Dictator)*, Fanatismo *Fanatism*, Fascismo *Fascism*, Liberticida *Tyrant*, Odocracia *Odocracy*, Presidio (Presidiario) *Prison* (*Inmate*), Preso *Prisoner*, Radicalismo *Extremism*, Tiranía (Tirano) *Tyranny* (*Tyrant*), Totalitarismo *Totalitarianism*.

15. IMPORTANCE VS. LACK OF IMPORTANCE (8 items):
REPUTATION. Negative: Degradación [military rank] *Downgrading*, Descrédito *Discredit*, Menosprecio *Contempt*

LEADERSHIP. Positive: Líder de opinion *Opinion leader.* SOCIAL CLASS. Positive: Abolengo *Noble ancestry*, Aristocracia *Aristocracy*, Élite *Elite*. Negative: Infraclase *Underclass*.
18. INTELLECT (7 items) Positive: Capacidad *Capacity*, Cultura *Culture*. Negative: Ignorancia *Ignorance*, Idiocia (Idiota) *Idiocy* (*Idiot*), Imbecilidad (Imbécil) *Imbecility* (*Imbecile*).
19. GENERIC EVALUATION [POSITIVE] (6 items) Benevolencia *Benevolence*, Mejor *Best*, Mejora/Mejoras *Improvement*, Mejorado *Improved*, Perfección *Perfection*, Second best
20. POLITENESS (2 items) Positive: Cortesía internacional *International comity*, *Gentlemen's agreement*.

Table 7. Remaining divisions of values.

4. Discussion of results

The distribution of entries among the axiological divisions in Table 1 clearly shows that the first group alone (DEVIANT BEHAVIOUR) accounts for a third of the whole corpus under scrutiny. Consequently this is the predominant group of values, regardless of its heterogeneous nature (16 different subdivisions). It is particularly rich in topics related to economic and property matters or personal offences (killing, violence, sexuality, etc.) on the one hand, and to national security on the other hand. The result may be predictable, given that law dictionaries, especially those including criminal law, must embrace all varieties of legal wrongs or deviant behaviour.

The next category is VITALITY GROUPS (11.5%) referring to disease or death. The weight of terms related to life, death and disease is mostly a contribution of forensic science and practice. The impact that diseases (natural or induced) have over legal cases (both civil or criminal) exerts a powerful influence also on dictionaries. Thus medicine plays a crucial part in the development of law.

COMPLIANCE WITH LEGAL OR MORAL NORMS (7.5%) is essentially different from the other divisions. The terms included here are mainly positively-loaded and embody some of the basic principles of law such as good faith, legality, legitimacy, law-abiding conduct, equity, balance, impartiality, justice or morality.

The combination of divisions such as ECONOMY (MATERIAL) / FUNCTION / PRAGMATISM AND REWARD VS PUNISHMENT accounts for 10% of the corpus and is directly or indirectly related to the impact of economic processes and practices in the legal world. The negative axis predominates here but positively-loaded terms were almost 40% of all entries. It is worth noting the strong link between law and economy, to the extent that the two disciplines cannot be separated in certain areas, such as economically related crimes.

Another interesting result is the low percentage of entries in three fields closely linked to the legal world and supposedly having a very strong axiological load: INNOCENCE VS. GUILTINESS (4%); DAMAGES, INJURIES AND MISFORTUNE (3.8%); and TRUTHFULNESS/ CERTAINTY VS FALSEHOOD/UNCERTAINTY (3.5%). A possible reason for this may be the criteria adopted for assigning concepts to different axiological divisions, although another explanation may be the considerable weight intuitively attached to certain legal topics to the detriment of others.

It would be unremarkable to observe that values linked to behaviour (such divisions as sex, work-related attitudes, attack or defence, causing death, emotional states, truth, freedom or authoritarism, generosity) dominate the axiological scenario, even if the percentage reached by these divisions individually is relatively modest. In fact, over 50% of all entries were directly connected with conduct or actions associated to behavioural responses.

5. Concluding remarks

The results summarised above provide a reliable estimate of axiological evidence (qualities and faults) in legal terminology as well as an account of the lexical and terminological resources used to denote the evaluative items in the dictionary under scrutiny. They measure the degree of coherence/contradiction between personal opinions presented in the theoretical literature on values, and qualities (or faults) explicitly mentioned in the legal world, where specialised dictionaries offer a good source for analysis.

Another advantage of this approach is that it helps to clarify the axiological mapping of relevant values in the discourse of legal sciences in Spanish, both globally and in their link to specific legal sectors, such as criminal law, constitutional law, legal administration, land law, forensics, etc. From a linguistic point of view, the overwhelming majority of nouns attached to legal terms and concepts (to the detriment of adjectives) provides plausible evidence that there is no reason to consider nouns as less of an axiological class than adjectives or adverbs, even if this has been the general belief of axiological studies (see Appendix).

In-depth interdisciplinary approaches of the kind demonstrate the existence of values linked to specific types of discourse, which normally go undetected in general classifications of values. The mapping of the most frequent axioms in legal terminology is a valuable tool not only for the linguist but also for those whose profession or studies require a sound knowledge of the law.

References

Cortés de los Ríos, Mª Enriqueta 2001. *Nuevas perspectivas lingüísticas en la publicidad impresa anglosajona.* Almería: University of Almería.

Cortés de los Ríos, Mª Enriqueta 2007. The Teaching of Metaphor and Vocabulary Used in Financial Advertising. *The ESPecialist* 28/1, 87-113.

Del Arco Torres, Miguel Ángel (ed.) 2004. *Diccionario básico jurídico.* Granada: Comares.

Felices Lago, Ángel 1991. *El componente axiológico en el lenguaje. Su configuración en los adjetivos que expresan emociones y conducta en la lengua inglesa*. PhD Thesis. Granada: University of Granada.

Felices Lago, Ángel 1992. The Integration Process of the Evaluation Classeme in a Dictionary. In Alvar Ezquerra, Manuel (ed.) *Proceedings From the IV Congress of EURALEX*. Barcelona: VOX-Biblograf, 349-358.

Felices Lago, Ángel 1996. Axioematic Analysis of Brand Names in English: A Semantico-Pragmatic Approach to Branding. In Budin, Gerhard (ed.) *Multilingualism in Specialist Communication*. Vienna: IITF/Infoterm, 991-1010.

Felices Lago, Ángel 1998. Axiological Analysis of Financial Terminology in Spanish. In Lunquist, Lita / Picht, Heribert / Qvistgaard, Jacques (eds) *LSP Identity and Interface. Research, Knowledge and Society*. Copenhagen: Copenhagen Business School, 290-299.

Felices Lago, Ángel 1999. Axiological Linguistics Applied to Branding: Analysis of Trade Names Related to Personal Care, Cloth and Footwear. *Unesco Alsed-LSP Newsletter* 22/2, 16-27.

Felices Lago, Ángel 2006. La codificación del parámetro axiológico en la terminología financiera y de inversión. In Calvi, Maria Vittoria / Chierichetti, Luisa (eds) *Nuevas tendencias en el discurso de especialidad*. Bern: Peter Lang, 203-222.

Felices Lago, Ángel 2008a. Las cualidades demandadas al solicitante de empleo en español frente al inglés. In Calvi, Maria Vittoria / Mapelli, Giovanna / Santos López, Javier (eds) *Lingue, culture, economia: comunicazione e pratiche discorsive*. Milan: Franco Angeli, 95-110.

Felices Lago, Ángel 2008b. Human Qualities and Faults in Terminological Contexts. In Sánchez Hernández, P. / Pérez-Paredes, P. / Aguado Jiménez, P. / Criado Sánchez, R. (eds) *Researching and Teaching Specialized Languages: New Contexts, New Challenges*. Murcia: Editum, 261-72.

Felices Lago, Ángel / Hewitt, Elaine 2004. Personal Qualities of Applicants in Job Advertisements. *LSP and Professional Communication* 4/2, 8-27.

Felices Lago, Ángel / Corral Hernández, Ana 2008. Axiological Analysis of Print Advertisements Related to Ecological Issues in *The Economist*. In Linde, Ángeles / Santana, Juan / Wallhead,

Celia (eds) *Studies in Honour of Neil McLaren.* Granada: University of Granada, 177-190.

Krzeszowski, Tomasz P. 1990. The Axiological Aspect of Idealized Cognitive Models. In Tomaszczyk, Jerzy / Lewandowska, Barbara (eds) *Meaning and Lexicography.* Amsterdam: John Benjamins, 135-165.

Krzeszowski, Tomasz P. 1993. The Axiological Parameter in Preconceptual Image Schemata. In Geiger, Richard A. / Rudzka-Ostyn, Brigida (eds) *Conceptualizations and Mental Processing in Language.* Berlin: Mouton de Gruyter, 307-330.

Krzeszowski, Tomasz P. 1997. *Angels and Devils in Hell. Elements of Axiology in Semantics.* Warsaw: Energeia.

Krzeszowski, Tomasz P. 2004. Metaphors of Discourse: Between Co-operative and Oppositional Discourses. In Duszak, Anna / Okulska, Urszula (eds) *Speaking from the Margin. Global English from a European Perspective*, Frankfurt am Main: Peter Lang, 107-116.

Lakoff, George 1987. *Women, Fire and Dangerous Things.* Chicago: The University of Chicago Press.

Langacker, Ronald 1988. A View of Linguistic Semantics. In Rudzka-Ostyn, Brigyda (ed.) *Topics in Cognitive Linguistics.* Amsterdam: John Benjamins, 49-90.

McArthur, Tom 1981. *Longman Lexicon of Contemporary English.* Harlow: Longman.

Martin, Elizabeth / Law, Jonathan [6]2006. *Oxford Dictionary of Law.* New York: Oxford University Press.

Münsterberg, Hugo 1908. *Philosophie der Werte.* Leipzig: Johann Ambrosius Barth.

Ortega y Gasset, José 1923. Introducción a una estimativa: ¿qué son los valores? *Revista de Occidente* 4/10, 315-335.

Osgood, Charles 1980. The Cognitive Dynamics of Synaesthesia and Metaphor. In Honnech, Richard P. / Hoffmann, Robert R. (eds) *Cognition and Figurative Language.* Hillsdale, NJ: Erlbaum, 203-238.

Osgood, Charles / Suci, George / Tannenbaum, Percy 1957. *The Measurement of Meaning.* Chicago: Illinois University Press.

Pauwels, Paul / Simon-Vandenbergen, Anne Marie 1993. Value Judgment in the Metaphorization of Linguistic Action. In Geiger, Richard A. / Rudzka-Ostyn, Brygida (eds) *Conceptualizations and Mental Processing in Language*. Berlin: Mouton de Gruyter, 331-367.
Pauwels, Paul / Simon-Vandenbergen, Anne Marie 1995. Body Parts in Linguistic Action. Amsterdam: John Benjamins, 71- 123.
Roget, Peter M. 1852. *Roget's Thesaurus of English Words and Phrases*. Harlow: Longman.
Scheler, Max 1941. *Nuevo ensayo de fundamentación de un personalismo ético*. Madrid: Revista de Occidente. Originally published in 1913-16 as *Der Formalismus in der Ethik und die Materiale Wertethik*.
Stati, Sorin 1979. *La sémantique des adjectifs: Essai d'analyse componentielle appliqué aux langues romanes*. Paris : Jean Favard.

Appendix

Outline of extralinguistic axiological classifications made by leading philosophers in different historical periods.

NEO-KANTIAN SCHOOL

Münsterberg (1908) - Pure values

Logical values. Values of existence (Things, Characters, Assessments); Values of connection (Nature, History, Reason).

Aesthetic values. Values of unity (Harmony, Love, Happiness); Values of beauty (Plastic arts, Poetry, Music).

Ethical values. Values of evolution (Growth, Progress, Self-growth); Values of qualified production (Economy, Law, Ethics).

Metaphysical values. Divine values (Creation, Revelation, Redemption, Salvation); Fundamental values (Universe, Mankind, Supra-ego).

Values of life (External world, Other world, Internal world).

Values of culture (External world, Other world, Internal world).

PHENOMENOLOGICAL AXIOLOGY

Max Scheler (1913-1916)
First step (lowest). Pleasantness/Unpleasantness.
Second step. Vital values (Physical strength, Death, Old age).
Third step. Spiritual values: Aesthetic (Ugly, Beautiful, Sublime, Ridiculous); Just/Unjust; Pure knowledge of truth (Philosophy, better than natural sciences).
Fourth step (highest). Divine versus Profane (Happiness, Despair).
This order is a moral imperative for Scheler. Ethical value is not included because it is the value that builds up the hierarchy.

Ortega y Gasset (1923) - Positive and negative values
Useful (able/unable, cheap/expensive, abundant/scarce).
Vital (healthy/ill, select/vulgar, energetic/idle, strong/weak).
Spiritual. Intellectual (knowledge/mistake, exact/approximate, evident/probable, etc.); Moral (good/bad, benevolent/cruel, just/unjust, scrupulous/indolent, loyal/disloyal); Aesthetic (beautiful/ugly, graceful/coarse, elegant/inelegant, harmonious/ inharmonious); Religious (holy/profane, divine/diabolic, supreme/derived, miraculous/ mechanical).

CHRISTOPHER GODDARD

Legal Linguists: As (In)substantial as Ghosts and True Love?

1. Introduction

This chapter[1] aims to establish whether the term 'legal linguist' contains substance; put differently, whether the profession of legal linguist exists in the shape of a set of identifiable skills which certain individuals possess, skills that respond to the needs of a market that in turn recognizes those skills as belonging to the profession of legal linguist. Is this an emerging profession or simply a set of non-eponymous skills deployed within other professions? What questions need to be framed – and answered – in order to provide clarification?

As an emerging discipline, legal linguistics needs to be effectively showcased for two related reasons. Firstly, marketing to potential applicants, employers, and stakeholders must show legal linguistics as having clear practical professional relevance. Secondly, legal linguistics programmes must be appropriately focused to respond to the needs of the discipline and the market. This would include establishing whether the discipline can be linked to the term 'legal linguist' and where and how legal linguistic skills can be applied.

This study begins by examining legal linguistics as a discipline, and the correlation between disciplines and professions. This is followed by a focus group survey questionnaire to establish whether the discipline of legal linguistics is matched by an eponymous profession with its own skills set. The survey was assembled and distributed, and its results are discussed here.

---

1 The title alludes to Maxim 76 in the Penguin Classics 1959 English translation of *Maxims* by François, Duc de la Rochefoucauld.

2. Legal linguistics: an emerging discipline

While linguistics as a discipline in the modern sense emerged in the early twentieth century, legal linguistics has only recently been establishing itself as a discipline. According to Mattila's (2006: 11) definition, legal linguistics "examines the development, characteristics, and usage of legal language". Salmi-Tolonen (2004: 1167) sees "law and all legal activity as communication", which implies a concurring statement of the purpose of the discipline as "to study the language of the law, in all its forms, and its development and usage in order to create new knowledge of the interplay between language, law and society" (2004: 1169). However, a variety of terms is in use to describe research into legal language. English, German, and French have two terms, respectively 'forensic linguistics' and 'law and language' – *Rechtslinguistik* and *Recht und Sprache*, *linguistique juridique* and *jurilinguistique* – while different terms are used or may not exist at all in other languages (Mattila 2006).· This suggests that international conceptual and terminological uniformity could be lacking.

2.1. Lawyers, translators, linguists, and legal linguistics

Today's and tomorrow's lawyers increasingly require some knowledge of legal languages other than their own in order to cooperate with foreign lawyers and other professionals, such as translators. Equally, translators can benefit from familiarity with legal linguistics matters. The process of European unification increasingly requires translations of legal texts, many of which involve linguist-translators rather than lawyers.

The "internationalization of legal life" (Zweigert/Kötz 1998: 21) involves the reality of non-native speakers of English operating as lawyers and legal translators in a professional context increasingly dominated by English. It is among this group in particular that purposive scientific study of language in legal contexts features prominently as a professional requirement. Interestingly, too, a significant overlap exists in the legal linguistic knowledge and skills needs of both groups (Goddard 2009).

While translators and linguists undoubtedly require some knowledge of law in order to work with legal texts, lawyers may easily be assumed to wield linguistic skills that they do not possess. Traditionally, lawyers become familiar with legal language by studying and writing about the law. In doing so, they absorb or adopt legal terms and legal style, if perhaps uncritically. However, the full grasp of legal language and its features that is vital for professional effectiveness requires purposive study, which may be lacking.

2.2. Specific problems addressed by legal linguistics

Constraints of space and topic-relatedness allow only a brief overview of the technical application of this discipline. In general, legal linguistics offers potential theoretical approaches to practical problems encountered in legal communication at national, international, and supranational levels. For example, legal linguistics may offer tools to drafters and translators working with legal texts.

At the national (monolingual) level, legal linguistics can address problems of text organisation and style. A good example would be 'translating' a standard form contract between a bank and its private customers from 'traditional' legal English to its plain modern counterpart. Thus

> The bank hereby expressly agrees that the account holder or any authorized user will not be liable hereunder for any unauthorized instruction insofar as such instruction was received after notification had been given to the bank by said account holder or authorized user that the password had become known to some third party or that the actions, negligence or other breach of security attributable to the bank has caused said unauthorized instruction.

becomes (my italics):

> 2.2 You will not be liable for instructions not authorised by a *User if*:
>
> 2.2.1 they are given after that *User* (or you) has notified us that they think the *Password* is known to someone else;

> 2.2.2 the *Security Codes* have become known through our actions or negligence;
> 2.2.3 the instruction was given as a result of some other breach of security, not caused by you or a User.
>
> (Source: Lloyds TSB)

In countries where two or more languages are officially in operation, legal linguistics would address problems of, for example, semantics in production of bilingual or multilingual legislation. Here, countries such as Canada, Switzerland, and Finland spring immediately to mind. A fascinating example is offered by production of the German-Italian legal dictionary for Alto Adige/Südtirol, which involved comparative legal linguistic study of terms in Austria, Switzerland, and Germany (Mattila 2006).

At the international and supranational levels, the chief hurdles for legal linguistics to address appear to be conceptual problems and absence of equivalence or presence of asymmetry between different legal languages and systems (Goddard 2009). Literal translation of the designations of legal terms may be meaningless or misleading to an individual from another legal system. This situation arises from what can perhaps be described as legal cultural reasons, here in the shape of each country's individual legal history, its legal cultural baggage. Although considerable difficulty exists with defining *legal culture* as a concept, given "the boundaries of jurisdiction, politics, and language, the nation state does make a convenient starting point for comparing legal culture" (Nelken 2004: 5). Examples of such problems are legion but would include, for example, designations of functionaries linked to the legal profession such as the French *maître* in front of the personal names of lawyers, or the English *Queen's/King's Counsel*. A literal translation of these titles is void (meaningless) for the outsider. Another problem is due to difficulties related to semantic field between two or more languages (Salmi-Tolonen 2004).

3. Disciplines and professions

It is probably true that at any point in time, the spectrum of disciplines and professions show some as nascent or emerging, others as established, with others as obsolescent or disappearing. As for whether disciplines are mirrored in eponymous professions (and vice-versa), the legal profession and law as a discipline offer contrasting examples from common law and civil law. In England, lawyers were traditionally initiated into a craft upheld and transmitted from generation to generation by a closely-knit corps of professional lawyers. Common law was seen, first of all, as a practice, with the notion of artificial reason justifying the craft-like education of future lawyers, so typical of common law (Postema 2003), so that it was not until the eighteenth century that Blackstone was given the first chair in English law at Oxford. While England built up its specific common-law culture, "on the Continent the revival of Roman law, with its institutional foundation in university-based legal scholarship and education, spawned a transnational legal culture and a transnational corps of learned lawyers" (Tuori 2007: Ch 2, my translation)

Disciplines impart skills that can be deployed in professions which may, but need not, eponymously echo their parent discipline. Thus, even if the discipline of legal linguistics is gaining recognition, it does not necessarily follow that the legal linguist exists at all.

4. The notion of 'legal linguist'

This section examines whether the legal linguist is definable as a profession, according to a focus group survey. To obtain perceptions of what constitutes a 'legal linguist', I designed a survey questionnaire sent by email to a focus group of academics, potential employers, legal translators, and past and potential students of the Riga Graduate School of Law's master's programme in legal linguistics. The questions were arranged to test the consistency of responses. Replies were received from the following:

- Four potential students, including two translators working with law firms.
- Two former students, one with a law qualification, the other without.
- One translator with the European Court of Justice.
- One lawyer-linguist from the European Council.
- Four academics.

In view of the limited number of respondents, this research should be seen as preliminary, though the author contends that this is justifiable due to constraints of time and space. All the responses collected appear in their original form, that is, the language has not been proofread. Only questions that relate to the topic dealt with in this chapter are shown here.

A. Does 'legal linguist' consist of specific identifiable skills? If so, what skills?

- Yes, domestic law, EU law, comparative law, cultural studies, LSP.
- I think a legal linguist should have skills in linguistic analysis, legal argumentation, semantics and at least two languages.
- Knowledge of foreign languages + knowledge of legal matters.
- Knowledge of linguistics and law; as to practical skills: legal translation/interpreting, legal drafting.
- Legal skills and language skills in particular.
- Has both legal and linguistic background. An understanding of special features of legal texts. Is aware of differences between legal systems.
- Exquisite and thorough understanding of legal texts, ability to improve them, make them reader-friendly and business-focused.
- Legal linguist definitely needs qualified skills both in Law and Linguistics and knowledge of at least one or two foreign languages.
- I am not very experienced translator of legal texts. However, I would say that this profession is an interdisciplinary profession where the attention has to be paid as to the specific language, as well legal aspects, such as: specific reading skills (knowledge of the different interpretation methods of legal texts, traditions of thought, knowledge of the specific culture i.e. German legal system, tradition), specific writing skills, also technical skills in order to know how to compose correctly legal texts, terminology knowledge and skills to build up new terms in target language, knowledge of legal documents types.

- Legal and linguistic skills combined.
- Yes. To my mind a legal linguist must have theoretical and practical background of both law and linguistics in the working languages (i.e. Latvian-English).
- Ability to understand and correctly use the language and its legal terminology.

B. Is legal linguist a recognised – or recognisable – profession?

- Neither – nor.
- Not yet, as far as I know.
- No.
- It is an emerging profession which is recognisable, but probably not recognised yet.
- No. Not really. In EU institutions we are called lawyer-linguists. Pure lawyers have little time for them and regard them as lawyers who are failures. Linguists have more respect for them.
- Yes – at least in the EU institutions.
- Certainly recognised among linguists, maybe less so among lawyers.
- Definitely recognisable as a profession, although there are some individuals possessing skills necessary for a legal linguist but without an academic degree (translators who work with legal texts on daily basis or lawyers working in an international environment or using at least two languages in their work).

C. If not, is legal linguist included under some other professional classification(s)?

- Not for the time being, but it should become a recognised and recognisable profession a.s.a.p.!
- Translators do some of the job, and specialised lawyers (although they tend not to do thorough linguist analysis.
- Legal translator.
- Legal translator, lawyer linguist.
- Not that I know of. We fall between two stools: not pure lawyers and not pure linguists, so that leads to a general neglect and lack of anyone to promote our viewpoint.
- Skills pertaining to legal linguists are separated among translators, editors, drafters, but none of them is required to make texts better.
- Nowadays it is indeed under some other professional classification such as Linguistics and Law, so individuals graduated from one of the mentioned faculties, or desirably having both professions are nowadays engaged in the field of legal linguistics as too few Universities can offer nowadays specific programmes at Master's or PhD or LLD level in legal linguistics.
- Generally tend to be linguists rather than lawyers.
- Translator.

D. Is a legal linguist the same as a lawyer linguist?

- No, 'lawyer linguist' is a lawyer with specialised linguistic skills and 'legal linguist' is a linguist with specialised skills in the field of law.
- Related – at least some legal training will be necessary.
- Yes.
- In my view, legal linguist is a wider term than lawyer linguist; it includes lawyer linguists, but also linguists who are not lawyers studying different aspects of the interface between language and law.
- Broadly yes. Lawyer-linguist is a job description in the EC institutions and basically means legal-linguistic reviser of legislative texts.
- This may be the case. To my mind, legal linguist may also refer to lawyers doing research on or working with questions related to the interrelationship between law and language.
- Legal linguist might not be the same as lawyer linguist, but in a small market it will turn out to be the same.
- No, it is not, as concept of Legal Linguist is of much wider sense than lawyer linguist's, as the engagement of the lawyer as a linguist is restricted in his/her specific field of Law, where she/he works.
- In Latvian language the actual translation is *jurists lingvists* (lawyer linguist). I perceive a difference in that way that the educational background of a lawyer linguist is lawyer as the primary qualification with a further professional education in linguistics. As to the legal linguist the case is vice versa.
- In real life, legal linguists' legal background and knowledge tends to be smaller than that of lawyer linguists.
- Lawyer linguist must have legal background, but legal linguist should have either legal or linguistic background supplemented by the missing knowledge.
- No. Lawyer linguist must be a lawyer, which is not necessary for Legal linguist. Both can work as translators, but the linguist cannot work as a lawyer.

L. Does the term legal linguist contain the same conceptual substance between different languages and legal cultures?

- No.
- I guess so, as the job does not yet exist.
- No, obviously. does this concept exist in all languages/legal cultures?
- No, the term may imply different types of competence.
- Do not know. balance between the two, but always one side predominates. Everyone is either first lawyer or first linguist. A good context needs both. cf ECJ translation depts.
- The term *legal linguist* is yet to be imported in different languages.
- Legal linguist is very often associated with legal translator which is not correct, though more or less I can admit that it contains the same conceptual substance in different languages.

- I have not enough knowledge to answer this question.
- Possibly yes.
- Yes.
- Yes, in general.

O. Is a legal linguist the same as a legal translator?

- No, a translator is not necessarily a skilled linguist, i.e. a linguist with large theoretical knowledge in the field of applied linguistics – speciality: LSP.
- No.
- At the CJ, yes. But legal linguist could in principle be someone who also drafts legal instruments.
- No, legal linguist may be a lawyer linguist etc.
- Broadly yes. Overlap. But depends on the types of text translated, or revised.
- Not necessarily. Legal translator may also be a linguist without a background in law.
- The market makes them the same; however, a legal linguist might focus on editing text more than translating them.
- No way, though legal linguist implies the qualification of legal translator but not vice versa as the general competence of legal linguist covers much more than that of legal translator.
- I think it is a broader term, it means also editing, composing, analysing.
- In my case, yes – however, a legal linguist may engage in a wider spectrum of activities/duties, such as maybe publishing, and other work outside law firms.
- Legal linguist can have either translator's background or lawyer's background, but legal translator should have translator's background supplemented by legal knowledge – it all depends on the base knowledge.
- Almost... translator is a linguist. A lawyer could be a translator if he is a linguist.

R. What does a legal linguist actually do?

- Legal linguist is supposed to understand and to be able to interpret linguistic issues of the legalese in general enabling the other specialists in the field of law to benefit from his/her professional judgements. He/she can also be employed as legal translator, court interpreter and work in terminology institutes as expert in the field of legal terminology.
- Analyse meanings of different language versions of legal texts written by the legal linguist himself/herself or by others.
- Here, at the CJ, they translated from FR into all the other languages of the EU.
- Translation/interpreting, drafting, research, teaching...
- Translate, revise, draft legal texts.
- A legal linguist might, for instance, work as a lawyer linguist, lawyer analyst, freelance translator, researcher, or in a ministry as a part of national lawdrafting

process etc.

- Edits texts.
- Translation of the legal documents, inspection ways of transposition of new concepts from source to target legal systems, expertise of the legal documents etc.
- Analysis, comparisons, editing, translation, composition of legal texts.
- Works with legal texts in a broad sense (including writing, editing and translation of legal texts).
- Translations.

S. How can legal linguistic skills be applied in practice?

- In many different ways: translations, interpretations, in /bilateral and multilateral/ comparative law activities, activities connected to EU law etc.
- As any other skills – by design and by chance.
- Translation, drafting, research, teaching.
- Translation, drafting, revision.
- In translating legal texts, such skills come useful.
- Legal linguists may invest their time in text improvement, clarification and market-adaption.
- By self-actualization of the all acquired skills and competence in the relevant field of engagement.
- Analysing contracts, legal agreements, notary acts etc.
- The 'linguistic' skills can be applied in translations; the 'legal' skills help to understand legal documents (both are useful even for reading an employment contract).

Additional comments and suggestions:

- The subject discussed here is extremely complex and future oriented. Both professions – lawyer linguist and legal linguist /I consider them as two professions with overlapping jobs/ need profiling and acknowledgment. The programmes offering an extensive and comprehensive training to both lawyer linguists and legal linguists are to be on the agenda everywhere. A step forward in that direction is for sure the proposed Tempus project "Language and Law in European Context". And now, a few words about 'the other one', i.e. lawyer linguist: the lawyer linguist (LL) is expected to represent an ideal balance of law and language and the key word is specialist knowledge in both disciplines. The most important issues regarding the profile of a LL are qualifications required for the job, tasks to be performed and goals to be achieved. On one hand the 'potential' employers don't agree on the scope of activities of a LL, and on the other hand, recruitment practices and qualifying criteria for the profession in question haven't been harmonized yet. Therefore, this new profession is to be introduced to a broad target audience as an expert who is capable of producing a legal document functioning properly as translated document in a different language and legal system.

- Add semiotics and discourse analysis; consider the team aspect where people reinforce each others' skills. There is a general ignorance about what JLs do and they tend to be looked down on, perhaps even despised by some. They are not aggressive and upwardly thrusting personalities. They none the less play an invisible but important role in keeping things going and ensuring the quality of the final legal/legislative product. I aim to talk about the revision aspect at Bergamo.
- Legal linguistics is a possibility to raise public awareness of text quality, language is a precise matter and language imprecision, lack of clarity not only annoys but may cause adverse consequences.
- Looking for implementation of legal linguistics education in a larger number of countries/higher education institutions.

The evidence collected here suggests the need, or at least the desire, for professional profiling and due professional acknowledgement of lawyer-linguists and legal linguists. The legal linguist as a profession is seen as possessing specific identifiable skills (Questions A, R, S). Though respondents were far from unanimous, skills included, for example, knowledge of domestic law, EU law, comparative law, cultural studies, LSP, linguistic analysis, legal argumentation, semantics and at least two languages, legal translation/interpreting, legal drafting, an understanding of special features of legal texts, semiotics and discourse analysis.

Practical deployment of legal linguistic skills is seen as including: legal translator, court interpreter and work in terminology institutes as expert in the field of legal terminology; drafting, research, revising and editing texts; inspecting ways of transposing new concepts from source to target legal systems; teaching.

However, while one respondent sees legal linguist as an emerging profession, which is recognisable but not yet recognised, many respondents think instead that the skills of legal linguists are separated from those of lawyer-linguists, (legal) translators, editors and drafters. (Questions B, C, D, O). As for the conceptual substance of the term 'legal linguist' in different languages, respondents' answers were inconclusive.

5. Conclusion

Although legal linguistics appears to be an emerging discipline, at the same time no common meaning or understanding of the term appears to exist between languages. Indeed, a variety of expressions are used, as we have seen in Section 2 of this chapter, and it has to be established whether these are parallel or overlapping disciplines. Moreover, responses to the questionnaire are somewhat unclear on this point. Research appears desirable in order to establish the scope of legal linguistics, with a view to establishing international conceptual and terminological uniformity.

It appears that a link does not necessarily exist between a discipline and an eponymous profession and vice-versa. Again, although the legal linguist may be an emerging profession, two important caveats remain. Firstly, the scope and skills of a legal linguist are not yet clear. Secondly, it remains to be seen whether those skills will be subsumed into and deployed in some profession.

In view of the limited number of respondents, this research should be seen as preliminary, though the author contends that this is justifiable due to constraints of time and space. However, research into concepts of legal linguist should delve into further sources, such as textbooks, dictionaries, and encyclopaedias. More importantly, research should cover the appearance of legal linguists and parallel professions (e.g. lawyer-linguist) in the European Union (EU) and other comparable bodies, such as the World Trade Organisation and the United Nations. In particular:

(a) How the profession of lawyer-linguist was created in the EU and what kind of discussion took place then regarding the need for this kind of profession and what kind of people should be recruited.
(b) How, in such discussions, a distinction (if any) appeared between 'legal linguist' and 'lawyer-linguist'.
(c) How lawyer-linguists are recruited in the EU today (e.g. qualification requirements, what kind of competitions are

arranged). What their exact tasks are in the EU and their relation to other similar professions in the EU (e.g. translators).

(d) Whether there are comparable professions in other international bodies where legal translation is widely carried out.

References

Goddard, Christopher 2009. Where Legal Cultures Meet: Translating Confrontation into Coexistence. *Investigationes Linguisticae* 17, 168-205. Available at <http://www.staff.amu.edu.pl/~inveling/index.php?direct=208>.

Mattila, Heikki E.S. 2006. *Comparative Legal Linguistics*. Aldershot: Ashgate.

Nelken, David 2004. Using the Concept of Legal Culture. *Australian Journal of Legal Philosophy* 29, 1-26.

Postema, Gerald J. 2003. Classical Common Law Jurisprudence (Part 2). *Oxford University Commonwealth Law Journal* 3/1, 1-28.

Salmi-Tolonen, Tarja 2004. Legal Linguistic Knowledge and Creating and Interpreting Law in Multilingual Environments. *Brooklyn Journal of International Law* 29/3, 1167-1191.

Tuori, Kaarlo. 2007. *Oikeuden Ratio ja Voluntas* [*The Ratio and Voluntas of Law*]. Helsinki: WSOYpro.

Zweigert, Konrad / Kötz, Hein ^{3}1998. *Introduction to Comparative Law*. Translated by Tony Weir. Oxford: Clarendon Press.

IULIA DANIELA NEGRU

Acceptability versus Accuracy in Courtroom Interpreting

1. Introduction

The conflict between acceptability and correctness or accuracy seems to have raised its controversial head again after just over fifty years since Chomsky (1957) attempted to define 'grammaticalness' as whether or not a linguistic structure is intuitively acceptable from a native speaker's perspective. He eventually separated accuracy from acceptability by distinguishing competence and performance – the former being a set of rules that are more of less fixed or at best slow-moving, whereas the latter is the language we actually use and as such it is dynamic, ephemeral and does not always correspond to what we would strictly define as correct.

However, far too many non-grammatical utterances are deemed acceptable by native speakers and, conversely, many syntactically 'correct' utterances were deemed unacceptable. There are simply too many variables involved when measuring acceptability, such as receiver typology (nationality, race, gender, age, profession and class) and text typology (some codes are very dynamic whereas others, like the law, are apparently much more static).

The aim of this chapter is to analyze how some of the variables are dealt with in oral interpreting, that is to say, in the language used by liaison interpreters in the courtroom, in 'real' as opposed to 'ideal' interpreting contexts. The study of such legal oral translation will not be language specific, in the sense that, even if Italian and Romanian are the languages submitted to analysis through the looking glass of English translation of conversations, the implications and the conclusions will most likely have some applications for any given language combination.

2. Legal discourse and interpreting

No other domain, not even scientific discourse, gives as much importance to its linguistic vehicle as does the law. Indeed, Mellinkoff (1963: 3), in his classic study of the language of the law, goes so far as to claim that "the law is a profession of words".

Certainly, it is the professional context *par excellence* in which the accuracy and the lack of ambiguity of an utterance determine the very substance of the profession itself. As Crystal (1987: 386) points out: "There is no other variety where the users place such store on the nuances of meaning conveyed by language, where unstated intentions are so disregarded". However, although the linguistic conservatism often characterised by archaisms, wordiness, dullness, pomposity and even, some would say, goobledegook, is certainly a general trait of the language of the law, it must also be pointed out in all fairness that not all the language of the law (or rather language in a legal context) fits this description.

In this chapter, legal language will refer to the language of and related to the law and legal process, which also includes language about law and language used in other communicative situations, such as courtroom interpreting, as Cao (2007) and Williams (2004) see it. Williams (2004: 111) is quick to avoid overly-simplistic sweeping categorisations that tend to be inaccurate and pedantic:

> Legal language is made up of several genres, each with its own specific, if often related, characteristics: It ranges from the spoken exchanges in a court between, say, lawyers and witnesses in a cross-examination, to the relatively standardized instructions given to jury members who are required to express a verdict in a court case, to the jargon employed by members of the legal profession in interpersonal communication, to the written language in case law, law reports and prescriptive legal texts.

Though Williams (2004: 112) is certainly correct when he says that "the actual language used [in the courtroom], for example by witnesses, may not differ radically from other genres of spoken discourse", one must not be led into thinking that it is all as 'easy' as we see on television. Indeed, it may be justified to say that courtroom proceedings could be considered even more complicated than even the highly-formulaic written mode because of so many language varieties at work simultaneously in the same professional context, especially for an interpreter who not only has to cope with rapid language switching but also with rapid genre switching (Cao 2007: 5):

> The legal translator's skills and tasks are very different from the lawyer's. The legal translator does not read and interpret the way a lawyer does. The legal translator does not write the law either. However, the legal translator needs to know how lawyers, including judges and lawmakers, think and write the way they do, and at the same time, to be sensitive to the intricacy, diversity and creativity of language as well as its limits and power.

Moving towards the oral mode, in a spoken context other numerous factors come into play, as the translator is no longer alone with the text, but s/he faces a communicative situation which, as Wadensjö (1998) suggests, is embedded with face-saving situations, and questions of footing (the interpreter is viewed as an equalizer, someone who will put litigants who do not speak the language of the proceedings on an equal footing with those who do), just to name a couple of the variables present in interaction.

Legal language is rather static, if compared to more dynamic 'innovative' varieties, to use Louis Trimble's (1985) distinction, but even so, it is hoped to show that interpreter performance and legal language competence may nevertheless be at some degree of variance without disrupting the message being transmitted in that particularly difficult linguistic context.

The main characteristics of written legal language, such as sentence length (recorded both in English and in Italian legal documents), the use of passive structures and other written language markers may or may not appear in the spoken discourse. They may appear because lawyers and prosecutors, for instance, come in with pre-

prepared speeches, spoken aloud often at the speed of sound so that neither interpreters nor the people they assist have the faintest idea of what is going on. Or, on the contrary, the oral mode may have a life of its own, since in hearings the rhythm and tone of conversation will mainly reflect those of a normal conversation, albeit with traps intended for those unaware of the unspoken rules of combat in court.

Clearly, there are things that participants are not allowed to say and if accidentally uttered will be struck from the records, such as expressing opinion, irony, hearsay evidence and the like, which are dealt with by the lawyers and judge through the use of particular linguistic formulae. It is worth examining interpreter behaviour in this case. Does the interpreter edit what was said to avoid disrupting the court proceedings or will s/he decide to reproduce faithfully everything that was being said? What if the mistakes on the part of the person assisted by the interpreter were due to stress and could clearly undermine what may follow in the legal proceedings? Should there be editing or not?

Obviously, the interpreter has to know the target language equivalent of the more formalised language being used but, when genre switching, s/he has to be careful not to omit in translation something as apparently casual as a *ritengo* or *eu cred* [I think] which would be a linguistic premise to inadmissible evidence, in that it is the expression of opinion and not fact.

The definition that authors give to legal interpretation offers a categorization according to which legal interpretation "is subdivided according to the legal setting into (a) quasi-judicial and (b) judicial interpreting or what is normally referred to as court interpreting" (Duenas Gonzales *et al.* 1991: 25-26). Interviews and hearings in out-of-court settings, administrative hearings and the like are part of (a) because the records of such communicative events may form the basis for a case or an appeal. The authors emphasize the need to have the same quality and precision in (a) as in (b), as they are both contexts where accuracy is paramount. Depositions, hearings, trials, sentencing and other judicial proceedings are part of (b), judicial interpreting proper.

The discourse features of legal language in the courtroom may vary depending on the field (Salvi 2002), that is, according to content (statutes, cases and comments etc), tenor, role of participants (relation between lawyers and legislative or juridical authority and intended readers) and mode (language and media used to convey the message).

3. Material and methodology

In this study, the communicative effect of interpreting will be analysed mainly with respect to the dynamics of Court hearings and interrogations and against the concept of 'acceptability' and 'accuracy'.

The interpreting corpus used for the present study consists of twelve interpretations, mostly interrogations. The language services were requested by the Prosecutor's Office, the Court or the Appeal Court and the interpreting setting was either at the above-mentioned offices, the Police Station or the prison. The translation and the interpreting corpus covers the period going from January 2006 up to December 2009.

The hypothesis is that, due to the complexity of the task and the multiplicity of variables at play in courtroom interpreting, what the interpreters provide is not an accurate rendering, but an 'acceptable' one. The process of research was carried out by means of recording interpreters where authorisation was given to do so, organising the data obtained according to the date of recording and eliminating interpretations which contained repetitive elements or interpretations which were too short to offer a basis for research. Hence from a starting point of about 20 interpretations, twelve were kept as their duration was superior to 10' of actual communication and interpreting time.

The method used to gather data was that of observation of the communicative event followed by the transcription of the recording. Conversation analysis (CA) was applied to the data in order to identify the internal logic of details, the sequential organization of action and reaction, or 'moves' (cf. Pallotti 2007). The methodological features include the way the data was selected (recording exchanges that take place independently of the investigator's need) and the data transcription. The transcription was done, however, in a more schematic manner than CA requires, since excessive detail (e.g. false starts, hesitations, intonation contours, etc.) implies looking away from the content, which was deemed more important than speech markers.

This study aims to be an analysis of 'real' as opposed to 'ideal' interpreting in a 'language for specific purposes' context with the intention of showing that even in such a highly-codified linguistic environment, acceptable translation is possible and even necessary and the belief that only legal experts can translate the law is fallacious.

4. Interpreter mediation in a legal context

The following material was obtained from recordings carried out in the Court of Law. Authorisation was obtained to transcribe and research this material provided all the personal references were removed and the resulting text was not 'traceable'. As a result, the actual sources are not cited and the names of the participants have been altered to avoid identification.

4.1. Acceptability in choice of language

The people present at the hearing are Sorin, the person under police investigation, Romanian citizen with some knowledge of the Italian language; next to the suspect Sorin there is the interpreter, Irina. In front of them there is a GIP or *Giudice per le indagini preliminari*, [Magistrate in charge of preliminary investigations], the secretary and, in a corner, the author of this chapter, recording the conversation on tape.

> Sorin: No. Non l'ho visto. Ho visto luce aperta. Io pensato [sic] Cristina
> *I didn't see him. I saw light open [sic]. I thought Cristina*
> e lui non... Dopo ha chiamato amico in piazza Garibaldi: "Nico,

and him not... After friend called in piazza Garibaldi: "Sorin,
ho preso sigarette. Vuoi pacco di sigarette?", "vengo subito". Mi
I got cigarettes. You want cigarette box?", "I'll be right there".
ha visto a San Giacomo. A San Giacomo mi ha dato tre pacco di
he saw me at San Giacomo. In San Giacomo he gave me three box
sigarette e 8.40 arrivato a casa. Arrivato a casa, guardo, nessuno.
of cigarettes and at 8.40 arrived home. Arrived home, I look, nobody.

GIP: gli dica che io faccio fatica a capire un po'. TU sei andato a
Tell him I have problems understanding him. YOU went to buy
comprare le sigarette?
the cigarettes?

Irina: Dumneavoastră ați mers să luați țigările?
It was you who went to get the cigarettes?

Sorin: Da.
yes

Irina: ha detto che è andato prendere le sigarette ed è tornato alle 8.40
He said he went to get the cigarettes and he came back at 8.40

Sorin: 8 e 35, 40.
8.35 – 8.40.

What kind of language are the interpreters and participants at this communicative event using? According to Cao (2007), it is all legal language, since the elements we have just seen, even though they could well be part of a normal day-to-day conversation, are transferred into the broad setting of legal language that was discussed above. In this case, the suspect is (re)telling ordinary events and answers ordinary questions. The special circumstances and conditions that apply to this setting (the suspect might be prosecuted if the evidence against him is considered sufficient) make the context a highly stressful and important one, where every word can make the difference between prison and freedom. This is probably why, as noticed above, Sorin keeps repeating words and phrases ("ho preso sigarette. Vuoi pacco di sigarette", "arrivato a casa. Arrivato a casa..."), as if in an attempt to add weight and truthfulness to his statement.

Firstly, the spoken legal language above sheds all traces of the kind of repetition inherent in typical written legal texts, such as contracts. As has been seen, repetition here has a different role, i.e. asserting truthfulness. At the beginning of the hearing, the GIP reads aloud the results of the investigation and the evidence the police have so far, which would normally be far from the oral mode of the above excerpt. The above fragment takes on a completely different tone. The legal 'touch' is not present – there are no multi-word prepositional structures overflowing from legal texts such as, for example, the legal document sent to lawyers in Italy to give notice about the end of investigation and the possibility of lawyers and defendants to consult the evidence. Such documents are lexically highly dense, a reason for complaint and vexation on the part of many legal translators who were consulted when talking about the typology and style of legal documents and performance in court.

The long complex phrases of such documents have been replaced with shorter direct instances of speech. Passive constructions give way to active speech in the form of dialogue interaction. The interpreter's task here is a difficult one. Indeed, Sorin speaks some Italian and prefers to communicate in Italian, although his competence is a source of miscommunication. This is a case when suspects create problems for themselves by considering language knowledge as a question of pride or sometimes as a way of feeling 'in control' of the interaction. Irina has the task to comprehend meaning from the standpoint of the entire culture and translate bad Italian through Romanian and back to Italian. It is nothing like the flow of interaction described by Wadensjö (1998) – the perfectibility of the theoretical ideal model of interaction contrasts heavily with the communicative situation proper.

The main point is that Irina decides to make some choices to the detriment of accuracy. Is she being less accurate but still manages to provide an acceptable interpretation that is true to the goal of legal interpreting, which according to Duenas Gonzales (1991) is legal equivalence?

The judge changes person from addressing Irina ("Tell him I have problems understanding him") to immediately changing addressee ("YOU went to buy"). Irina decides to leave out the question of incomprehensibility and she focuses on the core problem. She does not translate the fact that the judge has problems understanding Sorin, but rather the unclear fact ("It was you who went to get the cigarettes?"). This may well be a choice dictated not only by restraints of time but also a need to reduce pressure on the witness or cut the translation due to irrelevance – Sorin understands Italian and will have understood the reference of the judge at least in part. In the end, the sentence comes out clear and adapted albeit reduced.

The interpreter here is stripped of all power, as the role of control in communication is not with Irina, but with the GIP. Sorin too feels the need to complete the rendering by refining the time line ("8.35 – 8.40"). The so-called 'third party influence' on the part of the interpreter is non-existent or reduced to a minimum here. The interpreter does little or nothing to influence subtly the interaction by means of emphases and communicative devices. What she cannot control herself is the 'distance' factor – she uses the third person singular when talking about Sorin and describing his actions, instead of the usual 1st person, recommended by the literature.

4.2. Acceptability in choice of language turn

Early Saturday morning, there is an urgent call from the Prison. The same interpreter from the previous conversation is called to interpret for Ionuţ, who is being investigated for fraud and has been found outside his house while on house arrest. Ionuţ is accompanied by a lawyer and seems pretty calm, considering that the decision of the judge will probably send him to prison, since he has violated house arrest. The interpreter meets him only seconds before the hearing.

> Irina: Bună ziua, mă numesc Irina şi sunt interpret de limba română.
> *Good morning, my name is Irina and I'm an interpreter for Romanian.*
> Dacă aveţi nevoie de ajutor...
> *If you need help...*
> Judge: Buon giorno, allora possiamo cominciare
> *Good morning. So, let's start*

Irina:.... vă rog să îmi spuneţi, şi vă voi ajuta
Please tell me, and I will help you

Ionuţ: Da mulţumesc, da' cunosc italiana
Yeah, thanks but I know Italian

The judge continues by explaining the circumstances of the arrest, the date, the place. The interpreter's assistance is required on two further occasions, where Ionuţ did not know how to express two notions in Italian.

This is called 'stand-by' interpreting according to Colin/Morris (1996): the interpreter provides some help to facilitate the communication, without being truly necessary except in a couple of cases. This brings us back to the question formulated at the end of the second unit. Does Irina need to know how the system of law functions when her presence is barely necessary? Yes, the fact that she is of little use in this particular case does not mean that an interpreter should not be fully prepared if called on to deal with the terminology of the legal system.

The pre-established choice of turn in interpreter mediation is disrupted when the Judge interrupts Irina from expressing her goal and the purpose of her presence there. Necessity, time restraints, or rather the non-acknowledgment of the need of the interpreter to have a moment to present herself to Ionuţ makes the judge force his turn in the dialogue. However unwelcome, this often happens and participants frequently speak out of turn and even overlap. Accuracy is thus determined by power sharing and by an acceptable rather than ideal interaction whereby Ionuţ understands the interpreter and her purpose there, but grasps the urgency of 'getting down to business' on the part of the judge at the same time.

4.3. Acceptability in choice of quantity

In matters of serious offences (murder, drugs, counterfeiting and the like), phone tapping is used in Italy. The interpreters are all in a room with listening equipment and a software programme used to listen to, reply and analyze various segments of speech in telephone conversations. This is a field where, beyond the mere knowledge of a language, interpreters are asked to listen to telephone conversations of various lengths; they must understand if the chunk they are dealing with falls into one of the many legal aspects that the investigators are searching for and act upon the linguistic data they receive. It is, of course, the investigator's task further on in the investigation to transform the information from the summary provided by the interpreters into evidence for trial, but here the main task is again not guaranteeing accuracy of every word uttered but acceptability, but summarizing and identifying relevant pieces of information.

Acceptability here accounts for a specific necessity in interpreting, the gist of a conversation, instead of a 'close' translation. There is of course no context, no visual support and sometimes not even the necessary sound quality to work in ideal conditions.

4.4. Acceptability in the fluctuation to and from 'close' translation and interpreting

The following excerpt is from an interrogation. Dumitru is questioned about some events prior to the murder of a woman; the Prosecutor is trying to find as many details about what happened as possible before he can decide on whether to send the case to trial or not. Ilinka, the interpreter, is there to assist.

> Prosecutor: voglio chiedere una cosa. Questa sarebbe la sua quarta versione.
> *I want to ask something. This is your fourth version.*
>
> Dumitru: Eu.. ştiu da' eu, adică... eu încercam să îmi amintesc tot
> *I.. I know but, that is... I tried to remember everything*
> ce s-a întâmplat săptămâna aia, ştiţi… îi [sic, regional] prima
> *that happened that week, y'know... it's the first*
> dată când mi-s sunt adus la tribunal şi nu îmi amintesc chiar tot...
> *time that I'm brought to a court and I don't remember all...*
>
> Ilinka: lui dice che si rende conto. Lui cercava di
> *He says he realizes that. He was trying to*
> raccontare tutto quello che è successo in tutta la settimana,
> *tell everything that happened throughout the week,*

cercava di ricordarsi. è la prima volta che ha a che fare con
he was trying to remember. It's the first time he's
le forze dell'ordine e non si ricordava tutto.
had problems with the law and he didn't remember everything.

Prosecutor: ma insomma, lui l'ha spinta o non l'ha spinta?
Oh, come on, did he push her or not?

Dumitru: Noo, eu am lăsat-o acolo unde era, bea lângă masă.
No, I left her where she was, she was drinking next to the table
Altceva nu am vazut! Nu am vazut când s-o pus în pat. Nu am văzut!
I saw nothing else! I did not see when she went to bed. I didn't!

Ilinka: ha detto che l'ha lasciata a bere vicino alla tavola.
He said he left her drinking next to the table.
Non ha visto quando si è rimessa in letto. Non l'ha vista.
He did not see when she went back to bed. He didn't.

Prosecutor: non ho chiesto questo, ho chiesto se l'ha spinta lui o
I didn't ask that, I asked whether he pushed her or
non l'ha spinta.
he didn't push her.

Dumitru: Nu, da' nici nu aveam cum?! Când? Nu!
No, I had no way to do that?! When? No!

Ilinka: no.
No.

Interpreters in the courtroom are usually advised to 'translate' and not to interpret, but a word-for-word translation can only lead to misunderstandings and miscommunication as languages may not have a one-to-one replacement of words and expressions. However, such a requirement is understandable from the point of view of the representatives of the legal system aiming to have what a person is actually saying and requesting that interpreters do not take it upon themselves to speak for the witnesses. For example, interpreters echo the people who need their services as faithfully as they can; given the limits of language, they do not replace them. They certainly do not act as their advocates, nor do they give legal advice (cf. Colin/Morris 1996).

The understanding of the original meaning and the communicative intention must be grasped from the combination of words of the original utterance and such utterance should then be placed in context before conveying the final meaning into the target text. Here, the interpreter chooses to fluctuate between closeness and distance from the interpretation of the text. She opts for closeness when rendering the exact wording of the answer from Dumitru, although she realizes this was not the answer the GIP was waiting for. At the same time, distance from Dumitru and the text is taken as the interpreter prefers to use the 3rd person instead of the 1st and performs some interpretation which is not a word-for-word rendering. At the post-interrogation interview, she said she knew about the first person rule. However, under the stress and pressure of the situation she could not stop herself from using the 3rd person, especially since the case was a murder case and the stress of all the people in the room peaked when photos of a murdered woman were shown.

Ultimately, the responsibility of dealing with the traps of communication falls with the interpreter who may solve the dilemmas in the way s/he considers best, taking into consideration the setting and what is expected of them. The above interpretation, although not accurate, is a perfect example of acceptability. By being acceptable, but not accurate, it displays some of the 'mistakes' listed by Colin/ Morris (1996) when discussing the quality of the interpreter's performance. The interpreter may use more (or less) polite language than the original; inject or omit hesitation; use more formal or less formal language; eliminate or introduce ambiguities depending on the closeness or distance of the rendition.

Some of the mistakes are: Dumitru speaks in dialect, which can be a sign of lack of education, a signal which is lost when the interpreter goes into standard Italian. Far from expecting the interpreter to go into dialectal Italian, one still has to consider the fact that there is loss in terms of the defendant's level of education, attitude and respect towards what is happening. Irina chooses standard Italian, which is also more polite or at least would sound better to an Italian judge than dialect. She omits hesitations. What could have been done? The question is whether in this context, these are true mistakes. Against everything the interpreter books teach, Irina chose to facilitate communication in an already difficult setting by omitting hesitations, which are easily noticed anyway, even from body language and other non-verbal signals. In this respect, the tape inconveniently 'deletes' the original, non-verbal signals that can be relevant for further discussion of the dynamics of the situation.

Police officers are in charge of conducting and interviewing suspects; interpreters have the primary responsibility for the accuracy and completeness of the communication facilitated by them. Quite often the pressure on the witnesses during examination may result in false or presumably shaky argumentation which is not necessarily proof of guilt. Also, quite often, such stress may affect the completeness mentioned by the authors above. However, such requirements for accuracy should be flexible in that there are redundant elements that can and may be, intentionally or not, left out of the rendition, without affecting the message in the target text.

5. Conclusion

The interpreting situation hence is seen to be somewhat complex and even contradictory. On one side, there is the ideal selection of interpreters as sanctioned by the literature and, as can be seen, put into practice in countries like Australia (Cao 2007), where a sworn affidavit from the translator is necessary to certify the quality of the translation and the competence of the translator. Similar rules exist in other countries too, to regulate the choice of interpreters (Colin/ Morris 1996; Wadensjö 1998) according to accreditation and experience.

Such an ideal situation with an ideal amount of experience and competence is usually not even required in Italy, where interpreters are called to work for various legal institutions and in any case interpreters are certainly not even available on a large scale. It should, perhaps rather controversially, be added that the experienced competent interpreter is not even desirable for a question of costs. An AIIC interpreter would cost the Court of Law several hundred euros for a few hours' work, whereas the standard rate paid by the Italian Ministry of Justice is extremely low for each consecutive hour of work. How can one talk of a serious professional situation when, honestly speaking, the official rate of pay is more or less equivalent to that of a cleaner?

Having said that, responsibility is another key issue. The working relationship between interpreters and judges, magistrates, lawyers and administrators is not controlled by any given rules. There is hence no control on punctuality, availability, or credibility. There are no evaluation forms for the monitoring of interpreting performance. There are no coordinators to check and decide on the choice of interpreters, which is probably just as well since it does not seem that legal assistants or judges themselves are good 'judges' of standards in interpreting. As Colin/Morris argue (1996: 70):

> there is nobody who can be said to have full and final responsibility for the performance and quality of interpreting in the court. Is it the magistrate, is it the judge, is it the lawyer or is it actually the interpreter? Perhaps is it the person who engaged the interpreter?

Ideally, the interpreter should be aware of rules and ethics of interpreting. If the person chosen for the job is not a professional interpreter and just a native speaker, then there is little chance of him/her being aware of such rules. "The people engaged to interpret are not always skilled, experienced or fully competent" (Colin/Morris 1996: 15).

The contradiction mentioned above seems to be endemic in Italy. On the one hand, the legal system does not seem to be ready to handle and correctly select trained interpreters and certainly not to pay them properly. On the other, the literature on the subject recommends responsibility, detachment, interpersonal skills on top of the highest linguistic abilities.

So, in conclusion, as things stand, the practice is therefore still very far from the ideal model of accuracy. What is more, there seems to be no sign that any improvement is being made in an attempt to assure interpretation quality and interpretation quality control. Rather, the situation is moving ever more towards a functional model of acceptability by which is meant the best possible job considering the working conditions and context. Acceptability is not total accuracy but it is not necessarily a bad thing. It is doing the job as well as possible and whenever possible bearing the concept of accuracy in mind as an ideal if not a utopian target to be reached.

References

Cao, Deborah 2007. *Translating Law*. Clevedon: Multilingual Matters.

Chomsky, Noam 1957. *Syntactic Structures*. The Hague: Mouton.

Colin, Joan / Morris, Ruth 1996. *Interpreters and the Legal Process*. Winchester: Waterside Press.

Crystal David 1987. *The Cambridge Encyclopaedia of Language*. Cambridge: Cambridge University Press.

Crystal David / Davy Derek 1969. *Investigating English Style*. London: Longman.

Duenas Gonzales, Roseann / Vasquez, Victoria / Mikkelson, Holly 1991. *Fundamentals of Court Interpretation: Theory, Policy, and Practice*. Durham, NC: Carolina Academic Press.

Mellinkoff, David 1963. *The Language of the Law*. Boston: Little, Brown & Co.

Pallotti, Gabriele 2007. Conversation Analysis: Methodology, Machinery and Application to Specific Settings. In Bowles, Hugo / Seedhouse, Paul (eds) *Conversation Analysis and Language for Specific Purposes*. Bern: Peter Lang, 37-67.

Salvi, Rita 2002. *Traduttori e giuristi a confronto*. Bologna: CLUEB.

Trimble, Louis 1985. *English for Science and Technology*. Cambridge: Cambridge University Press.

Wadensjö, Cecilia 1998. *Interpreting as Interaction*. London: Longman.

Williams, Christopher 2004. Legal English and Plain Language: An Introduction. *ESP across Cultures* 1, 111-124.

FRANCISCO VIGIER

Legal Translation and Interpreting in the UK Today[1]

1. Introduction

Legal translation and interpreting in the United Kingdom (UK) have not received much attention from Translation Studies scholars, with only a few contributions tackling these professional areas (cf. Phillips 1999; Connell 2002; Corsellis 2003; Hickey 2005). Since the recent creation of a National Register for Public Service Interpreters (NRPSI), however, public service interpreting (which includes legal interpreting to a certain extent) has undergone a professionalisation process accompanied by an increase of research on the subject (for instance Townsley 2007; Corsellis 2008). This process, however, has not embraced translation, which retains a lack of regulation which allows anyone to work as a translator without any specific qualification or training.

The UK has two main translator and interpreter organisations, namely the Institute of Translation and Interpreting (ITI) and the Chartered Institute of Linguists (IoL), which are recognised by the government and committed to promote quality in translation and interpreting services. Nonetheless, a translator or interpreter willing to practise in Britain is not bound to belong to any of them, which makes the room for manoeuvre and activism on the part of these organisations rather limited.

1 Special thanks to Professor Tim Connell, Director of Language Studies at City University London and Vice-President of the Chartered Institute of Linguists, who supervised my research stay at City University (October-December 2008).

This chapter presents some of the results of a research project conducted at the City University London, with the aim of presenting as comprehensive an overview as possible of legal interpreting and translation in the UK taking into account different contexts and agents. The purpose of this study is therefore to survey the current situation of legal interpreting and translation in the UK, describing the country's present qualification and accreditation systems, as well as the working conditions and professional status of legal translators.

2. Legal interpreting in the UK

In the UK the scenario for *legal interpreting* (that is, court interpreting and interpreting in other legal areas) is fundamentally different from that of legal translation, as the former is involved in a professionalisation process initiated by the creation of the NRPSI in 1991. However, the NRPSI has only virtually influenced interpreting provision in criminal justice, and interpreting in civil settings lacks any form of regulation. In other words, the establishment of the NRPSI has affected the public sector but not the private one (Hickey 2005).

In fact, it is quite revealing that the Law Society of England and Wales, to which solicitors must belong in order to practise, has not subscribed to the NRPSI in spite of repeated attempts by the NRPSI, to make it available to Law Society members.[2] Thus, solicitors do not seem to pay much attention to translation and interpreting and usually commission these services to agencies or anyone they believe has a good command of foreign languages, while in civil law hearings they hire interpreters who may or may not be registered with the NRPSI.

Despite the profession's unquestionable importance, legal interpreting provision remain very uneven across the UK, and there is still a good deal of distrust and suspicion among other professionals who require such services:

2 Information provided by Mr Brooke Townsley, chair of the NRPSI, during a personal interview in November 2008.

> Until provision of interpreters is organised consistently across the public sector, interpreters will find administrative aggravations in addition to the stress of assignments themselves. Interpreters should be lobbying for best practice to be adopted by all – accurate and complete booking information, better and regular pay, regular support meetings backed up by counselling if needed, training for public service staff and above all professional recognition
> (Clegg 2002: 135)

The NRPSI, which emerged from various initiatives encouraged by the Nuffield Foundation (Corsellis 2008), has a twofold aim: to provide national access to professional interpreters for public services where they do not fully share a common language with a client or clients; and to provide a system for linguists to make their services available for public services.[3] As in other professional registers, there are selection criteria to be satisfied for membership, and members must abide by a Code of Conduct and are subject to Disciplinary Procedures if the code has been breached. To date, there are more than 2,000 interpreters in up to 100 languages registered throughout Britain.

The NRPSI, which is administered by a not-for-profit subsidiary of the IoL, is available for public service organisations and agencies via a yearly on-line subscription. Other agencies or companies may subscribe to the NRPSI as *bona fide* subscribers after providing evidence that they deal with the provision of public service interpreting. Individuals cannot access the information gathered by the NRPSI, which however is expected to become a public register in the long term (when more financing from the State is found). Currently, subscription rates for public service bodies amount to around £500 per annum, whereas fees for individual subscribers (i.e. interpreters) are around £140 p.a. for a first language and £95 for a second language.

The Criminal Justice System, which includes UK police forces and criminal courts, is by far the most important body working through the NRPSI, thanks to a *National Agreement on Arrangements for the Use of Interpreters, Translators and Language Service Professionals in Investigations and Proceedings within the Criminal*

3 See <http://www.nrpsi.co.uk/about/index.htm>.

Justice System.[4] According to this agreement, signed in 2002 and revised in 2007, interpreters working in criminal courts and police stations should be registered with the NRPSI. This has undoubtedly fostered an improvement in working conditions for interpreters in criminal justice, especially when compared to those working in other sectors, such as healthcare. For instance, interpreters must be paid at least £30 per hour (with a minimum fee of £84 per assignment regardless of the time they may have been eventually hired for). The agreement is normally observed in the criminal sector, and it is hoped it will be extended to the civil sector and produce similar agreements with other institutions, e.g. the National Health Service. However, it must be noted that it is not legally binding, as it is not statutory but contains mere recommendations.

Candidates for registration in the NRPSI must be at least of 18 years of age and eligible to work in the UK as self-employed individuals. There are three membership categories (full status, interim status, and rare language status) with different academic and professional criteria to be complied with,[5] but all interpreters are required to upgrade to full status within a certain timescale.

The diploma of reference for the NRPSI is the Diploma in Public Service Interpreting (DPSI) issued by the IoL. The DPSI, which originated as the Bilingual Skills Certificate in Community Interpreting (CCI), is today the UK's only qualification in the realm of public service interpreting[6] accredited by the Qualifications and Curriculum Authority and included in the National Qualifications Framework at Level 6, which amounts to a bachelor degree or a postgraduate certificate in the Framework for Higher Education Qualifications.

The DPSI is offered in four public service contexts: English Law, Scottish Law, Health, and Local Government. The DPSI examination comprises three units, on consecutive and whispered

---

4 Available online at <http://frontline.cjsonline.gov.uk/_includes/downloads/guidance/race-confidence-justice/National_Agreement_on_Use_of_Interpreters-August_2008.pdf>.

5 See <http://www.nrpsi.co.uk/pdf/CriteriaforEntry.pdf>.

6 See <http://www.iol.org.uk/qualifications/exams_dpsi.asp>.

interpreting, sight translation, and written translation [*sic*] respectively. The exams, held once a year in June, are organised and marked by the IoL Educational Trust, and DPSI is awarded to candidates who attain a pass in all the units. Successful applicants are then eligible for membership of the IoL and to be listed on the NRPSI.

3. Legal and official translation in the UK

Like translation in general, *legal translation* is a professional activity which has not yet been regulated in the UK:

> This [language provision for public services] is an activity which has not been previously regulated; it is an occupational area that has not had professional recognition; and it is a profession which has not had internal systems of support through examination, regulation by professional bodies or public standing.
>
> (Connell 2002: 148)

As in many other countries, no specific qualification is required to practise as a professional translator in Britain (Hickey 2005). Thus, contrary to other professions as varied as Law, Medicine and Surveying, translators do not have to belong to a professional body or union in order to practise. There are indeed prestigious, qualified translators, most of whom belong to one of the aforementioned professional bodies (the IoL or the ITI), however membership is not compulsory.

In the case of *official translation*, the scenario is even more unregulated in the UK compared to other countries, as no specific profession is authorised by the British government to perform translations of an official nature (while France has the *traducteur jurée/assermenté*, Germany the *ermächtigter Übersetzer* and Spain the *traductor-intérprete jurado*).

The situation of legal and official translation in Britain can thus be summarised as follows:

> Legal translators in England do not need to have their work approved by a governmental institution or body, nor do they have to take an examination. If a document needs to be sworn [*sic*], it can be done in front of a solicitor, commissioner for oaths or courts' officer. In some circumstances, such as when work is done through an agency, this is not considered necessary.
>
> (Rodríguez 2005: 159)

Obviously there are many situations where the translation of a given document must be certified or legalised for very various purposes (Mayoral 2003), in such a manner that the translator becomes accountable for its rendering. This may range from a university diploma (so that the holder can complete a postgraduate course in the UK) to a birth certificate (to be provided in a legal process). The UK has two main methods to certify such translations: self-certification by the translator or notarised translation.

Any translator may certify that their translation is accurate and faithful to the original. The ITI, as a professional association assessing the quality of its members, "has taken steps to establish itself as a body whose members can certify translations",[7] and offers eligible members (against payment) certifying seals. There are also recommendations for self-certified translations by an ITI member, e.g. that the translation should be verified by another ITI member, be subject to ITI's code of ethics and that the ITI seal be affixed to its first page and signed by the certifier. As far as the certification is concerned, the ITI suggests the following wording:

> I, the undersigned, [name], Member of the Institute of Translation and Interpreting, [other qualifications], declare that the translation of the attached documents [identifying particulars] is to the best of my knowledge and belief a true and faithful rendering of the original [language], done to the best of my ability as a professional translator [and verified by [name and ITI membership qualification]].

Translations with the ITI certification are accepted by many institutions, such as the Home Office, the Passport Office, many

7 From <http://www.iti.org.uk/indexMain.html>.

embassies and the security industry.[8] However, as the ITI suggests, if the client insists on a higher level of certification, they should be reminded of the existence of notarisation and referred to notaries.

In the UK, the profession of notary is quite different from its continental counterpart, as British notaries are almost exclusively concerned with foreign cases. Even if they have certain functions within the UK, they are nearly always required to authenticate a transaction or a document involving a foreign country. This may explain the relatively low number of practitioners in England and Wales (900 according to the Notaries Society)[9], while Spain, for instance, has almost 3,000 notaries. A notary's work normally includes, amongst other tasks, preparing powers of attorney for use overseas, dealing with the purchase of properties abroad, and authenticating personal documents for migration purposes.

Notaries are entitled to certify directly a translation they have carried out or just verify that the person appearing before them is the appropriate signatory. However, subject to certain notable exceptions, the majority of English notaries do not make and certify translations, and they most commonly certify the translator's signature.[10] In this case, notaries are not liable for the content of the translation.

As mentioned above, it is also common practice in the UK to *swear* a translation before a notary or solicitor (commissioner for oaths). This sort of certification merely legalises the translator's signature: i.e. solicitors satisfy themselves as to the translator's identity but do not certify his/her competence or monitor the quality of the translation. This certification is evidently more expensive, as fees are to be paid also to the commissioner for oaths. Therefore, since the English legal system is much less notarial and bureaucratic than civil law systems, it usually suffices that the translator adds a certification statement plus their signature, thus becoming accountable for the translation. However, as noted by Phillips (1998), this certification

8 Information provided by Ms Madeline Stewart, Office Administrator of the ITI, by personal correspondence in November 2008.

9 From <http://www.thenotariessociety.org.uk>.

10 Information provided by Mr Patrick O'Donnell, Notary Public in London, during a personal interview in November 2008.

may be considered invalid if presented before an authority in other countries, such as Spain, where the translation must be certified by a public authenticator (whether a sworn translator or a notary).

3.1. Qualifications related to the legal translation profession

The IoL is authorised to issue professional qualifications proving the holder's competence to undertake professional translating and interpreting tasks. Today one of the most prestigious qualifications is the Diploma in Translation (also known as DipTrans), which was first introduced in 1989 "as a benchmark of professional standards and has since continued to meet the needs for a high level professional translating qualification".[11] This is a postgraduate diploma accredited by the Qualifications and Curriculum Agency for entry into the National Qualifications Framework at Level 7 (equivalent to a master's degree or postgraduate diploma if mapped against the Framework for Higher Education Qualifications).

The DipTrans exam, held in January each year, is set and marked by the IoL Educational Trust. Its main purpose is to test the ability of candidates to translate from a source language into a (usually L1) target language to a professional standard. The examination consists of three units: general translation; semi-specialised options (Technology, Business or Literature); and semi-specialised options (Science, Social Science or Law). Therefore the DipTrans cannot be considered a specific qualification for legal translators.[12]

In order to gain qualified membership of the ITI, candidates must pass an examination as well as satisfy other entry criteria. This is aimed at testing candidates' ability to translate to a professional standard on a subject chosen from a list of great many specialisations (e.g. Agriculture and Horticulture, Biology, Defence, Law, Mining, and Textiles and Clothing). This examination consists of an assignment to be completed

---

11 See <http://www.iol.org.uk/qualifications/exams_diptrans.asp>.

12 According to Ducroquet (2005), the last semi-specialised option to be included in the DipTrans was precisely Law, which reveals once more the lack of attention that legal translation has so far received.

at home within a specific period of time (candidates are given a passage of about 1,000 words which they have to translate using the dictionaries, reference materials and equipment they would normally use as professional translators), plus a 500-1,000 word commentary on the linguistic, cultural and other issues presented by the text.

The main differences between the ITI exam and the DipTrans are the following:

> The ITI assessment is a tool to confirm that a working translator is producing work at the required professional level. The IOL [sic] Diploma in Translation, however, provides a qualification, which is widely recognised as a key to the profession. It allows anyone who wishes to become a translator to demonstrate that they have the necessary broad translation skills to enter the profession.
>
> (Ducroquet 2005: 61)

The UK has 61 undergraduate courses and 159 postgraduate courses in the field of Translation in general[13], but only one university programme specialised in legal translation: the Legal Translation PgDip/MA[14] offered by City University London as of 2008. For some this might indicate the beginning of a professionalisation of legal translation in Britain, as the programme will produce qualified, specialist legal translators with an academic education. They will certainly make a difference, as the market needs professional translators of this type.[15]

3.2. Legal translation in the private sector

In order to present a whole picture of legal translation in the UK, it seemed quite relevant to describe the role of legal translation in the private sphere, too, and more specifically in law firms operating with international clients and making transactions between two different legal systems and languages. Due to time limitations, the study

---

13 According to Careers Advice, cf. <http://careersadvice.direct.gov.uk>.

14 See <http://www.city.ac.uk/translation/courses/legal_translation>.

15 As suggested by Ann Corsellis in a personal interview in December 2008.

covered only a single language pair (Spanish-English) and a place (London), thus focusing on Spanish law firms operating in Britain and British law companies working for Spanish clients.[16]

For the first group, Cuatrecasas, Gonçalves Pereira, a highly reputed Spanish-Portuguese law firm with global operations, participated. Their London office, where commonly only issues relating to Spanish law normally come into play, works chiefly for leading international companies operating in London as a European base. The transactions carried out in this office often require legal actions initiated in the UK have legal effects in Spain, which is why Cuatrecasas provides these corporations with advice on aspects of Spanish law relating to such operations. In this context, translation evidently plays a very important role. Sometimes, monotonous or very urgent documents are translated by in-house staff (non-translators); however, when legal translations are of great importance, the commonest option is to outsource them to a Spanish translation agency, which also provides Cuatrecasas with sworn translations whenever required. The documents that most frequently need to be translated are powers of attorney. Nevertheless, there are many notaries in the world who issue bilingual versions, say in English and Spanish. When documents have been notarised in Spanish, there is no need for translation, as they have the same legal effects in Spain as in the country where they were drawn up.[17]

Edwin Coe is the British law firm operating with international clients that participated in our study. With about 30 partners and 100 employees, it is a medium-sized law firm for London. Of all its workload, 66% is UK-based and 33% is linked to international operations. As English is today's lingua franca for international legal and commercial matters, most of this firm's work with international clients is handled in English (most of their European partners use this language too). This means that only some 10% of all their international cases require translation services. In this firm, some of

---

16 A list of British law firms working for the Spanish Chamber of Commerce (London) was provided by the latter in November 2008.

17 Information provided by Mr Fernando Dancausa of Cuatrecasas (London) in November 2008.

the documents most commonly translated include company by-laws, leases, and articles of association. There are also two categories of translations: what are known as *friendly translations* (e.g. emails, letters, notices, and so forth), which are normally carried out by the firm's staff; and more formal translations, which are outsourced to agencies. The agency's certification is generally sufficient, but occasionally a further certification (for example, by diplomatic officers) may be required if the translation is to be effective in a particular country. In this case, the agency is vicariously liable for the service provided and there may be legal grounds to sue it for inaccuracy in the content of a translation.[18]

4. A survey of legal translators

In order to learn more about certain aspects of the profession in the UK, a small-scale survey was conducted among legal translators.[19] The first information was obtained in November 2008 through a personal interview with an IoL member listed on the Find-a-linguist service as a translator from English into Spanish in the Law category. With the qualitative data gathered, a questionnaire was devised for a small-scale survey. This included three parts: personal and professional profile (10 items), professional activity as a legal translator in the UK (9 items) and working conditions as a legal translator in the UK (7 items). The variables were expressed using both open and closed questions.

Two sources made up our sample. The first was the Find-a-linguist service[20] on the IoL website, where 60 translators from

18 Information provided by Mr Ronald Graham of Edwin Coe (London) in December 2008.

19 Our first intention was to organise focus groups with translators, but this was finally rejected as it proved impossible to find a date and a time which could suit all participants.

20 See <http://www.iol.org.uk/linguist>.

Spanish into English and 44 translators from English into Spanish were found, all working in the field of Law. The second was the ITI Directory of Members,[21] which was searched using the same criteria and produced 59 matches for legal translators from Spanish into English and 14 for translators from English into Spanish.

The questionnaire was administered via email in December 2008 and was returned completed by 30 translators from Spanish into English and 12 from English into Spanish, i.e. 27.5% and 25% of the sample respectively. Obviously this response rate does not allow us to generalise the results but the data nevertheless shed some light on a matter which has not been previously studied.

Some 70% of respondents were women and 67% were over 50 years of age, which confirms the *female* prevalence in the translation profession. The academic qualifications held by respondents are rather varied, with 30% claiming to hold either a Bachelor's or a Master's degree in Translation and 43% holding a Bachelor's or a Master's degree in Modern Languages. Other academic qualifications included options as different as a Postgraduate Diploma in Technical and Specialised Translation and an MA in Law. As far as their professional status is concerned, 30% were members of the IoL and 33% of the ITI, whereas the remaining 37% said that they belonged to both bodies, which suggests that a considerable number of professionals in Britain hold dual membership of these bodies.

Some of the results concerning their work as legal translators in the UK were highly revealing. When asked about their professional experience and commitment to translation, 64% of respondents said that they had a professional experience of more than 20 years, and 73% stated that translation was a full-time activity for them. With regard to specialism, legal translation constitutes 50% or more of their workload for only 37% of participants in the survey, which suggests that legal translators do not only work in this field but combine it with others. The legal documents which they most commonly translate are contracts and agreements (referred to by 65% or respondents), certificates (30%), and judgements and sentences (30%).

21 See <http://www.iti.org.uk/pages/directory/directory.asp>.

As regards the certification of translations, the figures speak for themselves, as 76% of respondents certify less than 10% of all documents they are required to translate (this being the lowest figure in the answers to this item). Whereas all participants mentioned certificates among the most commonly certified legal documents, only 12% referred to diplomas and academic qualifications. Almost all respondents (96%) stated that their translation had to be accompanied by notarisation in less than 10% of cases where certification is a requirement. When certifying a translation, 30% of respondents opt for self-certification, whereas 20% certify translations using the ITI seal.

Finally, with respect to working conditions, 45% of respondents said that over 60% of their work is for UK-based agencies and 30% answered that they charge £0.06 per word, while 20% are paid £0.07 per word. It must be stressed that this question had the lowest response rate in the questionnaire, as pay is always a sensitive issue (37% of people refused to answer). Nonetheless, 70% of respondents believe that working conditions for legal translators in the UK are good/very good and 75% consider that belonging to a professional body is a very good thing.

5. Conclusion

Whereas legal interpreting is witnessing an incipient regulation in the UK, the legal translation profession still lacks an arrangement of this sort. In the field of official translation, certification is not very frequently required; sworn translators do not exist in the English common law system, so normally the translator's self-certification is sufficient. Notarisation is an option of last resort, when a client believes that the translator's self-certification will not do or would like a document with a more official status. Having said this, there seems to be a tendency to assign important legal translations to professional legal translators, thus implicitly recognising their role and competence.

Evidently the study underlying this chapter constitutes a short-range research project and cannot provide answers to some of the most contentious issues regarding legal translation and interpreting in the UK. Therefore these areas need to be deeply researched in order to enhance the role of legal interpreting and translating and to know what is expected of a competent translator and interpreter in legal settings. These results should be taken into account when devising programmes aimed at training legal translators.

In any case, it is expected that the situation of British legal interpreters and translators will be influenced by EU legislation, which is binding throughout the UK. This is of special relevance in three issues: the recognition of professional qualifications issued in other member states (Directive 2005/36/EC), the internal market regulation and competitiveness within the EU (Directive 2006/123/EC) and the right to interpretation and translation in criminal proceedings, as stated in the new Proposal for a Council Framework Decision CNS/2009/0101.

References

Clegg, Nikki 2002. Hints for Would-Be PSIs. *The Linguist* 41/5, 133-135.

Connell, Tim 2002. The Professionalisation of the Individual When Translating and Interpreting for the Public Service. In Valero-Garcés, Carmen / Mancho-Barés, Guzmán (eds) *Community Interpreting and Translating: New Needs for New Realities.* Madrid: Universidad de Alcalá, 147-154.

Corsellis, Ann 2003. Interpreting and Translation in the UK Public Services: The Pursuit of Excellence versus, and via, Expediency. In Anderman, Gunilla / Rogers, Margaret (eds) *Translation Today: Trends and Perspectives.* Clevedon: Multilingual Matters.

Corsellis, Ann 2008. *Public Service Interpreting: The First Steps.* Basingstoke: Palgrave Macmillan.

Ducroquet, Lucile 2005. The IoL Diploma in Translation. A Constant in a Rapidly Developing Profession. In Kemble, Ian (ed.)

Translation Norms: What Is "Normal" in the Translation Profession? Portsmouth: University of Portsmouth, 59-69.

Hickey, Leo 2005. Interpretación jurídica en el sector público de Gran Bretaña. In Monzó-Nebot, Esther / Borja, Anabel (eds) *La traducción y la interpretación en las relaciones jurídicas internacionales,* Castellón de la Plana: Publicacions de la Universitat Jaume I, 181-196.

Mayoral, Roberto 2003. *Translating Official Documents.* Manchester: St. Jerome.

Phillips, Montserrat 1999. La profesión del traductor e intérprete autónomo: aspectos técnicos. *Aproximaciones a la traducción.* Madrid: Instituto Cervantes. Also available at <http://cvc.cervantes.es/obref/aproximaciones/phillips.htm>.

Rodríguez, Begoña 2005. What Norms Should Legal Translators Follow? In Kemble, Ian (ed.) *Translation Norms: What Is "Normal" in the Translation Profession?* Portsmouth: University of Portsmouth, 159-165.

Townsley, Brooke 2007. Interpreting in the UK Community: Some Reflections on Public Service Interpreting in the UK. *Language & Intercultural Communication* 7/2, 163-170.

ROCCO C. LOIACONO

The Translation of Bilateral Agreements between Australia and Italy: Linguistic or Functional?

1. Introduction

Italy is a civil law nation in the Roman tradition; Australia is a common law nation in the English tradition. Although the conceptual development of these two legal systems is vastly different, in order to maintain bilateral relations both countries have had to come to a solution, linguistically speaking, capable of bridging this legal and cultural divide. Interestingly, Australia has a large Italian immigrant community and Italian is the most widely spoken language after English. It is mainly for this reason that Italy and Australia have signed a series of bilateral agreements governing the rights of their respective citizens in the context of cultural and commercial exchanges between the two countries. Such agreements cover a range of subjects, including: extradition and mutual assistance on criminal matters; avoidance of double taxation; pensions and social security; cultural co-operation; co-operation in the production of films; economic and commercial co-operation. Each language version of an agreement has equal legal status, which means they are legally equivalent. The *Vienna Convention on the Law of Treaties* (1969) provides that multilingual texts are equally authoritative in each language.

The aim of this chapter can be summed up in the following question: what principles and strategies are adopted in the translation of the bilateral agreements in force between Italy and Australia? In attempting to answer this question, I will address potential problems in the translation of Italo-Australian agreements from one language to another. For this purpose, my study will consider the legal translation approaches adopted in other jurisdictions – the European Union (EU) and Canada – to establish differences and similarities with those observed in the agreements between Italy and Australia (which I will refer to in this chapter as the 'Italo-Australian agreements' or the 'Agreements').

2. Legal translation in the EU

According to Garzone (2000), the complexity of legal discourse helps explain why legal translation has historically focussed mainly on the preservation of the letter, rather than on the effective rendering of the target language: this is known as the linguistic or 'legal equivalence approach'. The alternative theory of legal translation is based on the notion that translation depends first and foremost on the intended function (*skopos*) of the target text as well as the nature of the source text: this is the 'functional approach'. Šarčević (1997) explains that translators are expected to preserve the unity of each legal instrument by producing a text that expresses the uniform intent, i.e. the original intent of the lawmakers or States. In other words, a reliable translation is one that expresses the intended meaning and leads to the intended results. Furthermore, it is assumed that all the parallel texts in a multilingual instrument express the same intent and that this is the original or true intent. In order to minimize misinterpretation and ambiguity, EU institutions prescribe a standard format for each type of parallel text.

The political-institutional structure of the EU (cf. Cosmai 2003) is based on the theoretical notion that legal texts are *drafted collectively* in the Union's 23 official languages and not translated, which resembles the Canadian co-drafting model. Cosmai (2003: 40) however, goes on to cite Braselman's (1992) claim that there *must* be an original version, with the consequence that all other language versions cannot be considered anything other than translations, inspired by the original text, and therefore irrelevant from an exegetic point of view. Nystedt (1999b: 200, my translation) is of the same view:

> One must be under no illusions, however: even if the text in each language itself provides that it is a 'version', and not a 'translation', it is in fact a translation, and not always undertaken under the best working conditions.

As far as legal terminology is concerned, the Joint Practical Guide for Persons Involved in the Drafting of Legislation within the Community Institutions (JPG 2003), adopted on 16 March 2000, recognises that certain expressions in one language – in particular quite common ones such as the French *sans préjudice* – have no equivalent in other Community languages. They can therefore only be translated using circumlocutions and approximations, which inevitably result in semantic divergences between the various language versions. Expressions which are too specific to one language should therefore be avoided as far as possible.

The consequence of this, according to Cosmai (2003), is that drafters are encouraged to adopt a generic terminology (hyperonyms) which is not linked to any particular legal tradition but ensures linguistic concordance amongst language versions. Thus the aim in drafting EU legislative texts appears to be that of guaranteeing the uniform intent of the single instrument, which results in application of the legal equivalence approach, rather than the functional approach.

3. Legal translation in Canada

Canada is not only a bilingual but also a bilegal (or bi-jural) nation, i.e., it is governed by two different legal systems (common law and civil law). At federal level, legislation follows the common law tradition and is officially bilingual. For over two centuries, translation from English into French was strictly literal; however, with the enactment of the *Official Languages Act* 1969, the Canadian Department of Justice acknowledged that literal translation violated the principle of equal language rights. In order to implement the principle of equal treatment, translators were granted freedom to produce target texts in the spirit of the French language (Šarčević 1997). This involved converting translators into co-drafters by incorporating them into the drafting process and granting them greater drafting responsibilities, allowing room for stylistic diversity in parallel texts. Thus the French federal legislation texts are drafted in a style more reminiscent of that of civil law jurisdictions.

According to Sullivan (2002), four different methods have been adopted for drafting bi-jural legislation in Canada:

- setting out in each language the preferred solution for each legal system;
- finding general French and English expressions that are comparable in scope and can be applied in roughly equivalent ways in the two systems;
- using common law terminology in the English version and analogous civil law terminology in the French one;
- drawing in the legal terminology of one of the legal systems and translating that into the language of the other system using ordinary, as opposed to, specialised legal language.

This ensures, as noted by Bastarache (2000), that all legal audiences in Canada are able to read federal statutes in the language of their choice and to find terms and wordings that are respectful of the concepts, notions and institutions proper to the legal tradition of their particular province or territory.

4. Translation strategies in Italo-Australian agreements

Is there a specific approach to the translation of the Italo-Australian agreements stemming from their drafting process, as in Canada? Information on how the Agreements were drafted and negotiated is hard to come by. My enquiries to relevant officials at the Australian

Department of Foreign Affairs and the Italian Ministry for Foreign Affairs suggest that initial drafts were produced in the language of the country that initiated negotiations. Successive translations were then made of the draft texts at each stage of negotiations until a final draft was agreed upon. The translations of that draft were then verified by officials of either side before being signed.

Looking at the Agreements themselves, it seems that the translation strategy adopted is more akin to that of the preparation of EU legislative texts, which focuses on the uniform intent of the single instrument (legal equivalence) rather than adopting a more functional approach (as in Canada). When the two language versions are compared, it is easy to notice that they are mirror images.

In my analysis, I have treated the Agreements as a single corpus, since there do not appear to be particular linguistic differences between individual Agreements, notwithstanding the different subject matter dealt with. The bilateral agreements in force between Italy and Australia number 21 in total. They take the form of either an 'exchange of notes' between embassies or ministers – e.g. the Exchange of Notes regarding Visas and Visa Fees (1951) – or the more traditional form akin to a bilateral treaty, signed by ministers of the respective governments. For this pilot study, I have selected for analysis this latter form of agreement, as it is more comparable to the form of multilingual legislation in the EU and bilingual legislation in Canada, thus allowing comparisons in translation approaches to be drawn. The first of the Agreements forming the subject of this study was signed in 1963, and the last in 1996. There are eleven of these Agreements:

- Agreement relating to air services / Accordo relativo ai servizi aerei (1963);
- Migration and settlement agreement / Accordo di emigrazione e stabilimento (1971);
- Agreement for the avoidance of double taxation of income derived from international air transport / Accordo per evitare la doppia imposizione sui redditi derivanti dall'esercizio del trasporto aereo internazionale (1972).
- Agreement of cultural co-operation / Accordo di cooperazione culturale (1975);

- Convention for the avoidance of double taxation and the prevention of fiscal evasion with respect to taxes on income / Convenzione per evitare le doppie imposizioni e prevenire le evasioni fiscali in materia di imposte sul reddito (1982);
- Treaty on economic and commercial co-operation / Trattato di cooperazione in materia di economia e commercio (1984);
- Treaty of extradition / Trattato di estradizione (1985);
- Reciprocal agreement in the matter of health assistance / Accordo di reciprocità in materia di assistenza sanitaria (1986);
- Treaty on mutual assistance in criminal matters / Trattato di mutua assistenza in material penale (1988);
- Social security agreement / Accordo in materia di sicurezza sociale (1993);
- Films co-production agreement / Accordo di coproduzione cinematografica (1996).

These vary in length between three pages and 18 pages, with an average length of nine pages.

Below I analyse the similarities between the translation strategy adopted in the Agreements and that used when drafting EU legislation. The examples cited compare what I believe to be the source text, followed by its translation. This decision was not a simple one, but was based on the following criteria: naturalness of language; appropriateness of lexical and syntactical choices; and communicative efficacy. In order to achieve homogeneity in the examples cited, the majority were chosen from the Agreements that deal with the functions of government, that is, the social security agreement, the convention for the avoidance of double taxation on income, the treaty of extradition, the treaty on mutual assistance in criminal matters and the migration and settlement agreement.

The examples have been organised adopting the categories developed by Cosmai (2003). As mentioned above, Italy and Australia have different legal traditions. Europe and Canada are no different where there is the need to accommodate the English common law tradition and the continental civil law tradition in the drafting of legal texts. Further, in the EU, the legal system of each Member State with its peculiar institutions and characteristics, as well as diverse linguistic and cultural considerations, provide difficulties for translators. This complicates the eternal problem of legal translation that a term in one particular legal system may not have a corresponding terminological equivalent in another. Further, as provided in the Joint Practical Guide, terms that are too specific to a particular legal system are to be avoided to facilitate translation in all the official languages.

By identifying categories of translation solutions adopted in the EU, Cosmai (2003) shows how the apparent untranslatability [*intraducibilità*] of terms across legal systems and cultures has been overcome. He has developed these categories along a continuum incorporating calques, generic or neutral terms, borrowings, and finally drafting quality. His taxonomy of categories provides a useful reference point for the analysis that is the subject of this pilot study.

The choice of examples below does not claim to be exhaustive, and in some cases, may be considered to be a random selection. The aim of this chapter, however, is not so much to present a complete analysis of the translation of the Agreements, but rather a preliminary sampling of the phenomena found in them. At the same time, this is an exercise in verifying the usefulness of Cosmai's (2003) taxonomy of categories for the description of this particular corpus.

4.1. Transparent translations and calques

This category accounts for translations which do not agree with the terminology of English legal language, and also provides examples of calques, which Cosmai (2003) identified as highly prevalent in the translation of EU legal texts. These solutions can be problematical where either the term in the target text resembles that adopted in the source text, but is used in the former to express a different concept, or where the translation chosen does not conform to normal language usage in the target language.

(1) Ministero di Grazia e Giustizia → Ministry of Grace and Justice

(2) Ministero delle Finanze → Ministry of Finance

In Australia a 'Ministry of Grace and Justice' does not exist. At both the State and Federal level (Australia, like Canada, is a federation) the department responsible for the administration of justice is the Department of the Attorney-General, the Attorney-General being the first law officer. A 'Minister of Justice' from time to time may be appointed to assist the Attorney-General in the running of certain sections of the Department, for example, prisons. As part of his or her ministerial duties the Minister of Justice may, depending on the government of the day, be requested to administer a 'Department of Justice', which, however, is generally a part of the Attorney-General's Department, and not autonomous. A translation such as 'Italy's Ministry of Justice' would have expressed the nature of the institution more effectively, as it would have referred to a concept familiar to an English-speaking reader (in the Australian context) and therefore would have conformed to normal language use. The second example is similar in this respect, as Australia does not have a 'Ministry of Finance': the equivalent government department is known as 'the Treasury'. The translations chosen have created nomenclatures that simply do not exist in the Australian context.

(3) Diritto al lavoro → Right of working

(4) Riunione delle famiglie → Reunion of families

(5) Una persona arrestata in seguito a domanda di arresto provvisorio dovrà essere rimessa in libertà → A person arrested upon such an application shall be set at liberty

The above examples have been chosen as they do not reflect an appropriate syntactical choice or communicative efficacy; a native English speaker would not use the translations chosen. In these three examples, it would be more authentic to say 'right to work', 'family reunions' and 'released'. Referring to Justice Bastarache's observation with respect to the translation of Canadian legislation, the Agreements do not appear to have been prepared so that citizens are able to understand them in the language of their choice.

(6) Italian workers shall be eligible [...] to be represented in Australian courts → I lavoratori italiani avranno diritto [...] ad essere rappresentati davanti alla magistratura Australiana;

Example (6) is particularly problematic since in Australia a magistrate performs functions that are quite different to those of an Italian magistrate. It would have been better to translate *Australian courts* as 'gli organi giudiziari australiani', which, as well as being a more faithful translation, would have effectively rendered the meaning of the functions performed by Australian courts.

(7) sottomettere il caso alle autorità competenti → submit the case to the competent authorities

Similarly problematic is (7) as, in English legal language, a court cannot be 'competent' to deal with certain matters. Competence relates solely to capability [*capacità*]. The more faithful translation would be 'relevant authorities', which would also work well from a communicative point of view.

4.2. Approximate equivalents and neutral terms

The next category contains approximate equivalents and neutral terms, applied where there is no corresponding terminological equivalent in the legal system of the target text, with the consequence that a completely new term has to be created in the translated version in order to achieve uniformity between the two language versions.

(8) counsel → difensore

The use of 'difensore' for *counsel* is not suitable because in legal English the latter means several things, depending on the party the counsel is acting for: counsel for the defence, for the prosecution, for the plaintiff, etc. 'Difensore' can only reasonably translate one of these terms – counsel for the defence. A term such as 'procuratore legale' would have been more precise, as it effectively renders the role of counsel in the Australian legal system.

(9) testimonial privilege → i diritti del testimone

(10) capofamiglia → head of a family

Conversely, in example (9), the translation of the English legal term *testimonial privilege* as 'i diritti del testimone' could be considered an appropriate choice, as, as far as I am aware, there is no literal equivalent in Italian legal language. In support of this, I cite Mastellone's *Legal and Commercial Dictionary: English/Italian* (1980: 119), where 'diritto esclusivo' is given as a translation for *privilege*. Also, the translation of *capofamiglia* as 'head of a family' in (10) is entirely appropriate, also on the basis that there is no literal equivalent for this term in English legal language.

(11) Se cause di forza maggiore impediscono a una delle Parti → If circumstances beyond its control prevent a Party

(12) Partner-related Australian benefits → Prestazioni australiane riguardanti il coniuge de jure o de facto

(13) Trusteeship Agreement → Accordo di Amministrazione fiduciaria

The translated Agreements also contain several 'neutral' terms which, though apparently having the corresponding legal term in the other language, may not effectively render the intended meaning. The first of these examples is *forza maggiore* (11), translated as 'circumstances beyond its control' rather than with the usual English legal term 'force majeure'. With reference to (12), the English word *Partner* has taken on a significance which encompasses both married and unmarried couples, so the Italian translation 'coniuge de jure o de facto' is a satisfactory neutral solution. In (13) the use of 'Accordo di Amministrazione fiduciaria' for *Trusteeship Agreement* may also be considered an appropriate solution for the concept of trusteeship, which is peculiar to the common law system. In fact, Mastellone (1980: 159) suggests 'amministratore fiduciario' as a translation for *trustee*, which would appear to indicate that the translational choice in (13) is a valid one.

4.3. Extreme fidelity to the source text

There are cases of extreme fidelity in the two languages. As in the previous categories, some examples may be considered acceptable while others are not.

(14) The Australian Government recognises the concern of the Italian Government [...] and agrees to use its best offices → Il governo australiano riconosce l'importanza che il governo italiano annette al fatto [...] e si dichiara d'accordo di dover interporre i suoi buoni uffici

(15) Norfolk Island → l'isola di Norfolk

(16) Christmas Island → l'isola di Natale

(17) Cocos (Keeling) Islands → le isole del Cocco (Keeling)

(18) Coral Sea Islands → le isole del Mar dei Coralli

In example (14) the translation of *agrees to use its best offices* as 'si dichiara d'accordo di dover interporre i suoi buoni uffici' is an obvious example of extreme fidelity. For the interpretation of examples (15-18), I refer to the website of the Italian Embassy in Australia (<http://www.ambcanberra.esteri.it>, accessed June 2009) in order to ascertain the names used officially by the Embassy to refer to territory over which it is responsible for the needs of Italian citizens present in that territory. The translation of the series of islands that lie off the Australian coast is particularly interesting: 'l'isola di Norfolk' is adopted as a translation by the Embassy, as is 'le isole del Mar dei Coralli'. 'L'isola di Natale' is not adopted by the Embassy, which refers to *L'isola Christmas* on its website, however, it could be considered acceptable, given 'Natale' is Italian for *Christmas*. However, 'le isole del Cocco (Keeling)' is incorrect because 'cocco' translates to *coconut* (not *Cocos*) in Italian. In fact, the website of the

Italian Embassy in Australia uses the term 'Isole Christmas e Cocos (Keeling)' when referring to its jurisdiction over these islands.

4.4. Untranslated terminology/borrowings

There are also instances in the Agreements of terminology that has not been translated, as well as borrowings.

(19) conspiracy to commit an offence [...] as provided by the law of Australia → la conspiracy per commettere uno dei reati [...] quale prevista dalla legge australiana

(20) (such as standards of speed and accommodation) → (fra cui la velocità ed il comfort)

(21) Proceedings for the resumption or expropriation for public purpose → Procedimenti di espropriazione o di 'resumption' per pubblica utilità

Example (19) has 'conspiracy' rather than the equivalent Italian term 'complotto' or 'associazione a delinquere'. This could possibly be attributed to different nuances in the Italian terms that may make them less appropriate as translations. In (20) there is another borrowing of an English word ('comfort') to translate *accommodation*, which would appear to be widely used in contemporary Italian (*Oxford-Paravia Italian-English Dictionary* 2001). Finally, (21) has the word 'resumption' in the Italian translation, significantly placed between inverted commas, which would imply that it is not a word that is frequently used in contemporary Italian. To investigate this further, I undertook a search of Italian dictionaries, namely Zingarelli (2008) and Treccani (1991), to see if 'resumption' appeared in those dictionaries, and it did not, which would seem to support the implication above.

4.5. Absence of consistency when expressing the same concept

There is occasionally a lack of consistency in translations that express the same concept in the same Agreement:

(22) Additional information → Informazioni complementari / informazioni integrative

(23) Each Contracting State → Ciascuno Stato Contraente / Ciascuno Stato

(24) The Requested State → Ciascuno Stato / Parte Richiesta

In this regard, *Additional information* (22) occurs consistently throughout the English version but appears in the Italian version as 'informazioni complementari' and then as 'informazioni integrative'. The second example (23) has *Each Contracting State* variously translated as 'Ciascuno Stato Contraente' and 'Ciascuno Stato'. In (24) *The Requested State* appears in the Italian version first as 'Ciascuno Stato' and then as 'Parte Richiesta'. Such examples give the impression of a document that has been patched together, rather than drafted taking into account the Canadian model for drafting bilingual legislation.

4.6. Drafting issues: long paragraphs

This category is referred to by Cosmai (2003) as drafting quality [*qualità redazionale*]. The Agreements are not always written to make their content easily understandable for ordinary readers. In this regard, the following long paragraph is particularly eloquent:

(25) Le parti contraenti convengono di istituire una Commissione Mista, composta in parte uguali, presieduta congiuntamente da funzionari responsabili del settore cinematografico di ciascun paese, assistiti da esperti designati dalle rispettivi autorità competenti, con il compito di esaminare le condizioni di applicazione del presente accordo, di risolvere le difficoltà che potranno presentarsi, di proporre alle autorità competenti dei due paesi, le modifiche all'accordo che saranno ritenute opportune. → There shall be a Mixed Commission equally composed of representatives of the Contracting Parties jointly chaired by officials from the Italian and Australian Film Industries and assisted by experts appointed by the respective competent authorities to supervise and review the working of this Agreement to resolve any difficulty which may arise and to make any proposals considered necessary for any modification of this Agreement.

The English text stands out as poorly drafted for many reasons. Firstly, there is the complete absence of punctuation. Secondly, it contains fewer finite verbs than the Italian text; in fact, there are only two: 'shall be' and 'may arise', and they occur in short relative clauses. All the other clauses contain non-finite verbs: *composed of, chaired by, appointed by, assisted by, considered necessary*. To be noted is also the high recurrence of past participles in the examples listed above. There are also several infinitives in the English text: *to supervise and review, to resolve any difficulty, to make any proposals*.

I therefore formed the view that the English text is a translation of the Italian as the use of 'competent authorities' for *autorità competenti* diminishes the communicative efficacy of the English text for the reasons outlined at example (7) above. This could also be considered another characteristic of poor drafting.

The quality of the drafting of the Italian text would seem superior to that of its English counterpart. Firstly, it contains punctuation. Secondly, participles in Italian agree with nouns and the morphological endings make cross-referencing easier to follow, for example: 'una Commissione Mista... presieduta'. Thirdly, the Italian text is more explicit: it contains fewer non-finite verbs (*considered necessary* is translated as 'che saranno ritenute opportune') and infinitives (*to supervise* → 'con il compito di esaminare').

5. Linguistic observations

I have included this section of additional observations on the register used in both language versions (albeit not a category considered in Cosmai 2003) as I believe it is an aspect of the drafting of the Agreements that deserves further study. A preliminary observation is that both language versions are written in the same register and style, with sectorial lexical choices, but not necessarily in the same items. Consequently, this impacts on the translation strategy employed.

5.1. Formal register

There is a high recourse to a more formal register in both languages; terms such as 'therein' (32) and 'herein' (31) are simply not present in everyday English language usage. Corresponding examples of this characteristic in Italian are 'qualsivoglia' (26), 'sarà parimenti necessario' (27), 'esperire presso gli organi giudiziari' (28) and 'vita natural durante' (30).

(26) any → qualsivoglia

(27) shall also be required → sarà parimenti necessario

(28) shall have the same rights to a review by administrative and judicial bodies → esperire presso gli organi giudiziari ed amministrativi [...] i ricorsi previsti

(29) engaged in the same or similar activities → svolgente attività identiche o analoghe

(30) during life → vita natural durante

(31) used but not defined herein → ivi usata, ma non definita

(32) situated therein → ivi situate

Example (29) illustrates another linguistic feature that denotes a more formal style of language, being the extensive use of the present participle in Italian: 'svolgente attività identiche o analoghe'. I also refer to (12) above in this regard: 'Prestazioni australiane *riguardanti* il coniuge de jure o de facto'. In terms of translation strategy, examples (26-28, 30-31) are instances where a less formal term in English has been translated with a more formal word in Italian. In examples (29) and (32), a formal term in English has been translated with a formal term in Italian. In fact, the translation never adopts a less formal term than the original.

5.2. Extensive use of the Italian future tense

As a final example of the recourse to a high register in the drafting of the Agreements, there is at (33) the extensive use of the future tense in the Italian versions to express a proscriptive function.

(33) shall lend their good offices and furnish assistances to one another, including the communication to each other of any necessary information → si adopereranno, si assisteranno e si scambieranno le necessarie informazioni

Example (6) above is also emblematic of this characteristic.

6. Conclusion

The strategy adopted in the translation of the Agreements would appear to be that of ensuring uniform intent of the instrument, opting for legal equivalence (cf. Garzone 2000) rather than the Canadian functional approach. Contrary to the latter, the translated text of the Agreements does not make any great effort to be easily comprehensible for either the Italian-speaking or English-speaking public. What appears to be of paramount importance is that both language versions produce the same interpretations, guaranteeing, in Cosmai's (2003) words, a concordance between the two. This is noticeable in the terminology and translation strategy adopted.

All of the above appears to indicate that the translations were not prepared with a person of an average level of education in mind. Unlike Canadian legislation, which is prepared taking into consideration each language group, the Agreements appear to have been drafted solely to be accessible to expert readers, that is to the bureaucrats responsible for administering them. To use Nystedt's (1999) words quoted earlier, the language versions of the Agreements are not 'versions' but would appear to be simply 'translations'.

Legal equivalence is chosen here because of the type of text the Agreements represent. They have been negotiated by officials of the ministries of foreign affairs of each nation in an extremely formal setting. Therefore the translation strategy adopted is unlike (one could say, light years removed from) that applied in the drafting of Canadian legislation. However, the normative effects of Canadian legislation impact on the daily lives of Canadians far more than the Agreements impact on the daily lives of Italians and Australians. The translation strategy applied in the Agreements is thus closer to that applied in the drafting of EU legislation. As illustrated in the application of Cosmai's (2003) taxonomy of categories above, there are similar characteristics identified in each, thus ensuring the uniform intent of a single legal instrument appears to be their main concern.

This pilot study has on one hand, confirmed Cosmai's taxonomy of categorisation of characteristics of translation of legal documentation, but also opens the door for further research in areas such as the translation of proper nouns, register and style, syntax, and morphological choices. Such research could be of great utility in attempting to further analyse and identify translation strategies employed in the translation of legal texts in a multilingual or bilegal context.

References

Bastarache, Michel 2000. Bijuralism in Canada. Paper presented at the Department of Justice Workshop on Bijuralism and the Legal Function (Ottawa, 4 February 2000). Retrieved from <http://www.justice.gc.ca> on 4 March 2009.

Braselman, Petra 1992. Der Richter als Linguist. Linguistische Überlegungen zu Sprachproblemen in Urteilen des europäischen Gerichtshofes. *Sprache und Literatur in Wissenschaft und Unterricht* 22/2, 68-85.

Cao, Deborah 2007. *Translating Law*. Clevedon: Multilingual Matters.

Cosmai, Domenico 2003. *Tradurre per l'Unione Europea. Problematiche e strategie operative*. Milan: Hoepli.

Garzone, Giuliana 2000. Legal Translation and Functionalist Approaches: A Contradiction in Terms? In *Actes du Colloque*

International 'La traduction juridique. Histoire, théorie(s) et pratique'. Geneva: Université de Genève, 395-414. Retrieved from <http://www.tradulex.org> on 16 October 2007.

[JPG] 2003. *Joint Practical Guide of the European Parliament, the Council and the Commission, for Persons Involved in the Drafting of Legislation within the Community Institutions.* Luxembourg: Office for Official Publications of the European Communities.

Mastellone, Luigi 1980. *Legal and Commercial Dictionary: English/ Italian*. Sydney: Butterworths.

Nystedt, Jane 1999. L'italiano che si scrive a Bruxelles. *Italiano e oltre* 14, 198-206.

Oxford-Paravia Dizionario Inglese-Italiano/Italiano-Inglese 2001. Turin: Paravia Bruno Mondadori / Oxford University Press.

Šarčević, Susan 1997. *New Approach to Legal Translation*. The Hague: Kluwer Law International.

Sullivan, Ruth 2002. *Sullivan and Drieger on the Construction of Statues*. Toronto: Butterworths.

[Treccani] 1991. *Vocabolario della lingua italiana*. Rome: Istituto della Enciclopedia Italiana.

[Zingarelli] 2008. *Lo Zingarelli: vocabolario della lingua italiana.* Bologna: Zanichelli.

CORNELIS J.W. BAAIJ

Translation in EU Legislative Procedure: A Receiver-Oriented Approach

1. Introduction

The overall approach to the translation of legislative texts in EU legislative bodies is source-oriented. Contemporary trends in legal translation theory indicate on the contrary that perhaps a receiver-oriented approach would be preferable. This chapter argues, however, that such a change of approach in EU legislative bodies is unlikely to happen.

Translation can be considered as the adhesive between two of the European Union's fundamental components: the objective of legal integration and the respect for linguistic diversity. On the one hand, one of the primary tasks of the European Union, in particular in the pillar of the European Community, is the unification and harmonization of the laws of its Member States. To this end, the Council, the Commission and the Parliament together adopt secondary legislation, such as directives and regulations. In order to achieve convergence between the laws of the Member States, these legislative instruments need to be interpreted in the same manner and produce the same legal effects in all Member States.[1]

On the other hand, the EU has from the outset committed itself to respect, protect and promote the diversity of language communities

1 Communication from the Commission to the Council and the European Parliament on European contract law, COM(2001) 398, p. 10; and Communication from the Commission to the European Parliament and the Council. A more coherent European Contract Law – An Action Plan, COM(2003) 68 final, p. 6.

in Europe. The Commission, Parliament and Council have referred to linguistic diversity as a 'core value', a 'basic principle' of the European Union and 'part and parcel of the European cultural identity'. Subsequent to the EU principle that decisions of EU institutions are taken as openly and as close to the citizens as possible, the respect for linguistic diversity implies that every EU citizen is to have equal access to EU institutions without language barriers.[2]

As a consequence of the concurrence of legal integration and linguistic diversity, EU legislation is issued today in 23 different language versions. These versions are considered equally authentic and are said to therefore require 'absolute concordance' (Lönroth 2008a). It follows that the requirements that EU legislation needs to be interpreted in a uniform manner and needs to achieve the same legal effects throughout the European Union, apply directly to the various language versions of a legislative instrument. In other words, these versions need to be interpreted and applied uniformly and it is the role of legal translation to reach this objective.

2. Appropriate translation methods in the EU

The question that arises is then *how* translation can secure a uniform interpretation and application of all language versions of EU legislation. On the one hand, due to the technical nature of legal language it is often believed that there is little room for the legal translator to divert from the form and content of the source text. For translation in EU legislative procedure, such a view on legal translation would mean that the grammar, syntax and style of the original legislative draft – the source text – should be followed as

2 See e.g. European Parliament Resolution on a New Framework Strategy for Multilingualism, 2006/2083(INI), Recital A; Council Resolution of 21 November 2008 on a European strategy for multilingualism (2008/C 320/01); Communication of the Commission, A New Framework Strategy for Multilingualism, 22 November 2005, COM(2005) 596 final, pp. 12-13.

close as possible in the other language versions – the target texts (Weisflog 1996; Šarčević 1997).

On the other hand, however, a different, more pragmatic approach to legal translation has emerged whereby legal translation is treated as an act of communication, as a part of legal discourse. In this view the main criterion for a successful legal translation is not whether the target text is semantically and syntactically a mirror image of the source text but rather whether the legal effect of the target text on its readers is equivalent to that of the source text on its readers. As a consequence, the translator is no longer considered a slave to the source text but an active participant in legal discourse. The legal translator is in this view someone who produces a new legislative text that satisfies the cultural expectations of the target audience of the target text (Šarčević 1997: 87, 129, 246).

In the light of these modern reflections on legal translation, it is suggested that the most appropriate translation for EU legislative procedure is receiver-oriented. It has been argued that translators in the EU should predict how the national courts will interpret and apply the respective language versions. This does not go as far as to say that legal translators should interpret the source text in the legal sense – interpretation of legislative texts is still a job for lawyers. Yet, the translator should adequately know what legal effect the source text is supposed to have and how to achieve the same legal effect through the particular language version that he/she is responsible for (cf. Varó 2002; Chromá 2004; Cao 2007).

The aim of this chapter is not to consider whether one approach to translation is to be preferred over the other. Rather, it is to explain why in EU legislative procedure the approach is prevalently source-oriented and why due to the nature of EU law it is unlikely that a receiver-oriented approach will be adopted.

3. Source-oriented translation in EU legislative procedure

The current manner of translation within EU legislative bodies can be said to be source-oriented in both form and content. With regard to form, it involves for example that the target texts have the same numbering of articles, paragraphs and titles as well as the same number of sentences as in the source text. With regard to content, two examples will next illustrate the current source-oriented approach employed in EU legislative bodies: the faithful translation of linguistic defects in source texts and the reluctance to give in to so-called 'language complaints'.[3]

3.1. Faithful translation of linguistic defects

Notwithstanding internal guidelines for clear and comprehensible drafting, poor language skills and political compromises made by drafters are often found to lead to ambiguities or vagueness.

On the one hand, political compromises may cause the original legislative draft-texts to be of poor quality. EU legislation is the end result of often difficult political negotiations and compromises reached by many different people in numerous working or consultative committees, groups of experts or national representatives of EU institutions and ultimately politicians. These compromises may easily lead to linguistic imperfections. In fact, it is said that imprecise or ambiguous wording is often intentional, serving as a political tool: when the text allows different preferred readings, Member States are more likely to accept the proposals.

---

3 My account of the approach to translation in EU legislative procedure in the remainder of this chapter is based on: the experiences of various translators, editors and jurist-linguists at the European Commission and the European Council, interviewed on 11, 12 and 26 June 2008 and 15 May 2009; the rules of procedure and guidelines of the respective institutions; various policy documents and articles of those involved in the drafting of EU legislation, such as Wagner *et al.* (2002), Robinson (2005), Gallas (2006) and Guggeis (2006).

On the other hand, the linguistic quality of the original draft-text may further be impaired due to the poor language skills of drafters. EU legislation is not drafted in all official EU languages simultaneously. For most of the legislative procedure, normally only one language version – the English version – of a legislative proposal is subject to linguistic, legal and political scrutiny. Partly – or perhaps primarily – due to cost restraints, translation into all the other official EU languages is conducted only at certain stages of the procedure. Throughout the legislative procedure, a proposal is more often than not examined, discussed and modified in only one language version. More than 95% of the legislative acts adopted in the co-decision procedure are originally drafted in English. Both the original draft-proposal as well as the amendments voted on by the Parliament are mostly prepared and drafted by lobbyists that are neither linguists nor lawyers. Also the working parties of the Council prepare the treatment of proposed legislation in a single language version, the so-called 'base text'. The use of a single language or a limited number of languages means that the proposal is drafted by people that work in a language that is not their mother tongue. As a consequence, the drafters may not always fully understand the draft-text or be able to express themselves adequately.

3.2. The freedom to correct linguistic defects

In principle translators and legal revisers are required to translate imprecise or ambiguous wording faithfully into other language versions rather than replacing them with one of possible meanings. Yet those involved in translating the original legislative texts in EU legislative institutions generally agree that this should not result in incomprehensible legislative texts. All drafters, including translators and legal revisers, are expected to avoid literal translations or jargon that would make the non-original language versions difficult to understand for the jurists that will interpret the legislative instrument.[4]

Is there then room for translators to diverge from the source text for the benefit of clear, precise language? Some argue that translators and revisers should be able to enhance the quality of the original legislative text by suggesting alternative wording to the drafters. Yet one could question to what extent translators can influence the original source text. It seems that generally individual translators feel reluctant or simply have no time to contact the drafting committee to ask questions, give feedback or make alternative suggestions. And if they do contact the drafters, it is often too late for suggestions because the Commission may have already formally adopted the draft-proposal, based on the texts in its three working languages (English, French and German) before the translator started producing his/her language version. And even if no final decision has been made, any textual modifications suggested by translators or legal revisers may prove difficult to implement since the original text is a distillate of numerous negotiations and compromises that took a long time to achieve.

Others argue that in any event the translators and revisers can and should improve the legislative text in the language version for which they are responsible. Karl-Johan Lönroth, Director-General of the Directorate-General for Translation of the Commission, observed that, due to poor linguistic quality of the original language versions of legislative drafts, the classical translator is slowly making place for a new profession, the 'treditor'. This is a translator that does not passively translate the original text, but rather edits and recreates it in a different language (Lönroth 2008b). It is doubtful, however, that the translators would actually have such independence. Translators may not be adequately aware of the legal consequences of his/her choice of wording because translators in EU legislative bodies are not required to have a professional or academic legal background. In addition, there is currently no legal revision of the individual language versions

---

4 Principle 5.4 of the 'Joint Practical Guide of the European Parliament, the Council and the Commission for Persons Involved in the Drafting of Legislation within the Community Institutions'. Retrieved on 15 October 2009 from <http://eur-lex.europa.eu/en/techleg/pdf/en.pdf>.

of the legislative proposals adopted by the Commission. Legal revision by the Commission's Legal Service is directed only at the original text before it is translated into other EU languages.

3.3. Language complaints

Those involved in the drafting of EU legislative acts are required to take into account the specific field of those to whom these acts apply and use language in a way that the intended recipients can understand. The question dealt with in the remainder of this section is whether such receiver-oriented drafting may extend to the use of specific national legal languages in different language versions.

The Council is primarily a political body where national interests play a significant role. Legislative proposals are here subject to extensive scrutiny and concessions by the many national representatives as well as the ambassadors of Member States to the European Union. As a consequence, the Council's jurist-linguists regularly deal with so-called 'language complaints' from national representatives or diplomats to adjust the wording of a particular language version in a certain way. These complaints may come up if for example certain phrasing would suit the requester's government. A language complaint may also be presented as a reason for a Member State for voting against a certain policy. In this sense, translation of the base-text of a legislative proposal may enable political compromise when there is a deadlock at the negotiating table.

Notwithstanding political pressure, however, jurist-linguists are expected not to give in to these language complaints too easily. Before the adoption of the Council's position on a legislative proposal, the Legal Service is only willing to accept a language request from a national representative if the legal scope of the language version remains unchanged and thus does not diverge from the base text. Jurist-linguists are expected to prevent that the language versions refer to certain national legal terms that may create national expectations. They must prevent certain language versions from leading a life of their own in various legal systems, possibly diverging from the meaning and legal scope of the original base-text. It must be noted, however, that jurist-linguists are not necessarily experts in every legal field and legal system that uses a particular language. It is therefore possible for a national representative to have certain expressions into the relevant language version introduced that may have certain desired national legal consequences that are not necessarily implied by the base-text or in other language versions.

4. The basis of the source-oriented approach

There are at least two reasons that explain why the current approach to legal translation in EU legislative bodies is source-oriented rather than receiver-oriented. These reasons can be found in the supranational status of the legal framework of the EU and the acknowledgment of an autonomous EU legal language, as well as the equal authenticity of language versions.

Throughout the legislative procedure, all those involved in drafting the text of a legislative instrument – including translators and legal revisers – are required not to use expressions that are too specific to the natural or legal languages belonging to individual Member States. The reason is that translators and legal revisers must adhere to the particular legal language that belongs to the EU's legal system. From the case law of the European Court of Justice, it is clear that the EU is a distinct, supranational legal order, for which the Member States in a number of fields have limited their sovereign rights, and which imposes *sui generis* obligations and rights not only on Member States but also on their citizens.[5] Further, according to the Court, EU law makes no express reference to national laws in order to determine its meaning and scope. It requires an autonomous and uniform

5 See above all Case C-26/62 *Van Gend en Loos,* [1963] ECR 00001, and Joined cases C-6/90 and C-9/90 *Frankovic*, [1991] ECR I-05357, par. 31.

interpretation of its meaning and scope throughout the EU.[6] As a result, translators and legal revisers in the EU are expected to take into account that legislative instruments are part of a supranational legal system with its own autonomous legal language. In particular, it is the task of the Council's jurist-linguists to replace any national terminology with supranational terminology belonging to the EU's own legal language.

In addition, as discussed, proponents of the receiver-oriented approach suggest that translators in EU legislative bodies should predict how national courts would interpret the target texts. This view seems to overlook the fact that the context of a language version is not merely the legal system in which a certain natural language is spoken. Since all language versions are equally authentic, every language version has each citizen of the EU as its recipient, regardless of the recipient's legal system or the legal language belonging to that legal system. For instance, the Portuguese language version has legal force in the legal system of the Czech Republic and Denmark as much as it has in Portugal.

5. Concluding remarks

The foregoing shows that a receiver-oriented approach to translation of legislative texts in EU legislative procedure is unlikely to be employed in EU legislative bodies. Especially when translators have no legal background and the target texts do not undergo legal revision, a receiver-oriented approach would run the risk of language versions diverging from the wording that the drafters of the source text

---

6 E.g. Case C-357/98 The Queen v Secretary of State for the Home Department ex parte: Nana Yaa Konadu Yiadom [2000] ECR-9265; C-287/98 Luxemburg v Linster [2000] ECR-6917; C-387/97 Commission v Greece [2000] ECR-5047; Case C-327/82 Ekro v Produktschap voor Vee en Vlees [1984] ECR I-107, Case C-373/97 Dionisios Diamantis v Elliniko Dimosio (Greek State), Organismos Ikonomikis Anasinkrotisis Epikhiriseon AE (OAE) [2000] ECR I-1705; C-441/93 Pafitis and Others v TKE and Others [1996] ECR I-1347.

intentionally and meticulously selected, as well as from the wording in the other language versions. A receiver-oriented approach would also contradict the notion that language versions of EU legislation take part in the supranational legal order of the EU and thus are intended to contain the legal language that belongs to the legal system of the EU. Lastly, a receiver-oriented approach toward translation in EU legislative procedure would prove impossible because, due to the equal authenticity of language versions, the legal context of every language version is the context of every national legal system in the EU.

It is not necessarily the opinion of the author that a receiver-oriented translation would not better serve the objective of a uniform interpretation and uniform application of EU secondary legislation. It was the aim of this chapter, however, to show that such an approach would be at odds with the supranational nature of the legal order of the EU, the acknowledgment of its autonomous legal language and the equal authenticity of language versions of EU legislation.

References

Cao, Deborah 2007. *Translating Law.* Clevedon Hall: Multilingual Matters

Chromá, Martha 2004. *Legal Translation and the Dictionary.* Tübingen: Max Niemeyer Verlag

Frame, Ian 2005. Linguistic Oddities in European Union Legislation: Don't Shoot the Translator. *Clarity* 21/53, 21-24

Gallas, Tito 2006. Understanding EC Law as 'Diplomatic Law' and its Language. In Pozzo, Barbara / Jacometti, Valentina (eds) *Multilingualism and the Harmonisation of European Law.* Alphen aan den Rijn: Kluwer Law International, 119-124

Guggeis, Manuela 2006. Multilingual Legislation and the Legal-linguistic Revision in the Council of the European Union. In Pozzo, Barbara / Jacometti, Valentina (eds) *Multilingualism and the Harmonisation of European Law.* Alphen: Kluwer Law International, 109-117.

Lönroth, Karl-Johan 2008a. Efficiency, Transparency and Openness: Translation in the European Union. Speech in Shanghai at the XVIII World Congress of the International Federation of Translators. Retrieved from <http://ec.europa.eu/dgs/translation/publications/presentations/speeches/20080801_shanghai_en.pdf> on 15 October 2009.

Lönroth, Karl-Johan 2008b. Language Technologies and the European Commission. Speech given in Rome at Lang Tech 2008. Retrieved from <http://ec.europa.eu/dgs/translation/publications/presentations/speeches/20080228_rome_langtech_en.pdf> on 15 October 2009.

Sager, Juan C. 1990. *A Practical Course in Terminology*. Amsterdam: John Benjamins.

Šarčević Susan 2000. *Legal Translation and Translation Theory: A Receiver-oriented Approach.* Genéve: Actes. Retrieved from <http://www.tradulex.org/Actes2000/sarcevic.pdf> on 15 October 2009.

Šarčević, Susan 1997. *New Approach to Legal Translation.* The Hague: Kluwer Law International.

Varó, Enrique A. / Hughes, Brian 2002. *Legal Translation Explained.* Manchester: St. Jerome Publishing.

Wagner, Emma / Bech, Svend / Martínez, Jesús M. 2002. *Translating for the European Union Institutions*. Manchester: St. Jerome Publishing.

Weisflog, Walter E. 1996. *Rechtsvergleichung und juristische Übersetzung*. Zürich: Schultess.

Notes on Contributors

CORNELIS J.W. BAAIJ is a PhD candidate at the Centre for the Study of European Contract Law (CSECL) of the University of Amsterdam's School of Law. He is conducting legal research into the impact of multilingualism on the harmonisation of private law in the EU. For this purpose he uses the philosophy of language to study the intersection of legal interpretation and translation and comparative legal research. He is also the founder of the Amsterdam Circle for Law and Language (ACLL), which offers an international platform for the exchange of research findings in the field of law and language.

ROSS CHARNOCK is *Maître de Conférences* in the University of Paris, where he specialises in the language of the law. After earning degrees at Exeter (UK), he received a doctorate in Linguistic Pragmatics in Paris during the early 1980s, under O. Ducrot. His research articles concentrate mainly on the rhetorical and semantic analysis of common law judgments. He also has research interests in pragmatics and argumentation as applied to language testing.

STEFANIA D'AVANZO is a Lecturer of English Language at the Faculty of Law of the University of Naples 'Federico II' and at the Faculty of Economics of the University of Sannio (Benevento). She holds a PhD in English for Special Purposes and a Master's degree in Linguistics and Sociolinguistics of European Languages from the University of Naples 'Federico II'. She is engaged in a National Research Project (PRIN) and her current research is mainly concerned with legal and institutional discourse, discourse analysis and teaching.

CHRISTOPHER GODDARD has a background in law, language, and education. Based at the Riga Graduate School of Law, where he led the team that established a Master's programme in Legal Linguistics, he is currently completing doctoral studies in legal linguistics at the

University of Lapland. In addition, through a UK-based company he provides legal linguistic services which include translating, editing and proofreading legal texts in English and delivering legal English courses.

STANISŁAW GOŹDŹ-ROSZKOWSKI received his MA and PhD in English Studies from the University of Łódź, where he is now Assistant Professor. His research interests are primarily in corpus-based analyses of variation in domain-specific genres and registers. His other academic interests include corpus linguistics and its application to phraseology, terminology and translation. He has recently completed a book titled *Textual Patterns of Variation in Legal English. A Corpus-based Study.*

SUSAN KERMAS is Associate Professor of English Language at the University of Salento (Faculty of Foreign Languages and Literatures). Her teaching and research interests focus primarily on lexicology, lexicography, specialized discourse and the history of English. Her work has appeared in the proceedings of numerous national and international conferences, including *Studies in Specialized Discourse* (eds J. Flowerdew and M. Gotti) and *Commonality and Individuality in Academic Discourse* (ed. M. Gotti). Her latest monographs are *World Englishes and the EFL Teacher: A Historical Perspective* (1998) and *English Lexis in a Changing World* (2003).

PATRICK LEROYER, PhD, is Associate Professor of French and Danish LSP and Business Communication at the Aarhus School of Business of Aarhus University and is attached to the Centre for Lexicography. His current research deals with theoretical lexicography in a broad, functional perspective and includes the development of specific theories for data access, selection and presentation in connection with communicative and cognitive functions in lexicographic information tools. He has published within the fields of LSP and business communication, specialised translation, terminography and lexicography.

ROCCO LOIACONO is a graduate of UWA, the University of Western Australia (Perth), where he received a combined degree in Law and

Languages with a specialisation in Italian. As well as working as a lawyer, he is currently completing a PhD at UWA on the legal translation of Italian-English in both directions. In 2008 he won an Italian Government Scholarship to undertake research at the Department of Translation Studies of the University of Bologna. He has also been awarded a teaching internship at UWA University for 2010-2011.

ESTRELLA MONTOLÍO DURÁN is a Lecturer of Spanish Linguistics at the University of Barcelona. Her work seeks to combine the theoretical and methodological aspects of grammar, pragmatics and discourse analysis, as applied to the study of academic and professional discourses. She has been a guest lecturer at numerous universities in Europe and the Americas and acts as advisor on matters of communication for several institutions and large corporations. Her latest research has appeared in *The Handbook of Business Discourse* (ed. F. Bargiela-Chiappini) and *Ideology and Ethics in Specialized Communication: A Discourse Perspective* (eds S. Sarangi and G. Garzone).

VANDA POLESE is Associate Professor of English Language and Linguistics at Naples University 'Federico II', where she is also a member of the PhD programme in English for Special Purposes. Her main research interests cover issues in ESP linguistics (particularly news discourse, pragmatics, translation, learning English with corpus tools, hybridisation, popularisation, and legal and institutional discourse). She is the author of *Language in the Spotlight: News Manufacturing and Discourse* (2004), editor of *La lingua e il testo* (2002), co-editor of *'Languaging' and Interculturality in EU Domains* (2005) and *Identity and Culture in English Domain-Specific Discourse* (2008).

KIRSTEN WØLCH RASMUSSEN is Associate Professor at the Department of Language and Business Communication of the Aarhus School of Business (Aarhus University), where she is a member of the ASB Research Group for Knowledge Communication. Her current research concerns quality assurance within the translation profession. She is engaged in a EU project titled 'Building Mutual Trust: A Framework Project for Implementing EU Common Standards in Legal Interpreting and Translation' and has published within the fields of legal communication, language, genre and discourse, and legal interpreting and translation.

JUDITH TURNBULL is a Foreign-Language Assistant at the Faculty of Economics of the University of Rome (La Sapienza). Her research interests include cross-cultural communication and discourse analysis in the fields of economics, law and translation studies. She has published several studies, most recently in *Point of View: Description and Evaluation across Discourses* (eds S. Radighieri and P. Tucker) and in the journal *Textus*.

FRANCISCO VIGIER is a PhD candidate at the University of Granada, where he graduated in Translation and Interpreting. His main research area is translator training and assessment, professional accreditation and official translation. As an active member of the AVANTI research group, he has participated in several collective projects dealing with career opportunities for translation graduates and the acquisition of intercultural competence. He is currently completing a doctoral thesis on the training of sworn interpreters-translators in Spain.

Linguistic Insights

Studies in Language and Communication

This series aims to promote specialist language studies in the fields of linguistic theory and applied linguistics, by publishing volumes that focus on specific aspects of language use in one or several languages and provide valuable insights into language and communication research. A cross-disciplinary approach is favoured and most European languages are accepted.

The series includes two types of books:

- **Monographs** – featuring in-depth studies on special aspects of language theory, language analysis or language teaching.
- **Collected papers** – assembling papers from workshops, conferences or symposia.

Each volume of the series is subjected to a double peer-reviewing process.

Vol. 1 Maurizio Gotti & Marina Dossena (eds)
Modality in Specialized Texts. Selected Papers of the 1st CERLIS Conference.
421 pages. 2001. ISBN 3-906767-10-8. US-ISBN 0-8204-5340-4

Vol. 2 Giuseppina Cortese & Philip Riley (eds)
Domain-specific English. Textual Practices across Communities and Classrooms.
420 pages. 2002. ISBN 3-906768-98-8. US-ISBN 0-8204-5884-8

Vol. 3 Maurizio Gotti, Dorothee Heller & Marina Dossena (eds)
Conflict and Negotiation in Specialized Texts. Selected Papers of the 2nd CERLIS Conference.
470 pages. 2002. ISBN 3-906769-12-7. US-ISBN 0-8204-5887-2

Editorial address:

Prof. Maurizio Gotti Università di Bergamo, Facoltà di Lingue e Letterature Straniere,
Via Salvecchio 19, 24129 Bergamo, Italy
Fax: 0039 035 2052789, E-Mail: m.gotti@unibg.it

Vol. 4 Maurizio Gotti, Marina Dossena, Richard Dury, Roberta Facchinetti & Maria Lima
Variation in Central Modals. A Repertoire of Forms and Types of Usage in Middle English and Early Modern English.
364 pages. 2002. ISBN 3-906769-84-4. US-ISBN 0-8204-5898-8

Vol. 5 Stefania Nuccorini (ed.)
Phrases and Phraseology. Data and Descriptions.
187 pages. 2002. ISBN 3-906770-08-7. US-ISBN 0-8204-5933-X

Vol. 6 Vijay Bhatia, Christopher N. Candlin & Maurizio Gotti (eds)
Legal Discourse in Multilingual and Multicultural Contexts. Arbitration Texts in Europe.
385 pages. 2003. ISBN 3-906770-85-0. US-ISBN 0-8204-6254-3

Vol. 7 Marina Dossena & Charles Jones (eds)
Insights into Late Modern English. 2nd edition.
378 pages. 2003, 2007.
ISBN 978-3-03911-257-9. US-ISBN 978-0-8204-8927-8

Vol. 8 Maurizio Gotti
Specialized Discourse. Linguistic Features and Changing Conventions.
351 pages. 2003, 2005.
ISBN 3-03910-606-6. US-ISBN 0-8204-7000-7

Vol. 9 Alan Partington, John Morley & Louann Haarman (eds)
Corpora and Discourse.
420 pages. 2004. ISBN 3-03910-026-2. US-ISBN 0-8204-6262-4

Vol. 10 Martina Möllering
The Acquisition of German Modal Particles. A Corpus-Based Approach.
290 pages. 2004. ISBN 3-03910-043-2. US-ISBN 0-8204-6273-X

Vol. 11 David Hart (ed.)
English Modality in Context. Diachronic Perspectives.
261 pages. 2003. ISBN 3-03910-046-7. US-ISBN 0-8204-6852-5

Vol. 12 Wendy Swanson
Modes of Co-reference as an Indicator of Genre.
430 pages. 2003. ISBN 3-03910-052-1. US-ISBN 0-8204-6855-X

Vol. 13 Gina Poncini
Discursive Strategies in Multicultural Business Meetings.
2nd edition. 338 pages. 2004, 2007.
ISBN 978-3-03911-296-8. US-ISBN 978-0-8204-8937-7

Vol. 14 Christopher N. Candlin & Maurizio Gotti (eds)
Intercultural Aspects of Specialized Communication.
2nd edition. 369 pages. 2004, 2007.
ISBN 978-3-03911-258-6. US-ISBN 978-0-8204-8926-1

Vol. 15 Gabriella Del Lungo Camiciotti & Elena Tognini Bonelli (eds)
Academic Discourse. New Insights into Evaluation.
234 pages. 2004. ISBN 3-03910-353-9. US-ISBN 0-8204-7016-3

Vol. 16 Marina Dossena & Roger Lass (eds)
Methods and Data in English Historical Dialectology.
405 pages. 2004. ISBN 3-03910-362-8. US-ISBN 0-8204-7018-X

Vol. 17 Judy Noguchi
The Science Review Article. An Opportune Genre in the Construction of Science.
274 pages. 2006. ISBN 3-03910-426-8. US-ISBN 0-8204-7034-1

Vol. 18 Giuseppina Cortese & Anna Duszak (eds)
Identity, Community, Discourse. English in Intercultural Settings.
495 pages. 2005. ISBN 3-03910-632-5. US-ISBN 0-8204-7163-1

Vol. 19 Anna Trosborg & Poul Erik Flyvholm Jørgensen (eds)
Business Discourse. Texts and Contexts.
250 pages. 2005. ISBN 3-03910-606-6. US-ISBN 0-8204-7000-7

Vol. 20 Christopher Williams
Tradition and Change in Legal English. Verbal Constructions in Prescriptive Texts.
2nd revised edition. 216 pages. 2005, 2007. ISBN 978-3-03911-444-3.

Vol. 21 Katarzyna Dziubalska-Kołaczyk & Joanna Przedlacka (eds)
English Pronunciation Models: A Changing Scene.
2nd edition. 476 pages. 2005, 2008. ISBN 978-3-03911-682-9.

Vol. 22 Christián Abello-Contesse, Rubén Chacón-Beltrán, M. Dolores López-Jiménez & M. Mar Torreblanca-López (eds)
Age in L2 Acquisition and Teaching.
214 pages. 2006. ISBN 3-03910-668-6. US-ISBN 0-8204-7174-7

Vol. 23 Vijay K. Bhatia, Maurizio Gotti, Jan Engberg & Dorothee Heller (eds)
Vagueness in Normative Texts.
474 pages. 2005. ISBN 3-03910-653-8. US-ISBN 0-8204-7169-0

Vol. 24 Paul Gillaerts & Maurizio Gotti (eds)
Genre Variation in Business Letters. 2nd printing.
407 pages. 2008. ISBN 978-3-03911-681-2.

Vol. 25 Ana María Hornero, María José Luzón & Silvia Murillo (eds)
Corpus Linguistics. Applications for the Study of English.
2nd printing. 526 pages. 2006, 2008. ISBN 978-3-03911-726-0

Vol. 26 J. Lachlan Mackenzie & María de los Ángeles Gómez-González (eds)
Studies in Functional Discourse Grammar.
259 pages. 2005. ISBN 3-03910-696-1 / US-ISBN 0-8204-7558-0

Vol. 27 Debbie G. E. Ho
Classroom Talk. Exploring the Sociocultural Structure of Formal ESL Learning.
2nd edition. 254 pages. 2006, 2007. ISBN 978-3-03911-434-4

Vol. 28 Javier Pérez-Guerra, Dolores González-Álvarez, Jorge L. Bueno-Alonso & Esperanza Rama-Martínez (eds)
'Of Varying Language and Opposing Creed': New Insights into Late Modern English.
455 pages. 2007. ISBN 978-3-03910-788-9

Vol. 29 Francesca Bargiela-Chiappini & Maurizio Gotti (eds)
Asian Business Discourse(s).
350 pages. 2005. ISBN 3-03910-804-2 / US-ISBN 0-8204-7574-2

Vol. 30 Nicholas Brownlees (ed.)
News Discourse in Early Modern Britain. Selected Papers of CHINED 2004.
300 pages. 2006. ISBN 3-03910-805-0 / US-ISBN 0-8204-8025-8

Vol. 31 Roberta Facchinetti & Matti Rissanen (eds)
Corpus-based Studies of Diachronic English.
300 pages. 2006. ISBN 3-03910-851-4 / US-ISBN 0-8204-8040-1

Vol. 32 Marina Dossena & Susan M. Fitzmaurice (eds)
Business and Official Correspondence: Historical Investigations.
209 pages. 2006. ISBN 3-03910-880-8 / US-ISBN 0-8204-8352-4

Vol. 33 Giuliana Garzone & Srikant Sarangi (eds)
Discourse, Ideology and Specialized Communication.
494 pages. 2007. ISBN 978-3-03910-888-6

Vol. 34 Giuliana Garzone & Cornelia Ilie (eds)
The Use of English in Institutional and Business Settings.
An Intercultural Perspective.
372 pages. 2007. ISBN 978-3-03910-889-3

Vol. 35 Vijay K. Bhatia & Maurizio Gotti (eds)
Explorations in Specialized Genres.
316 pages. 2006. ISBN 3-03910-995-2 / US-ISBN 0-8204-8372-9

Vol. 36 Heribert Picht (ed.)
Modern Approaches to Terminological Theories and Applications.
432 pages. 2006. ISBN 3-03911-156-6 / US-ISBN 0-8204-8380-X

Vol. 37 Anne Wagner & Sophie Cacciaguidi-Fahy (eds)
Legal Language and the Search for Clarity / Le langage juridique et la quête de clarté.
Practice and Tools / Pratiques et instruments.
487 pages. 2006. ISBN 3-03911-169-8 / US-ISBN 0-8388-5

Vol. 38 Juan Carlos Palmer-Silveira, Miguel F. Ruiz-Garrido &
Inmaculada Fortanet-Gómez (eds)
Intercultural and International Business Communication:
Theory, Research and Teaching.
2nd edition. 343 pages. 2006, 2008. ISBN 978-3-03911-680-5

Vol. 39 Christiane Dalton-Puffer, Dieter Kastovsky, Nikolaus Ritt &
Herbert Schendl (eds)
Syntax, Style and Grammatical Norms: English from 1500–2000.
250 pages. 2006. ISBN 3-03911-181-7 / US-ISBN 0-8204-8394-X

Vol. 40 Marina Dossena & Irma Taavitsainen (eds)
Diachronic Perspectives on Domain-Specific English.
280 pages. 2006. ISBN 3-03910-176-0 / US-ISBN 0-8204-8391-5

Vol. 41 John Flowerdew & Maurizio Gotti (eds)
Studies in Specialized Discourse.
293 pages. 2006. ISBN 3-03911-178-7

Vol. 42 Ken Hyland & Marina Bondi (eds)
Academic Discourse Across Disciplines.
320 pages. 2006. ISBN 3-03911-183-3 / US-ISBN 0-8204-8396-6

Vol. 43 Paul Gillaerts & Philip Shaw (eds)
The Map and the Landscape: Norms and Practices in Genre.
256 pages. 2006. ISBN 3-03911-182-5 / US-ISBN 0-8204-8395-4

Vol. 44 Maurizio Gotti & Davide Giannoni (eds)
New Trends in Specialized Discourse Analysis.
301 pages. 2006. ISBN 3-03911-184-1 / US-ISBN 0-8204-8381-8

Vol. 45 Maurizio Gotti & Françoise Salager-Meyer (eds)
Advances in Medical Discourse Analysis: Oral and Written Contexts.
492 pages. 2006. ISBN 3-03911-185-X / US-ISBN 0-8204-8382-6

Vol. 46 Maurizio Gotti & Susan Šarcević (eds)
Insights into Specialized Translation.
396 pages. 2006. ISBN 3-03911-186-8 / US-ISBN 0-8204-8383-4

Vol. 47 Khurshid Ahmad & Margaret Rogers (eds)
Evidence-based LSP: Translation, Text and Terminology.
584 pages. 2007. ISBN 978-3-03911-187-9

Vol. 48 Hao Sun & Dániel Z. Kádár (eds)
It's the Dragon's Turn: Chinese Institutional Discourses.
262 pages. 2008. ISBN 978-3-03911-175-6

Vol. 49 Cristina Suárez-Gómez
Relativization in Early English (950-1250): the Position of Relative Clauses.
149 pages. 2006. ISBN 3-03911-203-1 / US-ISBN 0-8204-8904-2

Vol. 50 Maria Vittoria Calvi & Luisa Chierichetti (eds)
Nuevas tendencias en el discurso de especialidad.
319 pages. 2006. ISBN 978-3-03911-261-6

Vol. 51 Mari Carmen Campoy & María José Luzón (eds)
Spoken Corpora in Applied Linguistics.
274 pages. 2008. ISBN 978-3-03911-275-3

Vol. 52 Konrad Ehlich & Dorothee Heller (Hrsg.)
Die Wissenschaft und ihre Sprachen.
323 pages. 2006. ISBN 978-3-03911-272-2

Vol. 53 Jingyu Zhang
The Semantic Salience Hierarchy Model: The L2 Acquisition of Psych Predicates
273 pages. 2007. ISBN 978-3-03911-300-2

Vol. 54 Norman Fairclough, Giuseppina Cortese & Patrizia Ardizzone (eds)
Discourse and Contemporary Social Change.
555 pages. 2007. ISBN 978-3-03911-276-0

Vol. 55 Jan Engberg, Marianne Grove Ditlevsen, Peter Kastberg & Martin Stegu (eds)
New Directions in LSP Teaching.
331 pages. 2007. ISBN 978-3-03911-433-7

Vol. 56 Dorothee Heller & Konrad Ehlich (Hrsg.)
Studien zur Rechtskommunikation.
322 pages. 2007. ISBN 978-3-03911-436-8

Vol. 57 Forthcoming.

Vol. 58 Carmen Frehner
Email – SMS – MMS
294 pages. 2008. ISBN 978-3-03911-451-1

Vol. 59 Isabel Balteiro
The Directionality of Conversion in English: A Dia-Synchronic Study.
276 pages. 2007. ISBN 978-3-03911-241-8

Vol. 60 Maria Milagros Del Saz Rubio
English Discourse Markers of Reformulation.
237 pages. 2007. ISBN 978-3-03911-196-1

Vol. 61 Sally Burgess & Pedro Martín-Martín (eds)
English as an Additional Language in Research Publication and Communication.
259 pages. 2008. ISBN 978-3-03911-462-7

Vol. 62 Sandrine Onillon
Pratiques et représentations de l'écrit.
458 pages. 2008. ISBN 978-3-03911-464-1

Vol. 63 Hugo Bowles & Paul Seedhouse (eds)
Conversation Analysis and Language for Specific Purposes.
2nd edition. 337 pages. 2007, 2009. ISBN 978-3-0343-0045-2

Vol. 64 Vijay K. Bhatia, Christopher N. Candlin & Paola Evangelisti Allori (eds)
Language, Culture and the Law.
The Formulation of Legal Concepts across Systems and Cultures.
342 pages. 2008. ISBN 978-3-03911-470-2

Vol. 65 Jonathan Culpeper & Dániel Z. Kádár (eds)
Historical (Im)politeness.
300 pages. 2010. ISBN 978-3-03911-496-2

Vol. 66 Linda Lombardo (ed.)
Using Corpora to Learn about Language and Discourse.
237 pages. 2009. ISBN 978-3-03911-522-8

Vol. 67 Natsumi Wakamoto
Extroversion/Introversion in Foreign Language Learning.
Interactions with Learner Strategy Use.
159 pages. 2009. ISBN 978-3-03911-596-9

Vol. 68 Eva Alcón-Soler (ed.)
Learning How to Request in an Instructed Language Learning Context.
260 pages. 2008. ISBN 978-3-03911-601-0

Vol. 69 Domenico Pezzini
The Translation of Religious Texts in the Middle Ages.
428 pages. 2008. ISBN 978-3-03911-600-3

Vol. 70 Tomoko Tode
Effects of Frequency in Classroom Second Language Learning.
Quasi-experiment and stimulated-recall analysis.
195 pages. 2008. ISBN 978-3-03911-602-7

Vol. 71 Egor Tsedryk
Fusion symétrique et alternances ditransitives.
211 pages. 2009. ISBN 978-3-03911-609-6

Vol. 72 Cynthia J. Kellett Bidoli & Elana Ochse (eds)
English in International Deaf Communication.
444 pages. 2008. ISBN 978-3-03911-610-2

Vol. 73 Joan C. Beal, Carmela Nocera & Massimo Sturiale (eds)
Perspectives on Prescriptivism.
269 pages. 2008. ISBN 978-3-03911-632-4

Vol. 74 Carol Taylor Torsello, Katherine Ackerley & Erik Castello (eds)
Corpora for University Language Teachers.
308 pages. 2008. ISBN 978-3-03911-639-3

Vol. 75 María Luisa Pérez Cañado (ed.)
English Language Teaching in the European Credit Transfer System:
Facing the Challenge.
251 pages. 2009. ISBN 978-3-03911-654-6

Vol. 76 Marina Dossena & Ingrid Tieken-Boon van Ostade (eds)
Studies in Late Modern English Correspondence. Methodology and Data.
291 pages. 2008. ISBN 978-3-03911-658-4

Vol. 77 Ingrid Tieken-Boon van Ostade & Wim van der Wurff (eds)
Current Issues in Late Modern English.
436 pages. 2009. ISBN 978-3-03911-660-7

Vol. 78 Marta Navarro Coy (ed.)
Practical Approaches to Foreign Language Teaching and Learning.
297 pages. 2009. ISBN 978-3-03911-661-4

Vol. 79 Qing Ma
Second Language Vocabulary Acquisition.
333 pages. 2009. ISBN 978-3-03911-666-9

Vol. 80 Martin Solly, Michelangelo Conoscenti & Sandra Campagna (eds)
Verbal/Visual Narrative Texts in Higher Education.
384 pages. 2008. ISBN 978-3-03911-672-0

Vol. 81 Meiko Matsumoto
From Simple Verbs to Periphrastic Expressions:
The Historical Development of Composite Predicates, Phrasal Verbs,
and Related Constructions in English.
235 pages. 2008. ISBN 978-3-03911-675-1

Vol. 82 Melinda Dooly
Doing Diversity. Teachers' Construction of Their Classroom Reality.
180 pages. 2009. ISBN 978-3-03911-687-4

Vol. 83 Victoria Guillén-Nieto, Carmen Marimón-Llorca & Chelo Vargas-Sierra (eds)
Intercultural Business Communication and
Simulation and Gaming Methodology.
392 pages. 2009. ISBN 978-3-03911-688-1

Vol. 84 Maria Grazia Guido
English as a Lingua Franca in Cross-cultural Immigration Domains.
285 pages. 2008. ISBN 978-3-03911-689-8

Vol. 85 Erik Castello
Text Complexity and Reading Comprehension Tests.
352 pages. 2008. ISBN 978-3-03911-717-8

Vol. 86 Maria-Lluisa Gea-Valor, Isabel García-Izquierdo & Maria-José Esteve (eds)
Linguistic and Translation Studies in Scientific Communication.
317 pages. 2010. ISBN 978-3-0343-0069-8

Vol. 87 Carmen Navarro, Rosa Mª Rodríguez Abella, Francesca Dalle Pezze
& Renzo Miotti (eds)
La comunicación especializada.
355 pages. 2008. ISBN 978-3-03911-733-8

Vol. 88 Kiriko Sato
The Development from Case-Forms to Prepositional Constructions
in Old English Prose.
231 pages. 2009. ISBN 978-3-03911-763-5

Vol. 89 Dorothee Heller (Hrsg.)
Formulierungsmuster in deutscher und italienischer Fachkommunikation.
Intra- und interlinguale Perspektiven.
315 pages. 2008. ISBN 978-3-03911-778-9

Vol. 90 Henning Bergenholtz, Sandro Nielsen & Sven Tarp (eds)
Lexicography at a Crossroads. Dictionaries and Encyclopedias Today,
Lexicographical Tools Tomorrow.
372 pages. 2009. ISBN 978-3-03911-799-4

Vol. 91 Manouchehr Moshtagh Khorasani
The Development of Controversies: From the Early Modern Period
to Online Discussion Forums.
317 pages. 2009. ISBN 978-3-3911-711-6

Vol. 92 María Luisa Carrió-Pastor (ed.)
Content and Language Integrated Learning: Cultural Diversity.
178 pages. 2009. ISBN 978-3-3911-818-2

Vol. 93-94 Forthcoming.

Vol. 95 Facchinetti Roberta, Crystal David, Seidlhofer Barbara (eds)
From International to Local English – And Back Again.
268 pages. 2010. ISBN 978-3-0343-0011-7

Vol. 96 Cesare Gagliardi & Alan Maley (eds)
EIL, ELF, Global English: Teaching and Learning Issues
376 pages. 2010. ISBN 978-3-0343-0010-0

Vol. 97 Sylvie Hancil (ed.)
The Role of Prosody in Affective Speech.
403 pages. 2009. ISBN 978-3-03911-696-6

Vol. 98 Marina Dossena & Roger Lass (eds)
Studies in English and European Historical Dialectology.
257 pages. 2009. ISBN 978-3-0343-0024-7

Vol. 99 Christine Béal
Les interactions quotidiennes en français et en anglais.
De l'approche comparative à l'analyse des situations interculturelles.
424 pages. 2010. ISBN 978-3-0343-0027-8

Vol. 100 Maurizio Gotti (ed.)
Commonality and Individuality in Academic Discourse.
398 pages. 2009. ISBN 978-3-0343-0023-0

Vol. 101 Javier E. Díaz Vera & Rosario Caballero (eds)
Textual Healing: Studies in Medieval English Medical, Scientific and Technical Texts.
213 pages. 2009. ISBN 978-3-03911-822-9

Vol. 102 Nuria Edo Marzá
The Specialised Lexicographical Approach: A Step further in Dictionary-making.
316 pages. 2009. ISBN 978-3-0343-0043-8

Vol. 103 Carlos Prado-Alonso, Lidia Gómez-García, Iria Pastor-Gómez & David Tizón-Couto (eds)
New Trends and Methodologies in Applied English Language Research. Diachronic, Diatopic and Contrastive Studies.
348 pages. 2009. ISBN 978-3-0343-0046-9

Vol. 104-108 Forthcoming.

Vol. 109 Ángeles Linde López & Rosalía Crespo Jiménez (eds)
Professional English in the European context: The EHEA challenge.
374 pages. 2010. ISBN 978-3-0343-0088-9

Vol. 110 Rosalía Rodríguez-Vázquez
The Rhythm of Speech, Verse and Vocal Music: A New Theory.
394 pages. 2010. ISBN 978-3-0343-0309-5

Vol. 111 Anastasios Tsangalidis & Roberta Facchinetti (eds)
Studies on English Modality. In Honour of Frank Palmer.
392 pages. 2009. ISBN 978-3-0343-0310-1

Vol. 115 Giuliana Garzone & Paola Catenaccio (eds)
Identities across Media and Modes: Discursive Perspectives.
379 pages. 2009. ISBN 978-3-0343-0386-6

Vol. 116 Elena Landone
Los marcadores del discurso y cortesía verbal en español.
390 pages. 2010. ISBN 978-3-0343-0413-9

Vol. 117 Maurizio Gotti & Christopher Williams (eds)
Legal Discourse across Languages and Cultures.
339 pages. 2010. ISBN 978-3-0343-0425-2

Vol. 118 David Hirsh
Academic Vocabulary in Context.
217 pages. 2010. ISBN 978-3-0343-0426-9

Vol. 119-120 Forthcoming.

Vol. 121 Davide Simone Giannoni & Celina Frade (eds)
Researching Language and the Law. Textual Features and Translation Issues.
278 pages. 2010. ISBN 978-3-0343-0443-6

Vol. 122 Forthcoming.

Vol. 123 Vijay K. Bhatia, Christopher N. Candlin & Maurizio Gotti (eds)
The Discourses of Dispute Resolution.
290 pages. 2010. ISBN 978-3-0343-0476-4